REAL ESTATE INVESTING FOR DOUBLE-DIGIT RETURNS

Petros S. Sivitanides, Ph.D.

© 2007 Petros S. Sivitanides, Ph.D.

All rights reserved. No part of this publication may be reproduced or transmitted in any form or by any means electronic or mechanical, including photocopy, recording, or any information storage and retrieval system, without permission in writing from both the copyright owner and the publisher.

Requests for permission to make copies of any part of this work should be mailed to Permissions Department, BookSurge Publishing, 7290 B Investment Drive, Charleston, SC 29418

ISBN: 1-4392-1386-0

Printed in the United States of America by BookSurge Publishing

*In memory of Rena,
my beloved wife, who showed me
what true love, self-sacrifice,
and strength of character means.*

PREFACE

Real estate investing is a venture of diligence and foresight, and investors with a good sense of where property rents and values are headed can be very successful. This book is about the foresight aspect of real estate investing. Although there have been many books written regarding due diligence and the analytical processes involved in assessing real estate investment opportunities, there are few books focusing on the foresight aspect of real estate investing. This book attempts to cover a portion of this gap with a focus on high-return, big-profit investment opportunities.

The most critical stage of the real estate investment process is the selection of specific properties in which to invest. Real estate is fixed at a given location and its modification is very costly; unless the chosen property has inherent potential, there is nothing the investor can do to make the investment profitable. Investing in real estate is not riskless, but the better investors understand the dynamics that trigger rent and property value increases, the smaller the risk that they will choose a property that will prove to be a poor performer.

Within this context, the book first uncovers circumstances that create opportunities for significant profits in real estate and then identifies general and specific categories of properties with significant profit potential. As such, it provides a valuable framework of reference to investors searching for highly profitable opportunities in real estate. The principles and conclusions presented in this book are universal and apply to any real estate market operating with the principle of free competition. Thus, the issues discussed in this book should be of great interest to property owners, investors, and real estate professionals residing in any free economy around the globe.

It should be emphasized that the thinking framework provided in this book in no way substitutes for the due diligence that needs to be carried out before committing funds to a specific property. Although the diligence aspect of real estate investing is extremely important, this book does not deal with analytical processes or the detailed calculations involved in evaluating whether a property represents a high-return opportunity; such issues are out of its scope. Investment decisions, however, should not be made without such analyses being performed by experts, to ensure they are done right and, most importantly, that the figures used are reasonable approximations of real costs, expenses, and expected revenues.

This book is not presenting a get-rich-quick scheme, nor is the author suggesting that profitable investing in real estate is a simple task. However, understanding and absorbing the contents of this book should give the reader an edge in identifying real estate investment opportunities with significant profit potential.

The discussion presented in this book is underscored by the author's deep understanding of real estate market dynamics and their impact on real estate investment performance, as cultivated through graduate and doctoral studies in urban and real estate economics, as well as through long professional experience in the field of real estate investment consulting and forecasting in one of the country's top real estate advisory and research firms. The material, however, is presented in a rather simplistic way so that people with non-economic background can understand it.

PETROS S. SIVITANIDES, PH.D.

TABLE OF CONTENTS

1. INTRODUCTION   1

The Thinking Framework   1
Factors That Trigger Capitalization-Rate Decreases and Property-Value Increases   5
Factors That Trigger Increases in Property Income and Values   9
Important Dimensions of Property Investments Targeting High Returns   14
Broader Categories of Properties with Big Profit Potential   14
Summary   16

2. ACHIEVING HIGH RETURNS BY RIDING THE REAL ESTATE CYCLE   18

The Real Estate Cycle and its Double-Positive Impact on Values   18
Achieving High Returns by Riding the Real Estate Cycle   19
Office Property Value Dynamics   25
Warehouse Property Value Dynamics   28
Retail Property Value Dynamics   30
Apartment Value Dynamics   34
Summary   36

3. BORROWING CAN HELP INVESTORS ATTAIN HIGH RETURNS   38

Financing the Purchase or Development of Real Estate with Borrowed Funds   38
Financing 100% of the Investment with Borrowed Funds   43
Summary   46

4. MARKET-DRIVEN VALUE INCREASES AND MARKET FUNDAMENTALS   48

Properties with Significant Market-Driven Value Increase Potential   48
How Property Rents and Prices are Determined   50
What May Cause Market Rents and Prices to Increase   54
The Supply of Real Estate   56

Growth Controls and Restrictive Zoning	63
The Demand/Supply Interaction in the Real Estate Market	65
How Much will Rents/Prices Increase in Response to a Surge in Demand	69
Summary	74

5. REAL ESTATE DEMAND AND VALUE INCREASES — 76

Components of Demand for Real Estate	76
The Concept of Utility and Demand	79
Changes in Demand and the Principle of Outbidding	81
Locational Dynamics, Locational Demand, and Value Increases	85
Summary	91

6. FORCES THAT TRIGGER INCREASES IN DEMAND FOR HOUSING — 93

Forces that Trigger Increases in Demand for Housing	93
Forces that Trigger Increases in Aggregate Market Demand for Housing	95
What may Cause Increases in Locational Demand for Housing	107
Summary	112

7. FORCES THAT TRIGGER INCREASES IN DEMAND FOR OFFICE SPACE — 113

What May Cause Increases in Aggregate Market Demand for Office Space	113
Prospects for Increases in Office Employment and Office Space Demand	119
Basics of Locational Demand for Office Space	120
Market-Driven Increases in Locational Demand for Office Space	123
What May Cause Development-Driven Increases in Locational Demand for Office Space	125
Summary	128

8. FORCES THAT TRIGGER INCREASES IN DEMAND FOR RETAIL SPACE — 130

Basics of Demand for Retail Space	130
Determinants of Aggregate Market Demand for Retail Space	132

What May Cause Increases in Aggregate Market Demand for Retail Space	140
What May Cause Increases in Locational Demand for Retail Space	145
Summary	149

9. SPECIFIC SUB-CATEGORIES OF PROPERTIES WITH SIGNIFICANT VALUE-INCREASE POTENTIAL — 150

1) Properties Located in Municipalities with Strong Population and/or Employment Growth Prospects and Restrained Supply — 151
2) High-Income Housing in Communities with Increasing Income, Restrained Supply, and Low Vacancy Rates — 158
3) Residential Properties in Neighborhoods About to Experience Significant Upgrading of their Environment — 159
4) Residential and Commercial Properties in Inner-City Neighborhoods About to Experience Significant Upgrading — 161
5) Properties with Compatibility Recovery Potential — 163
6) Properties with Complementarity Improvement Potential — 165
7) Properties with Potential for Significant Improvement of their Accessibility, Visibility, and Traffic Exposure — 169
8) Vacant Lots with Potential for Becoming Suitable for Development — 170
9) Properties with Potential for Upgrading Zoning Change — 170
10) Owner-Occupied Housing During Periods of Sharp Decreases in Interest Rates — 172
11) Monopoly Properties — 175

10. MISMANAGED PROPERTIES — 177
Mismanaged Properties — 177
Summary — 181

11. BARGAIN PROPERTIES — 183

Tax Delinquent Properties — 185
Foreclosure Properties — 186
Bankruptcy Sale Properties — 187
Summary — 188

12. BUILDING HIGH-RETURN PORTFOLIOS — 189

Applying Modern Portfolio Theory in Structuring High-Return Portfolios — 190
The Role of Sources of Profit Potential in Structuring High-Return Portfolios — 195
Summary — 198

GLOSSARY — 200

REFERENCES — 204

Chapter 1

Introduction

THE THINKING FRAMEWORK

As is the case for any investment, big profits in real estate can be made if one can sell considerably higher than the purchase price. Such strategy will be highly profitable since it will allow for large *capital gains* (the difference between sales and purchase price). Selling at a price that is considerably greater than the purchase price requires that:

a) The value of the property *increases considerably after its purchase*

b) The property is purchased *considerably below its market value*, because of a rushed sale or other special circumstances.

The above statements represent common sense and by no means qualify as a revelation. Of great interest, however, is how these statements can be translated in more specific terms in order to provide clues for identifying highly profitable real estate investment opportunities.

Besides capital gains, an additional source of profit for income-producing properties is the rental income received from the tenant. Strong increases in property income will give double bonus to a property owner because, all else equal, value will go up considerably too. The value of a property increases when the income it provides to its landlord goes up (all else being equal), because in the capital market, where asset prices are determined, there is a vital link between the market value of a property and the income it produces. This link is described by two formulas. Formula 1 postulates that property value is the ratio of the property's *net operating income* (NOI) over a rate referred to as the *market capitalization rate* (often referred to as the "cap rate"). Formula 2 clarifies that NOI represents the difference between the rental income produced by the property and its operating expenses, which typically include management fees, maintenance and repairs, salaries, utilities, insurance, supplies, advertising, and property taxes.

$$\text{Property Value} = \frac{\text{Property Net Operating Income (NOI)}}{\text{Market Capitalization Rate}} \quad (1)$$

or

$$\text{Property Value} = \frac{\text{Rental Income} - \text{Operating Expenses}}{\text{Market Capitalization Rate}} \quad (2)$$

Formulas 1 and 2 represent what is called in the appraisal literature the "simple income capitalization approach" in estimating property value. Historical data provided by the National Council of Real Estate Investment Fiduciaries (NCREIF) prove the validity of this rule. NCREIF collects and processes property income and value data from the largest institutional investors in real estate in the United States. Appraisal-based market capitalization rates for office properties, estimated from this database using the above formula for the period 1979-2004, have ranged between 6.3 and 9.6%. Similarly, over the same period, market capitalization rates for retail properties have ranged between 6.2 and 8.9%.

As Formula 2 indicates, if the rental income of a property increases significantly, the value of the property will increase significantly too (assuming that the market capitalization rate does not change). The rental income of a property is determined by two factors: the *rental rate* per square foot and *building occupancy*. For example, two office buildings that charge the same rent but have significantly different occupancy rates will have different rental income and NOI. Therefore, increases in the rental income of a property can be triggered by increases in the rental rate charged to tenants and increases in its occupancy rate.

By transforming Formula 1, we see that the market capitalization rate is actually the ratio of NOI over property value. Thus, in essence, the market capitalization rate represents the income return earned by investors active in the real estate marketplace.[1] We will discuss the capitalization rate and the factors that drive its movements in the following section.

To better understand how the two components of the formula (NOI and market capitalization rate) influence value, assume that you own an apartment, which you are renting to a tenant, and receive an annual NOI of $10,000. This represents the rental payments minus the yearly operating expenses associated with holding the property. Assuming a market capitalization rate of 8%, the value of your apartment can be calculated as:

$$V = \frac{\$10{,}000}{0.08} = \$125{,}000$$

Now, assume that during the second year you can charge higher rent so that property NOI increases by 5%. Assuming that market capitalization rates remain the same, the value of your apartment will also increase by 5% to $131,250:

$$V = \frac{\$10{,}500}{0.08} = \$131{,}250$$

Notice that if the market capitalization rate goes up, income increases may not necessarily result in property value increases. If we assume that at the same time the NOI of your apartment rises by 5%, the market capitalization rate increases to 8.5%, the value of your apartment will actually decrease slightly to $123,529:

$$V = \frac{\$10{,}500}{0.085} = \$123{,}529$$

---

[1] Investors evaluate the final price they pay for a property based not just on income return at the time of purchase, but on the total return they expect over a reasonable holding period, which is usually 5-7 years. Such evaluation is carried out using a complex model, the discounted cash-flow model (DCF), which takes into account not only the income the property is earning at the time of purchase, but also the anticipated income during every year of the assumed holding period, as well as profits or losses from changes in value over the holding period.

However, if we assume that at the same time the NOI of your apartment increases, the market capitalization rate *decreases*, the percentage increase in your apartment will be *considerably greater*. For example, assume that during the second year, not only does the NOI increase by 5%, but also the market capitalization rate drops from 8% to 7.5%. In such a case, the value of your property will climb to $140,000, representing a 12% increase over its original value of $125,000:

$$V = \frac{\$10,500}{0.075} = \$140,000$$

The conclusion is that robust property-value increases can be triggered by strong property-income increases, especially when they are combined with decreasing capitalization rates. Therefore, in searching for properties with significant profit potential, we need to identify *mechanisms, circumstances, and factors that trigger increases in property income and decreases in capitalization rates*.

I will examine such issues in great detail in following sections. For the time being, let me mention that rental income increases are triggered by the interaction of demand and supply in the space or user market where landlords offer their properties for leasing. In the case of owner-occupied housing, where there is no rent paid, price increases are triggered directly from the interaction between demand for and supply of owner-occupied housing units.

As explained in the next section, market capitalization rates tend to move downwards when interest rates dive to low levels, as they did during the early 2000's, triggering very strong increases in housing prices. In general, they decline when there are many investors in the market chasing few properties (demand exceeds supply in the investment market).

Within this framework, we will discuss the factors that trigger capitalization-rate decreases and property-income increases, the broader categories of properties with significant profit potential, how investors can take advantage of the cyclical nature of real estate markets and borrowing to achieve high returns, the price/rent determination mechanism in the investment and user market, and a host of factors and circumstances that trigger demand and property value increases for different property types. We will also review subcategories of properties with significant value-increase and profit potential, as well as issues regarding the structuring of high-return property portfolios.

FACTORS THAT TRIGGER CAPITALIZATION-RATE DECREASES AND PROPERTY-VALUE INCREASES

Capitalization rates represent *a required or acceptable* income return by investors. As such, they are determined by three factors (see Figure 1):

a) *Perceived risk* associated with the investment under consideration,

b) *Investor expectations for future property value increases* (appreciation)

c) *Required returns in alternative investment vehicles*, such as stocks and bonds

Risk is the uncertainty associated with the future income stream and/or capital gains expected from the investment.[2] For example, a government bond has zero risk, because there is no uncertainty regarding the *income* return on such an investment; the US Government guarantees interest payments on these bonds. On the contrary, corporate bonds are not considered as riskless since there is no guarantee that the company issuing the bond will be able to make the interest payments.

---

[2] Investment analysts tend to measure risk as the volatility of past historical performance. So stocks are considered as quite risky because their historical performance has been very volatile. Based on the same measure, bonds are considered less risky. The volatility of the performance of real estate investments, as reflected in the NCREIF data, is not directly comparable to the indices measuring stock and bond performance, because property values/prices are based on appraisals and not transactions, as is the case for stock and bond indices.

Figure 1 – Market Factors that Trigger Capitalization-Rate Decreases and Property-Value Increases

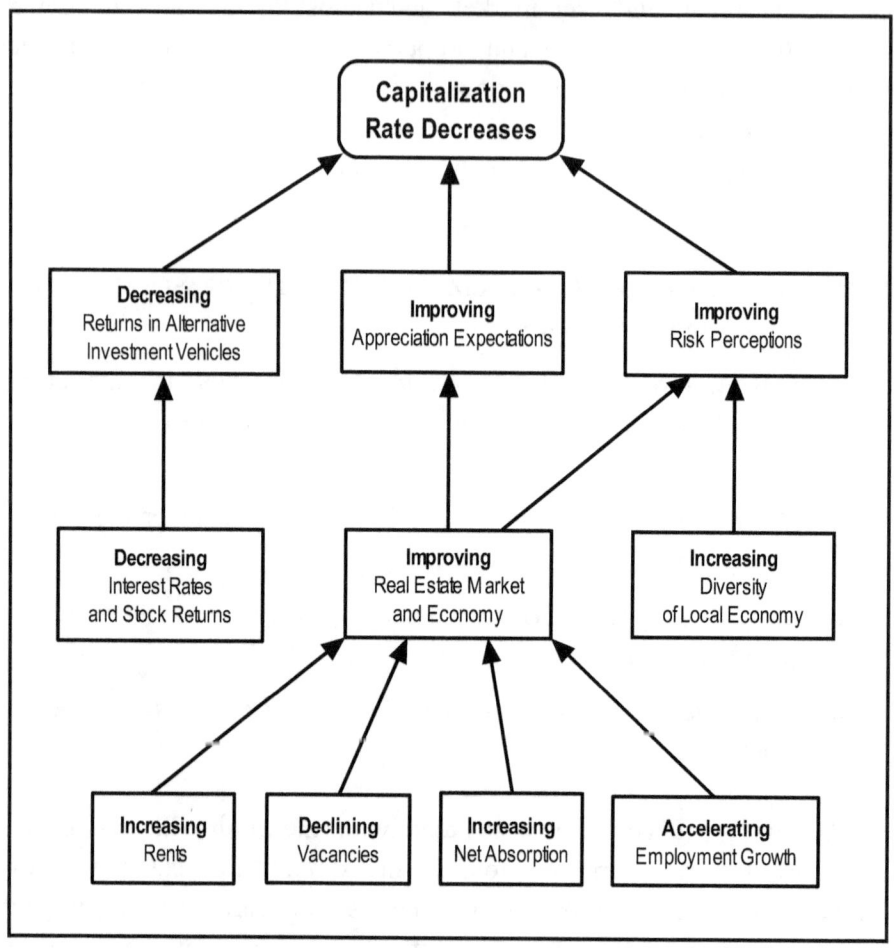

In real estate, risk can be defined as the uncertainty with respect to the property's income-earning capacity and value. Investors' risk perceptions regarding a property's prospects should be influenced by the economic and real estate market conditions prevailing at the time of the purchase. All else being equal, one would expect that when the real estate market is strong, with rising rents, high levels of absorption, and declining vacancies, investors will feel less uncertain about the property's future cash flows and appreciation prospects. This lower uncertainty will translate to a lower risk rating, allowing investors to accept lower returns and lower capitalization rates (see Figure 1). This proposition is supported by the findings of a study by Sivitanidou and

Sivitanides (1999), who verified empirically that when market conditions are strong, office capitalization rates are low.

As we will see in an upcoming section, the performance of a property is affected not only by the *broader market conditions* but also by *location and property-specific factors*. These location and property-specific factors also affect risk perceptions and the capitalization rate an investor may use to calculate the maximum price he/she is willing to pay for a property. For example, an investor may consider a 30-year-old property as riskier than a new one. I can think of many reasons why that would be true, such as the greater risk of functional obsolescence or greater overruns of maintenance expenses (beyond those normally accounted for buildings of this age).

Other location-specific factors that may affect an investor's risk perceptions have to do with the stage of development of an area. An investor may consider the purchase of a property in an area with little development, infrastructure, and supporting services as more risky, compared to a property located in a fully developed neighborhood. The former may have greater value appreciation potential, but if the neighborhood is in the early stage of development, there is also greater uncertainty as to whether development will intensify, and when. That is why new massive development in a mostly undeveloped area will decrease the risk of existing properties and contribute to decreases in the cap rate investors use to estimate the price they are willing to pay for such properties.

Sivitanidou and Sivitanides (1999) have confirmed the influence of another factor, which can be linked to the perceived risk of real estate investments. This factor has to do with the diversity of the local economy and office market. The term "diverse office markets" refers to markets in which office employment composition is *uniformly spread throughout several economic sectors*, as opposed to only a few sectors. The argument is that non-diverse office markets are more risky; if the sector in which most of the market's office employees are active takes a hit, there will be a significant negative effect on local office space demand, leading to declines in property income and values. Sivitanidou and Sivitanides found a strong statistical relationship between high diversity in an area's office tenant base and low capitalization rates. They also verified that markets with stable office-employment growth rates tend to have lower capitalization rates. Within the theoretical framework developed so far, this effect can only be linked to investor risk perceptions.

Another factor that may affect the investor's required rate of return, and therefore, the capitalization rate, is *expected appreciation*. Investors make their decisions based on the total expected return, which is the sum of income return and appreciation return. To understand how expected appreciation may affect the market capitalization rate, consider an investor who requires a total return of 12% on his/her investment. In evaluating a property for acquisition, the investor is told by a real estate advisor that the expected *appreciation rate* for the property is estimated at about 3%. Given the total return requirement of 12%, the investor will buy the property only if it is priced so that it offers a 9% (twelve percent minus three percent) income return, at least. If the investor's consultant estimates expected appreciation at 5%, the investor would be willing to accept a lower income return and buy the property at a price that corresponds to a capitalization rate of 7%.

The bottom line is that when market-wide expectations of value increases are *high*, market capitalization rates should be *low*; when the expectations for value appreciation are low, capitalization rates should be high. Notice that investor expectations regarding the future appreciation of a property are influenced by the same factors that influence risk perceptions, that is, indicators of market strength (see Figure 1).

Since real estate competes in the capital market for investment funds with alternative investment vehicles, such as stocks, corporate bonds, and government bonds, the level of returns offered by these vehicles should influence the return required by real estate investors. If returns in stocks and bonds decrease, relative to real estate, more capital will flow to real estate, pushing down required returns from property investments and capitalization rates. This is what has been happening in the last three or four years, after the stock market crash of the 2000 and the dive of interest rates (which influenced the return of bond instruments) to historic lows.[3] One of the major concerns of

---

[3] The 2000 stock market crash was triggered by the burst of the tech bubble and was reinforced by the September 11, 2001 terrorist attack. It started in January of 2000 and ended in October of 2002, after stocks registered a loss of 38%.

real estate investors in today's environment is the prospect of rising interest rates; such a scenario will most likely push capitalization rates up and hurt property values.

In sum, the factors and circumstances that trigger capitalization-rate declines and, therefore, *property-value increases* (assuming that everything else remains constant) include:

a) *Decreases in risk/uncertainty* regarding the future performance of a property due to:

- *Improving market conditions*, as measured by increasing rents, falling vacancy, high absorption levels, and accelerating employment growth
- *Significant developments* in the vicinity of a property, which improve its accessibility, supporting services, etc.

b) Expectations for *higher appreciation rate*s, which are influenced by the same factors as risk perceptions

c) *Decreases in interest rates* and stock/bond returns

Some of the factors mentioned above concern local market conditions and some concern macroeconomic forces that influence all markets at the same time. Based on the framework developed so far, it seems that investments in markets *expected to experience significant improvements in their supply-demand fundamentals, during periods of poor stock returns and low interest rates,* can take advantage of the most favorable circumstances for property-value increases, since they will boost property income and compress capitalization rates at the same time.

FACTORS THAT TRIGGER INCREASES IN PROPERTY INCOME AND VALUES[4]

The second set of forces that trigger property value increases relates to the property's income-earning capacity, or *market rents*. In thinking

---

[4] This section and Figure 2 have been taken from the unpublished book draft by Sivitanidou, M. R., *Market Analysis for Real Estate*.

about such forces it is important to distinguish two broader categories (see Figure 2):

1. *Macroeconomic forces* that affect market performance at the aggregate level and which can be classified into two sub-categories:

    a) General macroeconomic and metropolitan-specific forces that affect *all* property types, and

    b) Macroeconomic forces that drive the demand for and supply of *specific* property types, such as office, retail, or residential

2. *Location and property-specific* (or microeconomic) factors, which determine how individual property performance deviates from market performance.

1.a. General Macroeconomic/Metropolitan Growth Forces

These forces include developments that may affect the economy of a metropolitan area and all its property markets. Some examples of such developments include increasing global competition and technological advancements that may undermine an area's major industries; significant changes in exchange rates that may render foreign imports less attractive in favor of domestic industries; changes in the economic well-being of America's major trading partners that can have a significant impact on export-oriented metropolitan economies; or changes in interest rates that may influence demand and the volume of new construction, and, therefore, the supply of all property types nationally.

The effect of general macroeconomic forces is usually powerful and widespread to many locations of a country or a region but it varies from metropolitan area to metropolitan area in terms of size and timing, due to differences in industrial structures and the sectoral composition of local economies. One force that changes the pace of economic growth in many European countries is the European Union. Property values registered huge gains in countries like Ireland and Poland just after their admission in the European Union.

Figure 2 – Property Profitability Influences[4]

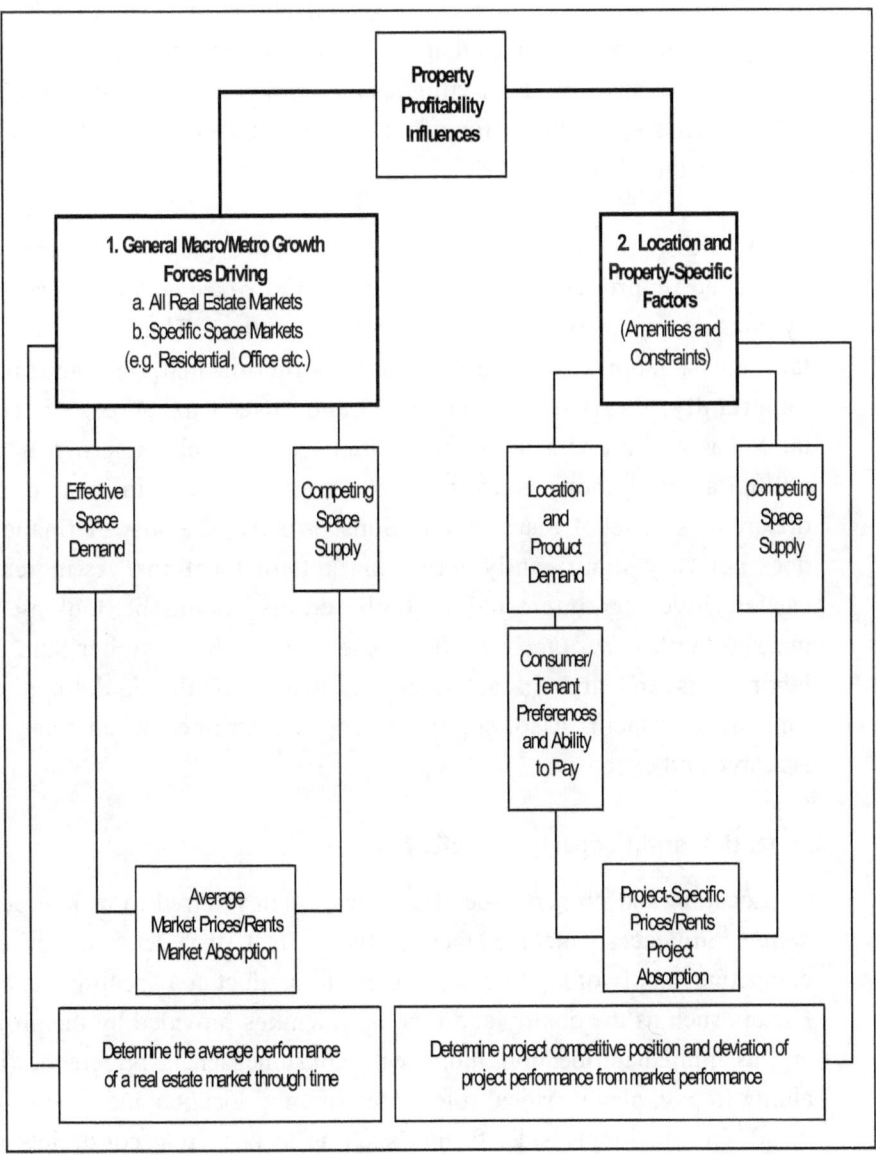

1.b. Macroeconomic Forces that Drive the Demand for and Supply of Specific Property Types

A number of studies have shown that the demand for industrial space is driven by employment in specific sectors of the economy. For example, Wheaton and Torto (1990) have shown that demand for industrial space is driven primarily by employment in manufacturing and wholesale trade. Thus, macroeconomic forces that affect employment only in these sectors will have an impact on the local industrial market, but not on the local office market since demand for office space is driven by employment in service sectors (Wheaton, 1987).

On the supply side, the major factors that drive new construction for a specific property type include potential *revenues* (as determined by market prices/rents) and *development costs*. The latter include land costs, labor costs, the cost of construction materials and, most importantly, the cost of financing. Land costs vary across different land uses within the same metropolitan area, as well as across metropolitan areas. Labor costs vary also across metropolitan areas due to differences in labor market conditions. Finally, the cost of financing does not vary significantly across markets or locations. As indicated earlier, investors interested in high returns should be looking for markets with *restrained supply*. These markets have higher land and labor costs and are characterized by strict growth regulations that limit development. Also, supply is more constrained when financing is scarce and expensive.

2. Location and Property-Specific Factors

Location and property-specific forces, often referred to as *microeconomic* influences, include factors that affect the demand for and competing supply of a particular real estate product at a specific location. Factors such as the quality and type of amenities provided by the project and its immediate location, along with consumer/tenant preferences and ability to pay, play a critical role in determining location and product demand. On the supply side, factors such as local zoning constraints and growth controls may create supply shortages and limit competition. Furthermore, the spatial distribution of existing and new comparable properties plays a key role in determining the intensity of the competition faced by a specific property at a given location, especially in the case of retail. These factors shape the competitive position of a project within its market area, which plays a crucial role in determining the level of rents/prices and absorption it can achieve, relative to the average market rent and total market absorption.

To better understand the difference between macroeconomic and microeconomic influences on real estate markets, consider that the *time path* of achievable rents for two properties within the same market is mostly similar. However, there maybe differences in the *rent level* each property commands, which persist through time. Differences in performance through time are due to changes in macroeconomic forces, which influence a metropolitan area's economy and affect all locations/properties similarly. Differences in performance across properties and locations *at the same point* in time (referred to as "cross-sectional differences") are due to differences in locational/property characteristics (amenity levels and/or constraints).

Changes in rent differences across projects/locations within the same market can occur due to changes in amenity/constraint differentials or changes in the way such differentials are valued. For example, it is argued that dispersion of economic activity in the suburbs, induced by advances in information and communication technologies, is narrowing locational differentials in office space rents, as the value of locational proximity has declined (Sivitanidou, 1997).

The conclusion of this section is that powerful macroeconomic and location/property-specific factors jointly shape the performance of a specific property. The primary objective of the sections that follow is to help the reader get a better grasp of the changes in macroeconomic, location, and property-specific factors that can *trigger value increases*. Such understanding will be instrumental in sharpening one's ability to identify circumstances and properties that allow for significant real estate profits.

IMPORTANT DIMENSIONS OF PROPERTY INVESTMENTS TARGETING HIGH RETURNS: TIMING, PROPERTY TYPE, AND LOCATION

Based on the discussion in this chapter, we can detect three major elements, which need to be incorporated in strategies aiming at achieving high real estate investment returns:

1) *Favorable timing*, to take advantage of global, macroeconomic, regional and metro-wide forces that are expected to exert strong positive influences on local markets and boost property incomes and values

2) *Property types* that will benefit from anticipated positive macroeconomic trends and potential shifts of household and firm demand

3) *Locations* that will capitalize the benefits of expected macroeconomic developments and economic growth by attracting the additional space demands of firms and households, as well as shifting demand patterns due to income increases. In the case of national investors, the location choice incorporates two basic dimensions, which are consistent with the macro and micro nature of forces that influence property performance:

    1) Selection of market/metropolitan area
    2) Selection of sub-market/community within a given market

All three dimensions are important, and if combined so that each dimension contributes in its own way to property-value increases, their combined effect on property values and the investor's return will be quite strong.

BROADER CATEGORIES OF PROPERTIES WITH BIG PROFIT POTENTIAL

Based on the discussion so far, we can distinguish two broad categories and four sub-categories of properties with significant profit potential (see Figure 3):

Figure 3 – Categories of Properties with Big Profit Potential

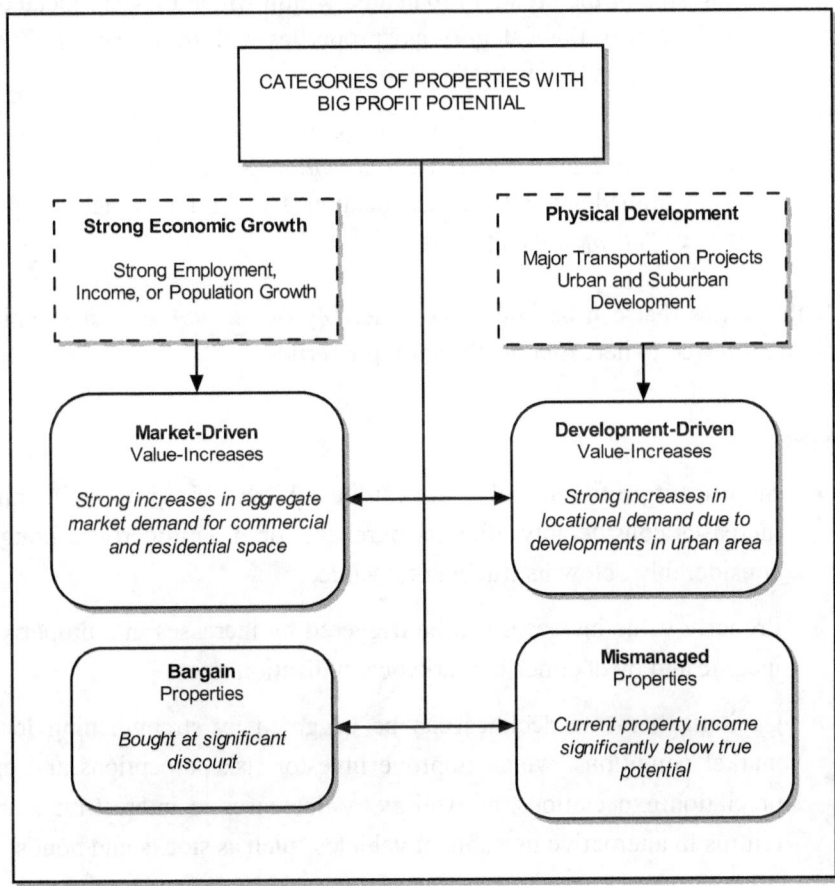

A) Properties with *prospects for robust property-income and value increases*, which can be classified in three sub-categories:

    A.1. Properties about to experience significant rental income and/or value increases due to *strong economic growth* of the metropolitan market within which they are located, or other favorable changes in broader macroeconomic forces. I will refer to this category as "properties with *market-driven* value-increase potential".

    A.2. Properties about to experience strong rental income and/or value increases due to *significant improvements in their locational ad-*

15

vantages as a result of significant developments in their surrounding area or the broader urban area within which they are located. I will refer to this category as "properties with *development-driven* value-increase potential".

- A.3. Properties that, due to mismanagement, are currently earning an *income well below their true potential*, given the advantages of their immediate and broader location. I will refer to these properties as "*mismanaged* properties".

B) Properties that can be bought considerably *below market value*, which are referred to hereafter as "*bargain* properties".

SUMMARY

- ➢ Significant profits in real estate can be achieved if a property's value increases considerably after its purchase, or if a property is bought considerably below its true market value.
- ➢ Property value increases can be triggered by increases in a property's income and by declines in market capitalization rates.
- ➢ Capitalization-rate declines can be triggered by strengthening local market conditions, which improve investor risk perceptions and appreciation expectations, as well as by decreases in interest rates and returns in alternative investment vehicles, such as stocks and bonds.
- ➢ Property-income increases can be triggered by macroeconomic factors, which influence the demand and supply for all property types or a specific property type, and by microeconomic and location-specific forces.
- ➢ The three crucial components of real estate investment decisions targeting high returns include appropriate timing, property type, and location. These need to be chosen in a way that will maximize the investor's benefit from macroeconomic and locational forces expected to significantly boost property income and values.
- ➢ Properties with big profit potential can be classified into four broad categories depending on the source of the expected value growth: 1) properties with market-driven value-increase potential, 2) properties

with development-driven value-increase potential, 3) mismanaged properties, and 4) bargain properties.

Chapter 2

Achieving High Returns by Riding the Real Estate Cycle

Real estate investors can use an important attribute of real estate market behavior to maximize their returns and profits. As it will be seen in the discussion that follows, timing the movements of rents and prices in real estate markets may be less difficult and, perhaps, less risky compared to stock and bond markets. Due to the rigidities regulating the behavior of the real estate market, and the (by nature) slow response of property supply to favorable and unfavorable economic shocks, property rents and values move mostly in a slow and smooth fashion, as opposed to the irregular and unpredictable movements of stocks and bond prices.

The Real Estate Cycle and its Double-Positive Impact on Values

It has been shown empirically (Wheaton, 1987) that the office space market is characterized by cyclical movements with long periodicity due to a number of idiosyncrasies. These idiosyncrasies include the sluggishness of the supply response (that is, the construction of new buildings) to changes in demand and prices, as well as the slow adjustments of market rents/prices and demand, due to long-term rental contracts, which prevent tenants from changing their consumption of space when market conditions change. As Figure 4 shows, the periodicity of a cycle is the time it takes to move from peak to peak, while amplitude is the difference between the price/rent level at the peak of the cycle and the price/rent level at the trough of the cycle.

Having in mind how market capitalization rates move (see Chapter 1), and looking at real estate cycles from the perspective of value increases, it appears that property values and sales prices get a *double boost* as the market moves from trough to peak. As the market improves, occupancy, rental income, and property income increase (see Figure 5). Increasing property income, in turn, exerts upward pressures on property values. Improved occupancy and rising rents reduce risk in the eyes of investors and reinforce expectations for continuing market improvements. These perceptions exert downward pressures on market capitalization rates, which start to decrease, pushing values further up. Thus, when the market reaches a peak, property income climbs to its highest level, while capitalization rates drop to their lowest level. Within this context, property values get a double boost when the market is strong, and a double hit when the market is soft (see Figure 4).

Figure 4 – The Real Estate Cycle and Capitalization Rates

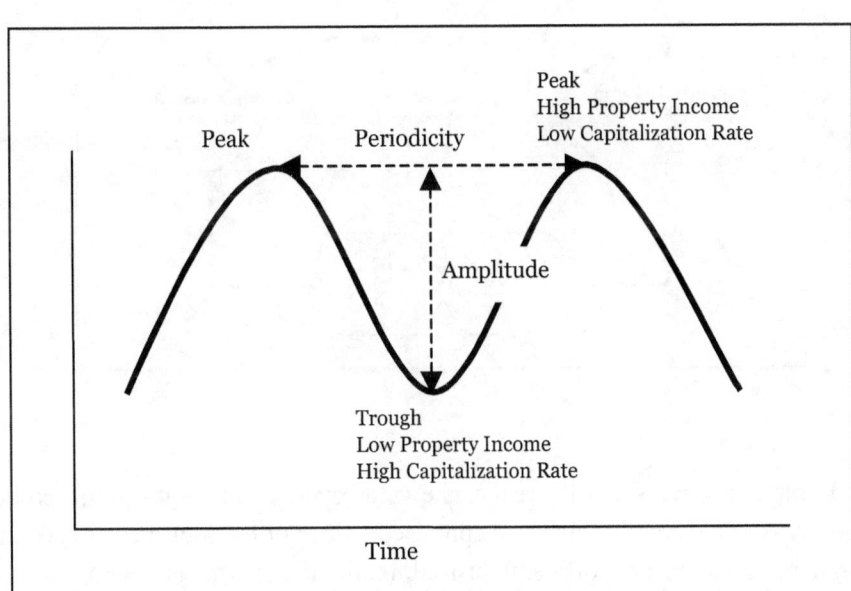

ACHIEVING HIGH RETURNS BY RIDING THE REAL ESTATE CYCLE

Based on the simplistic representation of the real estate cycle in Figure 4, it seems that real estate investors who buy at the bottom of the market and sell at the top can achieve high investment returns. In the discussion that follows, I will refer to this strategy as the *BBST* (buy at bottom, sell at top) strategy. Understanding the property value cycle can help real estate investors devise strategies to take advantage of the cyclical behavior of real estate markets and maximize their profits.

Figure 5 – Values Get Double Boost from Improving Market Fundamentals

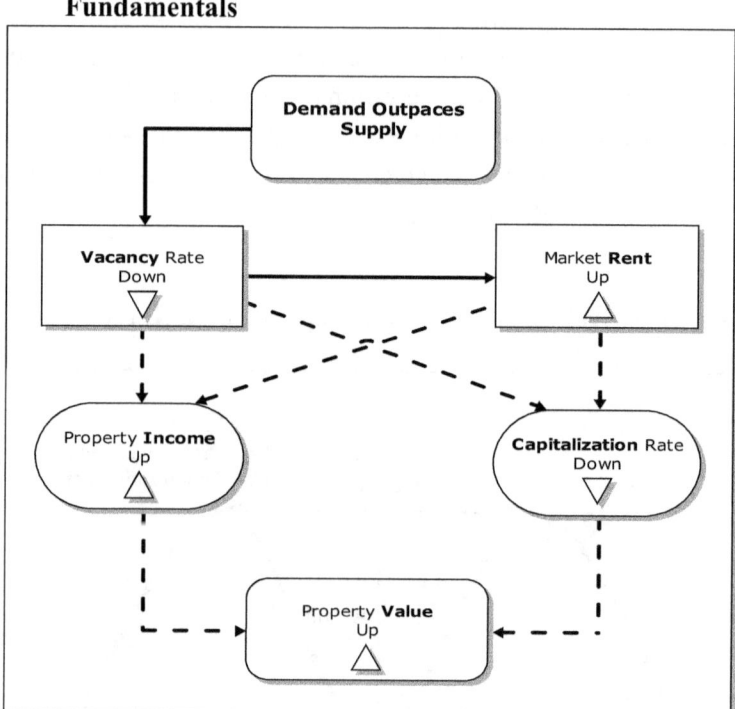

In order to understand the real estate value cycle and how it differs across property types, we will review the appraised values of the four major types of commercial real estate—office, industrial, retail, and apartments, with a focus on the pattern of movements and the types of strategies that can earn the highest return for property investors.

Figure 6 contrasts historical value indices for four property types over the period 1978-2004 (apartment data start from 1984), as reflected in NCREIF's data on appraised property values.[5] These indices, which have 1978 as base year (100), except apartments, reflect historical trends in average values for each property type. This means that some individual properties within each property type must have registered value increases even greater than the averages portrayed in the graph. With these in mind, we can draw the following conclusions:

Figure 6 – The Value Cycle for Four Property Types

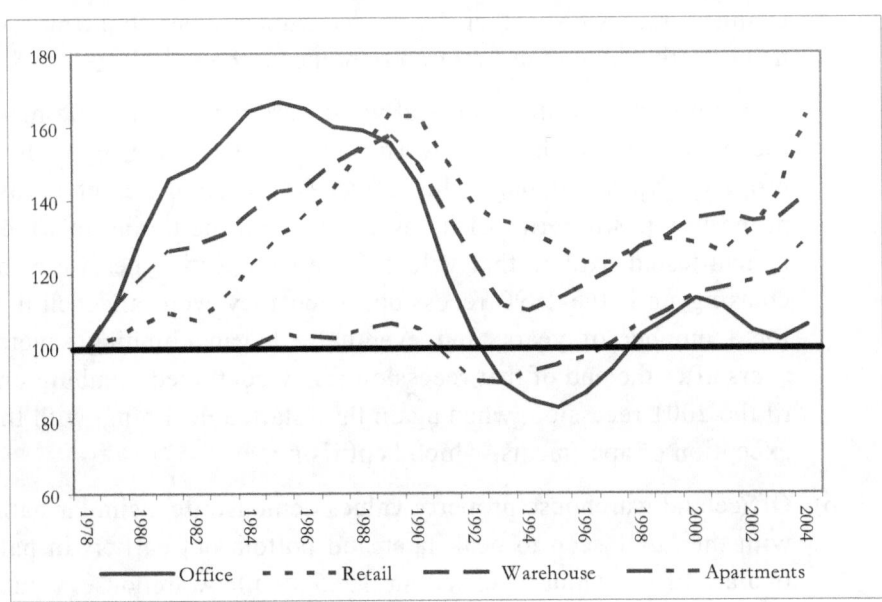

Source: NCREIF

a) All property types, except apartments, indicate some cyclical behavior, with common characteristic the acceleration of property value declines after 1990, which marked the start of the national recession. Office property value declines seem to have started earlier (since 1986), but rapidly accelerated in 1990 and thereafter. Furthermore, property values for all types continued declining for some years, and then turned upwards sometime be-

---

[5] Although NCREIF values are based on appraisals and not transactions, they should still reflect reasonably accurately trends in transaction prices. Empirical studies have found a very strong correlation between movements in appraised values and movements in transaction prices.

tween 1994 and 1997. The 2001 recession triggered another cycle of value declines in three of the four property types, but these declines were considerably smaller than those triggered by the 1990 recession.

The effect of the 2001 recession was considerably less damaging for property values because of the very low interest rates, which pushed capitalization rates down, thus mitigating property value losses due to decreases in rental income. Retail and apartment property values were the least affected by this recession because it was a business recession, rather than a consumer recession; employment declined, but consumption remained strong.

The similarities in the historical value patterns indicate that macroeconomic forces had a powerful and similar effect on all four property types, although this effect has been different across property types in terms of its magnitude and the timing in which it manifested. Notice that values for all property types were increasing until the 1990 recession. Then they were all declining for a number of years, and eventually began climbing several years after the end of that recession. They continued climbing until the 2001 recession, when again they started declining, with the exception of apartments, which kept rising.

b) Office and warehouse property values demonstrate a similar path, with the latter seen to peak later and bottom out earlier. In particular, office values peaked in 1985, while warehouse values peaked in 1989. Office values bottomed out in 1995, while warehouse values bottomed out in 1994.

c) The office property value cycle registered the largest fluctuations, rising almost 70% (somewhat higher than the increases registered by retail and warehouse properties) over the period 1978-1985 and then dropping 50% over the period 1985-1995.

d) Retail property values declined the least, about 25% from peak to bottom. It should be noted though that the value pattern presented in Figure 6 is the composite of the four major retail development formats—neighborhood, community, regional, and super-regional centers. As it will be shown later, this pattern seems similar to the value pattern of super-regional centers. This is understandable since super-regional centers represent considerably larger developments in scale and value compared to the other four formats included in the NCREIF total retail index. During the first quarter of 2005, super-regional centers accounted for 35% of the value of all retail properties in the index.

e) Average apartment values took a quite smaller hit during the 1990 recession, compared to the other property types.[6] Moreover, in contrast to the other three property types, the 2001 recession did not trigger any decrease in values or further cyclical fluctuations. As a result, apartment values stayed on a climbing path for 11 years in a row (1994-2004). The resilience of apartment values during the 2001 recession is most likely due to very low interest rates and the significant drop in apartment capitalization rates. Although low interest rates and capitalization rates influenced positively the values of the other three property types as well (as indicated by their small cyclical fluctuation during the 2001 recession), the effect on apartments was stronger due, perhaps, to the smaller percentage of NOI accounted for by capital expenditures (see Box 1 for a discussion of how lower capital expenditures are linked to capitalization rates and prices).

The overall conclusion from Figure 6 is that the real estate cycle does exist, and that it applies to office, retail, and warehouse properties, but it is not clear whether it applies to apartments. Office property values seem to have registered a considerably deeper downturn than the other property types, but at the same time, the up cycle gave investors opportunities for higher rates of return and bigger profits. In general, the value behavior of all property types over the period 1978-2004 shows that national economic recessions trigger value declines as real estate demand decreases, but economic growth leads eventually to trend reversal and value growth. These common influences from macroeconomic forces seem to have affected value patterns in all property types similarly in terms of direction (with the exception of apartments) but differently in terms of the exact timing and magnitude of the effect.

---

[6] Historical data on apartment values starts from 1984, and not from 1978, as is the case for the other three property types because of the lack of sufficient data.

BOX 1 – NOI, CAPITAL EXPENDITURES, AND VALUE

As indicated earlier, the income return is usually calculated as the ratio of the NOI of a property over its value. The cash flow, however, that eventually goes into the owner's pocket, is what is left after capital expenditures are deducted from NOI. Capital expenditures refer mostly to improvements landlords need to undertake when a new tenant enters the building. The ratio of cash flow over property value is referred to as *yield* and represents the true income return of the property. So, the smaller the capital expenditure of a property as percent of NOI is, the higher the yield the investors earn.

To understand what this has to do with property values, remember that the ratio of NOI over value represents the capitalization rate. Furthermore, consider the example of an office building and an apartment building that are bought at the same NOI/value ratio (capitalization rate). If the apartment building has lower capital expenditure as a percentage of NOI, it should provide a higher yield than the office building. Let's see an example with numbers, taking into account that, according to the NCREIF data as of the first quarter of 2005, the average capital expenditure for apartments is 18% of NOI and for office space 34% of NOI. Let's consider an office building and an apartment building, both producing an annual NOI of 100,000 and bought at an 8% capitalization rate:

Annual NOI = $100,000

Purchase price for each building = $100,000 / 0.08 = $1,250,000

Cash flow for Apartment Building = (100%-18%) x $100,000 = $82,000

Cash flow for Office Building = (100%-34%) *100,000 = $66,000

Yield for Apartment Building = $82,000 /$1,250,000 = **6.6%**

Yield for Office Building = $66,000 /$1,250,000 = **5.3%**

Price at which Apartment would provide
 same yield as Office = $82,000/5.3% = $1,547,170

Implied capitalization rate for Apartment price
 that provides same yield as the Office building = 100,000/1,547,170 = **6,4%**

As the example shows, the apartment building could be bought at a 6.4% capitalization rate and still allow the same yield as the office building. This provides an explanation as to why apartment capitalization rates dropped more than capitalization rates in other property types, holding values on an upward path, despite the ongoing economic downturn.

Office, warehouse, and retail properties have considerably higher capital expenditures as percent of NOI, due to costly tenant improvements that landlords undertake when a new tenant enters the building.

One important observation is that appraised values follow a *smooth* pattern of multi-year upward and downward movements without irregular fluctuations (especially in the case of office and warehouse properties). However, as Geltner (1991), has pointed out, this is the result of the smoothing bias introduced by appraisers, who tend to adjust values slowly and with some time lag relative to actual market price changes.

Geltner's argument implies that the time path of actual market values is less smooth than the patterns of appraised values reviewed in this chapter. Although there is little doubt about this, it should be noted that several transaction rent indices based on signed lease contracts suggest that market rents move quite smoothly. Furthermore, data suggest that the other major determinant of property values, the capitalization rate, moves also smoothly. Since the two major determinants of real estate market values move smoothly, it is only logical to assume that real estate market values should also have a relatively smooth pattern.

OFFICE PROPERTY VALUE DYNAMICS

Having established that there are indeed cycles, at least in terms of appraised values, we turn our attention to the kind of returns BBST strategies provide and to the question of whether there are alternative strategies that can provide higher returns and profits to real estate investors. Examining the property value patterns registered by the four property types from this perspective yields an interesting and not-so-obvious conclusion.

As Figure 7 indicates, from 1978 until 2004, office property values registered two cycles, with the first significantly larger in amplitude and periodicity than the second. The long duration and large amplitude of the first cycle was due to the large flows of capital to real estate from institutional investors, who not only inflated significantly office property values until 1986, but also were reluctant to exit the market when the national office vacancy rate shot to the high teens, weakening the fundamentals of the office space market.

Figure 7 – The Office Property Value Cycle

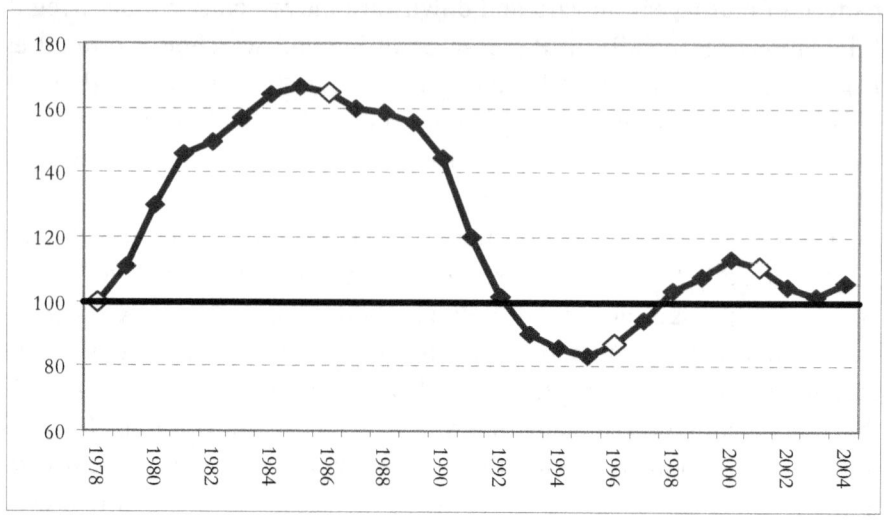

Source: NCREIF

During 1978-2004, office property values peaked twice, in 1985, and 15 years later, in 2000. This pattern would have allowed real estate investors to apply the BBST strategy twice. In applying a BBST strategy, there is an issue: how does one identify when the market is at the bottom or at a peak? Since both a bottom and a peak are, by definition, turning points, and no investor can know for sure in advance when there will be a trend reversal, such points can be identified with certainty only after the facts. Thus, the bottom can be identified only after values turn up after a series of declines; the peak can be identified only after values turn down after a series of increases.

Within this context, I am assuming that an investor applying the BBST strategy enters the market in the year during which values register their first increase after a period of declines. Since the data starts in 1978 and traces a long upward leg of the first cycle, I will use that year as the first entry point in applying the buy-at-the-bottom principle. The exit point of this strategy would be 1986, when values registered their first decline after seven years of increases. This first decline would serve as a sign that the peak had been reached. Based on this rationale, investors applying the BBST strategy would enter again in 1996 and exit in 2001.

The NCREIF data on values and income indicate that these strategies would yield quite high returns for investors. In particular, the 1978-1986 strategy would earn investors an annual return of **15.4%**, while the 1996-2001 strategy would earn an annual return of **14.5%**. These are very good returns, but are they the highest obtainable? Could a different strategy provide higher returns?

Taking into account that return is generally higher when appreciation gains (increases in value) are received sooner than later, it is likely that a short-term hold strategy, such as three years, may yield higher returns for investors, in the case BBST strategies dictate holding the property for many years. Furthermore, the three-year hold is supported by the way property values increase after bottoming out. For example, the historical data on value increases for both office and warehouse properties show that values increase at an *accelerating rate in the first 2-4 years* after bottoming out. After that, value-growth slows down. This behavior is understandable and probably unavoidable, due to the synergy of two powerful forces at that particular point of the economic and real estate cycle:

a) First, the economy, and demand for commercial real estate, *grows the fastest* when it comes out of the recession

b) Second, real estate supply coming out of the down cycle *does not have much steam* and can only react slowly to such rapid increases in demand due to the development/construction lag

Within this context, a "buy at bottom, sell soon" strategy, or *BBSS* strategy, may provide even higher returns than BBST strategies with long holding periods. Another advantage of this strategy is that it allows the investor to sell the property while values are *still rising* and eliminates the need to include one year of declining values in the holding period to verify that the top has been reached.

Application of the BBSS strategy in the case of the office property value cycle indicates that it is clearly more profitable than the BBST strategy. In particular, an investor who bought an office asset in 1978 and sold it in 1991 made a **22.2%** annual return, which is far higher than the 15.4% return produced by the BBST strategy with same year of entry! Similarly, an investor who bought an office asset in 1996 and sold it in 1999 made a **16.9%** return, which is clearly higher than the 14.5% return produced by the BBST strategy with the same year of entry.

Having big profits in mind, it is important to emphasize that the levels of returns just mentioned represent the average of the performances of all office properties included in the NCREIF database. This means some properties provided returns even higher than these averages. What kind of properties performed better than average? Office properties located at the most desirable and supply-constrained markets and submarkets are likely the ones that performed the best.

If property values continue to behave as they have in the past, these results indicate that office investors can earn high returns by applying BBST strategies. Furthermore, BBSS strategies may provide even higher returns to commercial real estate investors. These results are consistent with the argument I often repeat in this book—the greater value increases should occur in the first 2-3 years after a demand shock occurs, due to the construction lag and the delayed response of supply.

These conclusions are based on the behavior that office property values registered over the period 1978-2004. The future behavior of office property values could be different because of changing forces that may render the office market more efficient and less cyclical, with smoother downturns and upturns. Some analysts argue that after the real estate crash of the 1990s, financing for commercial real estate is more restrained, contributing to more balanced responses of supply to demand increases, and, therefore, to a less cyclical market. Furthermore, it is argued that the increasing role of real estate investment trusts (REITs) and public markets has contributed to a more efficient and smoothly operating real estate market. Although the quite smaller cyclical fluctuation of office property values during their second cycle (1995-2003) may be an indication of such a smoother behavior, my opinion is that such behavior was mostly due to the coincidence of record-low interest rates, which pushed down cap rates, rather than the market becoming less cyclical.

WAREHOUSE PROPERTY VALUE DYNAMICS

The industrial component of the NCREIF index includes different types of industrial space, such as flex, R&D, warehouse, and others. I am focusing on the warehouse index because warehouse and distribution (W&D) buildings are the popular investment vehicles in the industrial market for institutional investors. As Figure 8 demonstrates, W&D property values have registered clear cyclical movements during 1978-2004. It is interesting to note the 11-year, uninterrupted climb of warehouse property values during 1978-1989. During that period values increased by almost 60%. It is also interesting to note the very small negative effect of the 2001 recession, which hardly qualifies as a downturn.

Figure 8 – The Warehouse Property Value Cycle

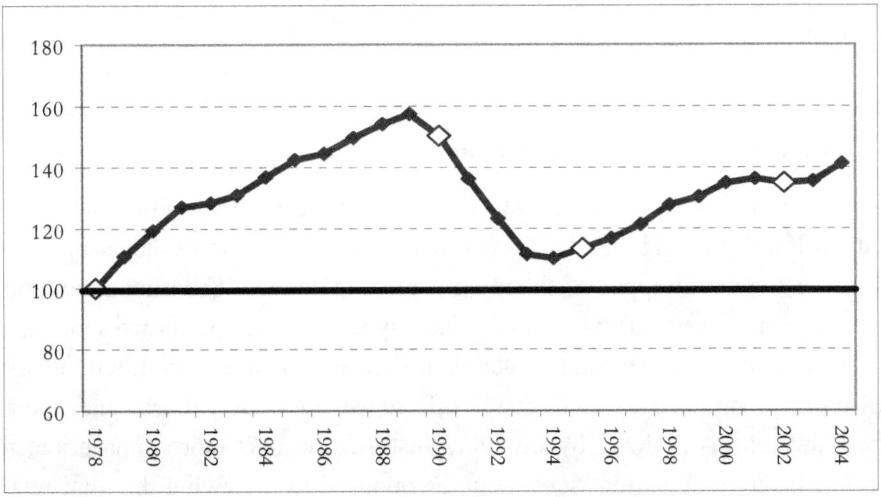

Source: NCREIF

As was the case for office properties, the warehouse value cycle allows the application of a BBST strategy twice. Following the rationale developed in the case of office properties, an investor could first apply this strategy by buying a warehouse property in 1978 and selling it in 1990, when the first decline in warehouse values would signal that the peak had been reached. Investors could apply this strategy for a second time by buying a warehouse asset in 1995, just after values bottomed out, and selling it in 2002, just after warehouse values peaked. Investors that applied this strategy over the period 1978-1990 earned a **12.6%** annual return. That's not bad at all, if it is taken into account that the investment was held for eleven years. Usually, the longer the holding period, the smaller the annual return (all else being equal). Investors who applied the BBST strategy over the period 1995-2002 earned an annual return of **12.2%**, which is definitely attractive.

Evaluation of the performance of the BBSS strategy in the warehouse value cycle reveals its superiority in terms of providing higher returns than the BBST strategy, reinforcing the conclusion reached in the case of office properties. For example, investors who applied the BBSS strategy by buying a warehouse asset in 1978 and selling it in 1981 made an annual return of **17.5%** (compared to the **12.7%** achieved with the BBST strategy with the same entry year). Investors who bought a warehouse property in 1978 and sold it in 1981 made an annual return of **13.8%** (compared to the **12.2%** return achieved by the BBST strategy with the same entry year).

RETAIL PROPERTY VALUE DYNAMICS

As we will discuss later, retail developments can be classified in several categories, depending on size, format, tenant mix, and the area they serve. The four most common types of shopping centers include neighborhood, community, regional, and super-regional. Each type of retail performs somewhat differently, although strong broader economic and income growth will benefit all types in similar ways. Given the differences in value patterns and, therefore, the returns realized by investors historically, it is more appropriate to review each value pattern separately, as opposed to reviewing the total retail index.

The path of property values for neighborhood shopping centers seems to have been smoother than the office and warehouse value cycles, with fluctuations from peak to trough and trough to peak ranging between 20% and 30% (see Figure 9). With the exception of a few one-year irregularities, this pattern consists of three multi-year parts—two increasing and one decreasing. The first long climb of retail property values (putting aside two minimal down steps in 1982 and 1987) started in 1978 and ended in 1988, followed by a downward movement that lasted from 1989 until 1996. From 1997 to 2004, neighborhood centers embarked on an uninterrupted ascent that pushed values up by more than 30%.

Figure 9. The Value Cycle for Neighborhood Shopping Centers

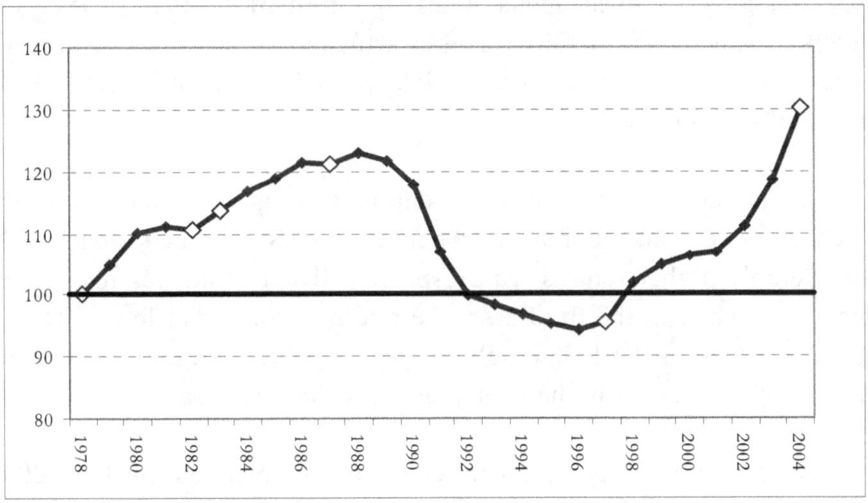

Source: NCREIF

Applying a BBST strategy to the neighborhood-center value pattern is somewhat problematic, particularly in 1982, when only a one-year decline was registered. According to our rule, this decline, which was preceded by a series of value increases over the period 1978-1981, should trigger the exit of an investor applying a BBST strategy. However, the sharp increase in values in the next year (1983) should trigger the beginning of another BBST strategy. Thus, this pattern would lead an investor to exit the market in one year and reenter in the next.

Following the rules used to apply the BBST strategy to office and warehouse, the neighborhood center value pattern allows for the application of such a strategy three times. The first application would involve buying a retail asset in 1978 and selling it in 1982; the second application would involve buying a retail asset in 1983 and selling it in 1987; and the third application would involve an acquisition of a retail property in 1997 and a resale in 2004. The 1997-2004 hold does not represent a strict application of the rules used so far in applying the BBST strategy since by 2004, neighborhood center values did not turn down. However, it will be very interesting to see what kind of return an investor would have earned after such a multi-year climb in values. Estimation of the rate of return for the three strategies indicates that investors who applied these entry-exit strategies achieved annual rates of return of **12.2%**, **10.1%**, and **13.8%**, respectively. BBSS strategies with the same year of entry and three-year holding periods would yield annual returns of **13.2%**, **11%** and **13.4%**, respectively.

It is interesting to note that, in contrast to what we discovered in the case of office and warehouse properties, BBSS strategies don't yield considerably higher returns than respective BBST strategies in the first two cases, while in the third case, the return is somewhat lower. This is because values in the BBST holding period, which is quite longer than three years, rise faster in the later years than the early years.

The path of property values for community centers during 1979-2004 was similar to that of neighborhood centers, with values practically rising for a decade (1979-1989), then declining for seven years (1990-1996), and then going back to a mostly upward trend (with the exception of 2000 and 2001), with values almost returning to their 1989 peak level in 2004 (see Figure 10). Ignoring the short fluctuation in values between 1979 and 1982, the first BBST strategy could be applied by buying a community shopping center in 1983, when values registered a strong increase after a slight decline in 1982, and liquidating in 1990, just after the peak was reached.

The second BBST strategy could be applied by buying in 1997 and selling in 2000, when a slight decline was registered. One could argue that this is not really a BBST strategy, since selling in 2000 does not seem to be selling at the top, but at the middle of the upward leg of the cycle, as additional sharp increases took place after 2000. Such an argument is valid only because we are looking at this pattern ex-post (that is, after the facts), but practically, an investor facing value declines in 2000 would have no way of knowing that these value declines would not continue and that strong gains would follow very soon. Of course, investors could take advantage of the sharp value increases between 2002 and 2004 by entering in 2002, when the first sharp increase occurred after the two-year period of value stagnation.

Figure 10 – The Value Cycle for Community Shopping Centers

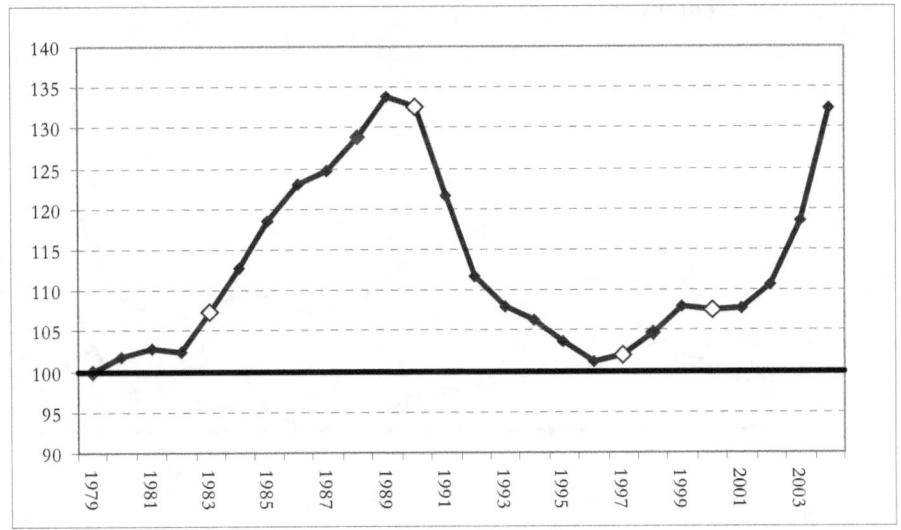

Source: NCREIF

The two BBST strategies just described would provide annual returns of **11.2%** and **11.3%** respectively, while a 1983 community center acquisition with a three-year hold would provide an annual return of **13.2%**, 200 basis points higher than the respective BBST strategy with the same year of entry. The second application of the BBST strategy, which has a three-year holding period, also qualifies as a BBSS strategy.

Property values for super-regional and regional shopping centers moved similarly, with the former *rising much faster* than the latter between 1983 and 1989. After 1989, however, values for these two types of shopping centers moved on a parallel path (see Figure 11), registering a long decline until 1997, and then a short cyclical fluctuation, followed by a sharp rise during 2002-2004. This value pattern would allow investors to apply the BBST strategy just once. A second BBST strategy could start in 2002 for both types, but the exit year can not be identified since values kept rising until 2004.

Figure 11 – The Value Cycle for Regional and Super-Regional Shopping Centers

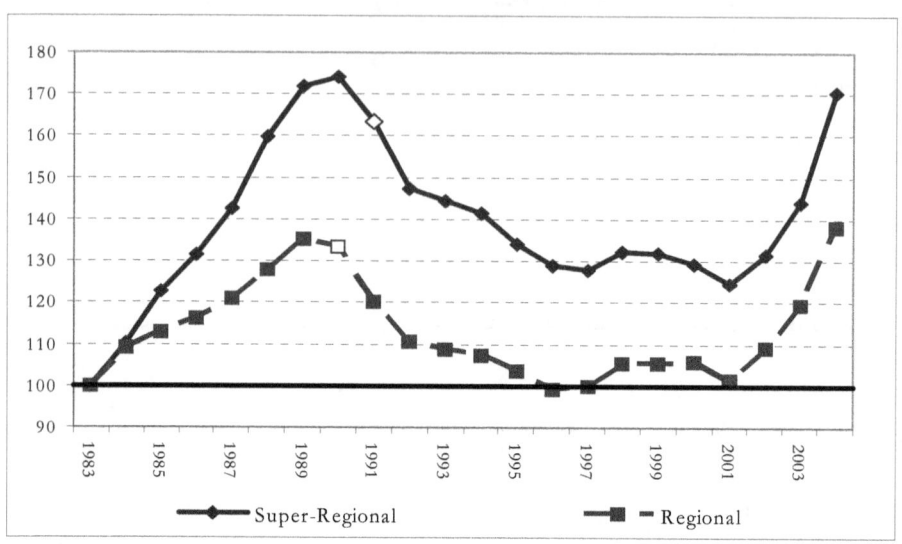

Source: NCREIF

In the case of super-regional centers, the BBST strategy could be applied by buying in 1983 and selling in 1991, while in the case of regional centers, it could be applied by buying in 1983 and selling in 1990. These timing strategies would provide real estate investors with annual returns of **14.5%**, in the case of super-regional centers, and **11.5%** in the case of regional centers. Respective BBSS strategies would again prove more profitable, providing annual returns of **18.3%** in the case of super-regional centers and **13%** in the case of regional centers.

APARTMENT VALUE DYNAMICS

Although value patterns for office, warehouse, and retail have shown an undeniably cyclical behavior, apartment values haven't presented a clear-cut case of cyclical movements over the period 1984-2004 (Figure 12).[7] In particular, apartment values followed a slightly fluctuating pattern between 1984 and 1989, with mostly an upward trend, but not clearly tracing the upward leg

---

[7] Sufficient historical data for apartments is available only from 1984.

of a cyclical movement. In 1990, as the recession hit, apartment values turned down and stayed on this path until 1992, tracing a smooth, downward cyclical movement. After remaining flat in 1993, apartment values started rising and continued climbing until 2004, marking, perhaps, the upward leg of a long up cycle. Looking forward, from a high-return perspective, the question is whether this up cycle will end any time soon.

Figure 12 – The Apartment Value Cycle

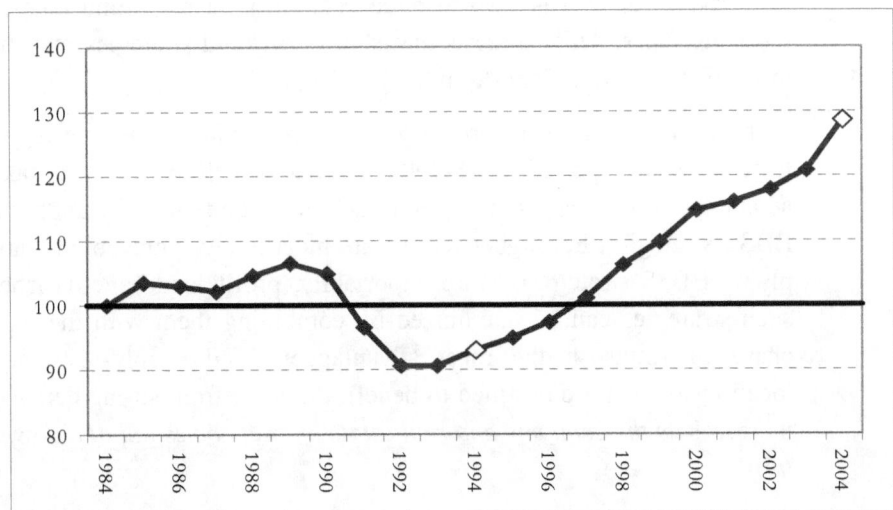

Source: NCREIF

The historical pattern of apartment values does not allow the full application of a BBST strategy because a point of investment entry can be identified (1994, when apartment values started rising after the end of the down cycle), but the exit point cannot be identified, since values kept rising until 2004 when available data ends. Although we don't know whether 2004 represents the top of the cycle, for the sake of assessing the profitability of this strategy we will assume that the property is sold during that year. Such a strategy would provide the investor with an annual return of **11.7%**, which is quite good if we consider that the holding period of this strategy is 10 years. A three-year hold, starting in 1994 would provide the investor with an annual return of **12.5%**.

SUMMARY

- Office, warehouse, and retail property values have exhibited a clearly cyclical behavior over the period 1978-2004, while apartment values have not yet registered a clear cyclical pattern. Whether the long ascent of apartment values (between 1994 and 2004) is shaping the upward leg of a clear cyclical movement is yet to be seen.

- When property values start rising, just after they bottom out, they keep rising for at least two to three years at an accelerating rate, in most instances. This suggests that short-term hold strategies may be more profitable than long-term hold strategies.

- If the future behavior of property values is similar to the one registered over the period 1978-2004, investors will be able to take advantage of the real estate cycle to achieve high returns by applying BBST strategies, but higher returns are most likely achievable by applying BBSS strategies. More importantly, profits and benefits from such strategies can be maximized by combining them with the purchase of assets at the most advantageous and supply-restrained locations, which are destined to benefit the most from strong demand increases *as the economy and real estate market comes out of a downturn.*

- Application of BBST strategies in the past would have provided investors with double-digit annual returns ranging between **13%** and **15%**, in the case of office buildings and super-regional shopping centers, and between **11%** and **13%**, in the case of warehouse buildings, apartments, and neighborhood and community shopping centers.

- Application of BBSS strategies would have produced even better results. In the case of office and warehouse properties, as well as super-regional centers, such strategies would have achieved considerably higher annual returns, ranging between **15%** and **20%**. In the case of neighborhood and community centers, the superiority of BBSS strategies over BBST strategies is not consistent; in the case of apartments, it is small.

- Cyclical movements triggered by the most recent recession were shorter, indicating, perhaps, that the real estate market is becoming more efficient and less cyclical. It is quite likely, however, that the mild impact of the 2001 recession on property values was due primarily to the very low interest rates prevailing during that period, rather than a reduction of the inherent cyclicality of the real estate market.

- The shortening of real estate cycles, especially its climbing phase, if indeed such is happening, is another reason why BBSS strategies should be preferred over BBST strategies.
- Understanding what stage of the real estate cycle the market is at can provide important clues with respect to the potential of significant value gains ahead.

CHAPTER 3

BORROWING CAN HELP INVESTORS ATTAIN HIGH RETURNS

Borrowing is of great importance for investors aggressively pursuing high returns and big profits. Borrowing funds to finance real estate investments is a common practice because of the benefits that such a strategy can provide to investors. First, borrowing can reduce significantly capital requirements for purchasing a property, allowing many cash-constrained investors to become active in the real estate marketplace. Actually, there are financing techniques that allow investors to acquire properties without using their own money. Second, under certain circumstances, borrowing can increase the investor's rate of return dramatically. Borrowing to finance the purchase or development of real estate, however, is not without risks. This risk becomes even greater when adjustable-rate financing is used.

FINANCING THE PURCHASE OR DEVELOPMENT OF REAL ESTATE WITH BORROWED FUNDS

Using borrowed funds (debt) to finance the purchase of a property or a development project can significantly increase the rate of return of an investment under certain conditions. Using debt to finance a real estate investment is referred to as *leverage*. By default, a real estate investment that does not involve the use of borrowed funds is referred to as *unleveraged*.

Wurtzebach and Miles (1994) indicate that the use of debt will increase the return of a real estate investment if the *mortgage constant*, which reflects the cost of financing in percentage terms, is *smaller than the unleveraged return offered by the investment*. Otherwise, leverage will have a negative effect. The mortgage constant applies to fixed-rate loans and represents the percentage of the original amount borrowed by the investor that needs to be paid periodically in order to completely repay the principal (the original loan amount) and interest over the term of the loan. The formula for calculating the mortgage constant for a fixed-rate loan is:

$$\text{Mortg. Const.} = \frac{\text{Interest Rate}}{1 - [1/(1+\text{Interest Rate})^n]} \quad (3)$$

The term *interest rate* refers to the loan rate, and *n* refers to the term of the loan in number of periods. For example, if one wants to estimate the monthly mortgage constant, *n* would represent the term of the loan in months. Depending on the type of period, the mortgage constant can reflect the monthly, quarterly, or annual percentage of the loan that needs to be paid during each period. Notice that the mortgage constant has nothing to do with the amount of the loan, just the rate. For example, for a loan at an interest rate of 6% and term of 20 years, the annual mortgage constant would be:

$$\text{Mortg. Const} = \frac{6\%}{1-[1/(1.06)^{20}]} = 8.72\% \quad (4)$$

The second element needed in order to evaluate whether leverage will enhance returns is the *unleveraged return* expected from the investment. This is calculated as the ratio of NOI over the purchase price, or total investment cost in the case of development:

$$\text{Unleveraged Return} = \frac{\text{NOI}}{\text{Purchase Price}} \quad (5)$$

Consider, for example, that you purchase an apartment with an annual NOI of $30,000 for $300,000. Enticed by the low mortgage rates, you want to examine whether a loan at an interest rate of 6% and term of 20 years, which as calculated above, has an annual mortgage constant of 8.72%, will have a positive or negative effect on the return of your investment. In order to answer your question, you first need to calculate the unleveraged return of the investment as:

$$\text{Unleveraged Return} = \frac{30{,}000}{300{,}000} = 10\%$$

The unleveraged return of the investment is 10%, which is higher than the mortgage constant, in this case 8.72%. This suggests that under the particular assumptions, with respect to the loan rate and the unleveraged return of the investment, borrowing will indeed help the investor achieve a higher return, assuming that NOI will not decrease during the holding period. Since we are focusing on properties with prospects for strong rent increases, the chances of decreasing NOI are, in theory, small.

The comparison of the unleveraged return and the mortgage constant can help the investor evaluate whether leverage will increase the rate of return of the investment, but not by how much. In order to evaluate how much, we need to calculate the investment's leveraged return, which takes into account the borrowed funds and the payment made periodically to service the debt (debt service). The one-period, leveraged income return of an investment can be calculated as follows:

$$\text{Leveraged Return} = \frac{\text{Before Tax Equity Cash Flow}}{\text{Investor's Equity}} \qquad (6)$$

$$\text{Leveraged Return} = \frac{\text{NOI} - \text{Debt Service}}{\text{Purchase Price} - \text{Loan Amount}} \qquad (7)$$

In order to demonstrate the effect of positive leverage on the return of a real estate investment, let's continue our example with the apartment that was purchased for $300,000, assuming that the investor financed 30% of the purchase price with a 20-year loan at a 6% fixed interest rate. The calculations are shown below:

Purchase Price = $300,000
NOI = $30,000
Loan Amount = $300,000 x 30% = $90,000
Investor's Equity = $300,000 - $90,000 = $210,000
Annual Debt Service = $90,000 x 8.72% = $7,848
Leveraged Before-Tax Equity Cash Flow = $30,000 - $7,848 = $22,152
Unleveraged Income Return = $30,000 ÷ $300,000 = 10%
Leveraged Income Return = $22,152 ÷ $210,000 = 10.5%

These calculations show that by financing 30% of the purchase price, the return on equity invested, which is the amount of the investor's own money used for carrying out the purchase, increased from 10% (the return of the investment without using any borrowed money) to 10.5%. This increase in this case is quite small. One major reason for this is that the investor financed only a small percentage of the purchase price with borrowed funds.

In general, when positive leverage is possible, that is, when the mortgage constant of the loan is smaller than the investment's unleveraged return, the greater the amount of the loan, the greater the increase in the investor's leveraged return (on a before-tax basis). To demonstrate this point, let us assume the investor finances 80% of the purchase price with borrowed funds. Because the loan amount will be a higher percentage of the value of the property, the interest rate will be higher, since the lender assumes a greater risk.[8] So let's assume the investor secures a 20-year fixed-rate loan at 6.5% to finance 80% of the purchase price. The annual mortgage constant for this loan is 9.08%, which should have a positive effect on the investor's return, since the unleveraged return is 10%. Let's see how much better the leveraged return is compared to the unleveraged return under these new assumptions:

Loan Amount = $300,000 x 80% = $240,000
Investor's Equity = $300,000 - $240,000 = $60,000

---

[8] The percentage of the purchase price or value of the property that is financed with borrowed funds is referred to as loan-to-value ratio (LTV).

Annual Debt Service = $240,000 x 9.08% = $21,792
Leveraged Before-Tax Equity Cash Flow = $30,000 - $21,792 = $8,208
Unleveraged Income Return = $30,000 ÷ $300,000 = 10%
Leveraged Income Return = $8,208 ÷ $60,000 = 13.7%

As these calculations demonstrate, by borrowing 80% of the purchase price, the investor's return increases considerably—from 10% to 13.7%. Notice that Formulas 6 and 7 refer to the *income* return, since it ignores any appreciation gains, that is, any increases in property value. To calculate the one-period *total return* on the investment, we need to add in Formula 6 any increase or decrease in price.

$$\text{Total Leveraged Return} = \frac{\text{NOI - Debt Service + Change in Value}}{\text{Purchase Price - Loan Amount}} \quad (8)$$

To see how this formula is applied, let's continue our example with the assumption that the property is worth 5% more one year after its purchase. In such a case, the calculations change as follows:

Appreciation = $300,000 x 5% = $15,000
Unleveraged Before-Tax Equity Cash Flow = $30,000 + $15,000 = $45,000
Leveraged Before-Tax Equity Cash Flow = $30,000 - $21,972 + $15,000 = $23,208
Unleveraged Total Return = $45,000 ÷ $300,000 = 15%
Leveraged Total Return = $23,208 ÷ $60,000 = 38.7%

This example demonstrates that, taking into account reasonable value gains, the use of leverage dramatically increases the investor's return and profits (in percentage terms). As these calculations show, the combination of positive leverage, the high percentage of borrowing relative to the purchase price, and a decent increase in value significantly improve the investor's return from 15% to 38.7%.

Notice that Formulas 6, 7, and 8 refer to the calculation of the *one-period* return. The calculation of the multi-period rate of return of an investment, which is referred to as internal rate of return (IRR), involves the use of a more complex mathematical formula, based on the *discounted cash-flow approach*.

The model and the mathematics involved in its application are out of the scope of this book, but it is discussed briefly in a footnote.[9] It suffices to say that the combination of positive leverage and increases in value contribute to equally impressive increases of the investor's return within a multi-period context as well. It should be emphasized, however, that, usually, the sooner the property-value gains are obtained, the greater the IRR. From a strategic point of view, this means that a property needs to be resold as soon as the investor has no reason to believe that significant value gains will be realized in the future.

FINANCING 100% OF THE INVESTMENT WITH BORROWED FUNDS

The example discussed in the previous section demonstrated that when there is positive leverage, the smaller the amount of the investor's money (equity) used to acquire the property, the more dramatic the investor's benefit in terms of total return (on a before-tax basis). The immediate question that comes to mind is whether the investor can finance 100% of the purchase with borrowed funds, thus using none of his/her own money. This can be done by using a second loan (second mortgage) to finance the down payment.

The investor can use the same property as collateral for the second loan, but in this case, the lender will require a considerably higher interest rate. In such a case, the use of borrowed funds may result in negative leverage, that is, losses as opposed to gains. Let's see how this strategy

---

[9] The discounted cash-flow approach estimates the periodic (annual, quarterly, etc.) total rate of return of a multi-period investment as the discount rate that equalizes the present value of future cash flows with the investor's total cost or purchase price. This rate of return is referred to as *internal rate of return* (IRR). Notice that the periodicity reflected by the estimated internal rate of return will depend on the periodicity of the cash flows used to calculate it. For example, if annual cash flows are used, the estimated IRR will reflect the annual rate of return of the investment; if quarterly cash flows are used, the estimated IRR will reflect the quarterly rate of return of the investment. Greer and Farrell (1993) point out that there are two problems with respect to the IRR calculation. The first involves the assumption that all cash flows received during the period the investment is held are reinvested at the same rate as the IRR. For example, if the estimated IRR for a real estate investment is 20%, this return estimate incorporates the assumption that all cash flows received during the holding period are re-invested with a return of 20% until the liquidation of the property. This assumption may be unrealistic, since it is difficult to find real-world investment opportunities with a 20% return. If the re-investment rate of cash flows received during the holding period is lower than the estimated IRR, the true rate of return will be lower. The second issue with respect to the IRR calculation is that it may give multiple solutions if the cash-flow stream includes not only positive but also negative cash flows.

may work in the example we have worked with so far. In particular, let's assume the remaining 20% of the purchase price, which otherwise would be paid by the investor's own money, is also financed through a second mortgage, with an interest rate of 12%. In such a case, the calculations will change as follows:

Purchase Price = $300,000
First Mortgage = $300,000 x 80% = $240,000
Second Mortgage = $300,000 - $240,000 = $60,000
Annual Debt Service for First Mortgage = $240,000 x 9.08% = $21,792
Mortgage Constant for Second Mortgage = 13.39%
Annual Debt Service for Both Loans = $21,792 + ($60,000 x 13.39%)
= $21,792 + $8,034 = $29,826
Leveraged Before-Tax Equity Cash Flow = $30,000 - $29,826 = $174

The above calculations demonstrate that the use of a second mortgage at a high rate leaves the owner with a miniscule positive net cash flow of $174, which does not provide any benefit to the owner for getting so heavily indebted. Furthermore, the borrower's risk increases exponentially since, at the event of even a minimal decline in property income, NOI will not be sufficient to cover the loan payment. Unless the investor can secure a second mortgage at a significantly lower rate, which is unlikely, the second mortgage makes the deal quite risky. Although the case presented is just an example, it reveals the typical problem with using a second mortgage on the property bought, which is the drain of NOI.

Although a second mortgage may not be the solution to financing 100% of the purchase price, it may be possible for an investor to use a second low-rate loan to finance the down payment by using as collateral another property, which is not burdened by any loan. Thus, the second loan is really a first, and not second, mortgage on another property, which allows the investor to borrow the money for the down payment at a low rate. For the simplification of calculations, assume that the down payment ($60,000) is 80% of the value of the second property used as collateral to secure the loan. This assumption will allow us to use the same interest rate for both loans in the calculations below. Let's see how the calculations change under these assumptions. I also assume that the investor uses $1,000 from his own money to be able to calculate the investment's leveraged return.

Purchase Price = $300,000
Borrowed Funds (Both Loans) = $300,000 - $1,000 (Investor's Equity) = $299,000
Mortgage Constant for Both Loans = 9.08%
Annual Debt Service = $299,000 x 9.08% = $27,149
Leveraged Before-Tax Equity Cash Flow = $30,000 - $27,149 = $2,851
Unleveraged Income Return = $30,000 ÷ $300,000 = 10%
Leveraged Income Return = $2,851/$1,000 = 285.1%
Leveraged Total Return = ($2,851+$15,000)/$1,000 = $17,851/$1,000 = 1,785%

In sum, financing the down payment with borrowed money can make the investor's rate of return skyrocket, *if a loan can be obtained at a sufficiently low rate.* The best and most profitable way to finance the down payment is a second loan using as collateral a property not burdened by another loan. This will allow the investor to borrow money at the lowest possible interest rate, maximizing the property's leveraged return. If a second mortgage can be found so that the total payment for both loans is covered with some comfort by the property's NOI, and the investor can still get a decent positive cash flow, that would be another profitable venue to finance the down payment.

In concluding the above example, I would like to bring the reader's attention to the assumption of a 10% first-year unleveraged return, which was a critical number in determining whether the investor's return benefits from borrowing. Such an assumption may be optimistic if we take into account that it really represents the NOI/value ratio. As I indicated in an earlier discussion, this ratio represents the market capitalization rate, which for an apartment ranges mostly between 6% and 8%, according to NCREIF data. Thus, finding an apartment at a price that would allow a 10% first-year return may not be that easy, but certainly not impossible.

Although the benefits of using leverage are very enticing, funding most of or the entire purchase price with borrowed money entails risks. The risks come from the potential for future NOI and value decreases, which may force the investor to come up with the funds to pay a portion of the debt service. Such circumstances will result in negative leverage, which will reduce the investor's overall return and could lead to losses. In the worst case, in which the investor cannot make the required debt payments, it could result in a complete loss of investment capital, with the property or properties (if the collateral for the second loan is a different property) taken over by the lender.

It should be noted that the risk of negative leverage due to fluctuations in the property's NOI is small when property income comes from *long-term leases by credit tenants* and solid companies. In such cases, the benefits of leverage can be used with lower risk on the part of the investor, as long as fixed-rate financing is used. If an adjustable-rate mortgage is used, the risk of borrowing increases considerably. As the name implies, adjustable-rate mortgages are loans with variable rates that adjust during the term of the loan, depending on market interest rates.

Wurtzebach and Miles (1994) argue that negative leverage may not be necessarily bad, as some investors may be willing to take that risk in anticipation of significant tax shelter benefits and capital gains upon the sale of the property, especially in an inflationary economic environment. Investors can use tax shelters in the case of improved properties by subtracting depreciation from taxable income, thereby achieving tax savings. In essence, such tax savings increase the property's cash flow.

SUMMARY

- Using borrowed funds to finance the purchase or development of a property is referred to as *leverage*.
- Leverage can increase the investor's return significantly under certain conditions, in which case is referred to as *positive leverage*.
- In the case of fixed-rate loans, for leverage to have a positive effect on the investor's return, the mortgage constant, which represents the annual debt payment (or some other periodic payment) as a percent of the loan, should be smaller than the annual return the property provides, without the use of debt (unleveraged return).
- If this condition does not hold, borrowing funds will reduce the investor's return, a situation referred to as *negative leverage*.
- When the loan terms and the income of the property allow for positive leverage, the greater the percentage of the purchase price that is fi-

nanced with borrowed funds (at a fixed rate), the more dramatic the increase in the investor's rate of return (on a before-tax basis) when compared to the return achieved if no borrowed funds were used.

- Real estate investors can finance 100% of the purchase price using a second loan on the property about to be purchased, but they will have to pay a quite higher interest rate for such a loan; this will result in negative leverage or put the property's cash flow under tremendous strain, leaving little margin for NOI to cover debt service.

- Investors can avoid the high rates of a second mortgage and still finance the down payment for the purchase of a property by using as collateral for the second loan another property that is not burdened with a loan; this will allow investors to finance 100% of the purchase price at the lowest rate possible.

- Borrowing is not without risk due to potential fluctuations in market rents and decreases in property NOI (as existing leases expire) to levels that not only may be inadequate to cover the debt service, but also may reduce property value below the balance of the loan.

- In the case of properties with long-term leases to credit tenants, the risk of borrowing is lower.

CHAPTER 4

MARKET-DRIVEN VALUE INCREASES AND MARKET FUNDAMENTALS

In the first chapter, I identified four categories of properties with significant profit potential. The first category includes what I labeled as properties with significant market-driven value-increase potential due to broader market forces. In this chapter, I focus on the broader market processes and mechanisms that trigger such value increases.

PROPERTIES WITH SIGNIFICANT MARKET-DRIVEN VALUE-INCREASE POTENTIAL

Properties with market-driven value-increase potential are buildings expected to register significant increases in their income-earning capacity and value in the near future, because of strong economic/employment growth in the urban area in which they are located. Obviously, if such properties are bought before the expected value increases take place and resold after they occur, they will allow for high returns and big profits.

Usually, properties with significant value-increase potential are located in neighborhoods and submarkets with relatively low vacancy rates and are not threatened by the development of incompatible uses, such as heavy industrial uses, or other developments that will undermine their value. Properties in markets and submarkets with high vacancies are risky and should be viewed with extreme caution because they are prone to market rent declines, which will eventually result in NOI and value declines. This is not to exclude *buildings with high vacancies* in submarkets where *the average vacancy rate is low*. In fact, such properties may offer opportunities for big profits, if their higher vacancy is due to mismanagement, rather than property characteristics that make it less attractive.

It is obvious from this discussion that the potential for achieving high profits in real estate depends on how well one can identify properties with good *prospects for strong value increases* within reasonable time. Investors, seeking to enhance their ability to identify properties with significant profit potential, need to understand very well the price determination mechanism, the broader principles of property value and rent increases, and the specific factors that trigger such increases. The purpose of the material that follows is to help the reader develop such an understanding and acquire a solid background for inspiration and guidance when searching for profitable real estate investment opportunities. For this reason, I will discuss in this and following chapters the laws that regulate the functioning of the real estate market, the mechanism by which property prices and rents are determined, and the specific factors that trigger rent and property value increases for different property types.

It should be emphasized that the clues and information provided for identifying properties that may have significant profit potential are no substitute for the due diligence that needs to be carried out in evaluating a specific property. The ideal process of assessing and quantifying prospects for rent and therefore, property value increases, involves econometric modeling and empirical analysis at the broader market level and the submarket level. Furthermore, when the conclusions from such analyses are applied to a specific property they need to be adjusted according to its characteristics and peculiarities, as well as its advantages and disadvantages.

Some professional firms produce econometric forecasts of expected rent movements in the nation's major real estate markets. Such forecasts can be quite useful to investors aggressively pursuing high returns and big profits. When applying such forecasts to a specific property, one needs to be very careful, since its income will mostly depend on existing leases—in particular, the quoted contract rate, adjustment terms, and rollover schedule--rather than market rents. Thus, the path of market rents will influence a property's income, depending on how many leases expire, how many are renewed, and how many are replaced by new leases.

How Property Prices and Rents are Determined

In order to identify what may cause rents and property values to rise, one needs to understand how property rents and sales prices are determined in a free, competitive market. According to conventional economic theory, price in a competitive market is the result of the interaction between buyers, who represent the demand side of the market, and sellers, who represent the supply side.

The fundamental process by which the market mechanism works in a free economy is that prices/rents adjust until demand (or the quantity demanded) and supply (or the quantity supplied) change as much as needed in order to become equal. The crucial element of this mechanism is how demand and supply behave in response to price/rent increases. This is where the fundamental laws of demand and supply enter the picture. As much as I want to refrain from economic and technical language, I cannot avoid discussing these laws since the supply-demand framework is the theoretical foundation of the specific discussion in this book.

The law of demand postulates that quantity demanded decreases as prices increase. For example, if office rents rise, the demand for office space should decrease (all else being equal). Thus, the demand curve is graphed in the quantity-price space as a downward-slopping curve (see Figure 13).

The law of supply postulates that quantity supplied increases as prices increase. For example, if property values and prices rise developers will construct and bring into the market more space (all else being equal). Thus, the supply curve is graphed in the quantity-price space as an upward-slopping curve. As Figure 13 demonstrates, the price at which the demand and supply curves intersect (P_E) is the price that equalizes the quantity demanded with the quantity supplied.

Before proceeding to the more specific discussion of the price/rent determination mechanism in the real estate market, it is important to clarify that at any point in time, there are two markets operating at different, but quite interlinked levels (see Figure 14):

a) The *asset market*, where properties are offered for sale, and

b) The *rental market*, where properties and space are offered for lease.

Figure 13 – A Simple Graphic Illustration of the Demand-Supply Framework

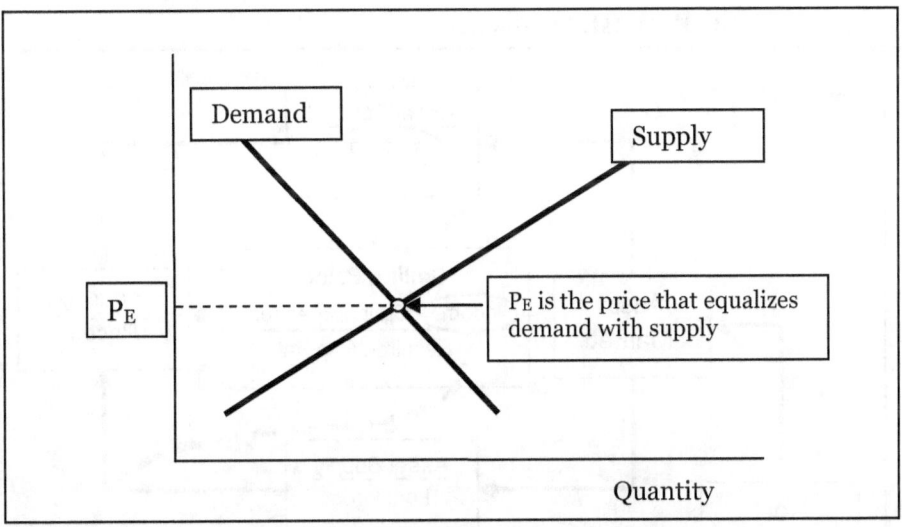

The buyers in the asset market are investors (and households, in the case of owner-occupied housing), and the sellers are landlords, or investors liquidating their investments. The buyers in the rental market are firms and households, while the sellers are landlords/investors. Notice that the interaction of demand and supply in the asset market determines property *prices*, and therefore property values, while the interaction of demand and supply in the rental market determines lease contract rates, that is, *market rents*, and *occupancy rates*.

As Figure 14 shows, there is an important link between the asset and the rental market, which I have discussed in Chapter 1. In particular, rental-income levels, which are determined in the rental market, determine a property's NOI (rental income – operating expenses), which along with capitalization rates, determine the prices investors are willing to pay in the asset market. Notice that

51

each investor may be using a different required income return. Investors with higher required income returns will have a lower ceiling price, while investors with a lower required income return will have a higher ceiling price. The role of the ceiling price investors are willing to pay in order to acquire a property will become clearer in the discussion that follows.

Figure 14 – The Price and Rent Determination Mechanism in the Real Estate Market

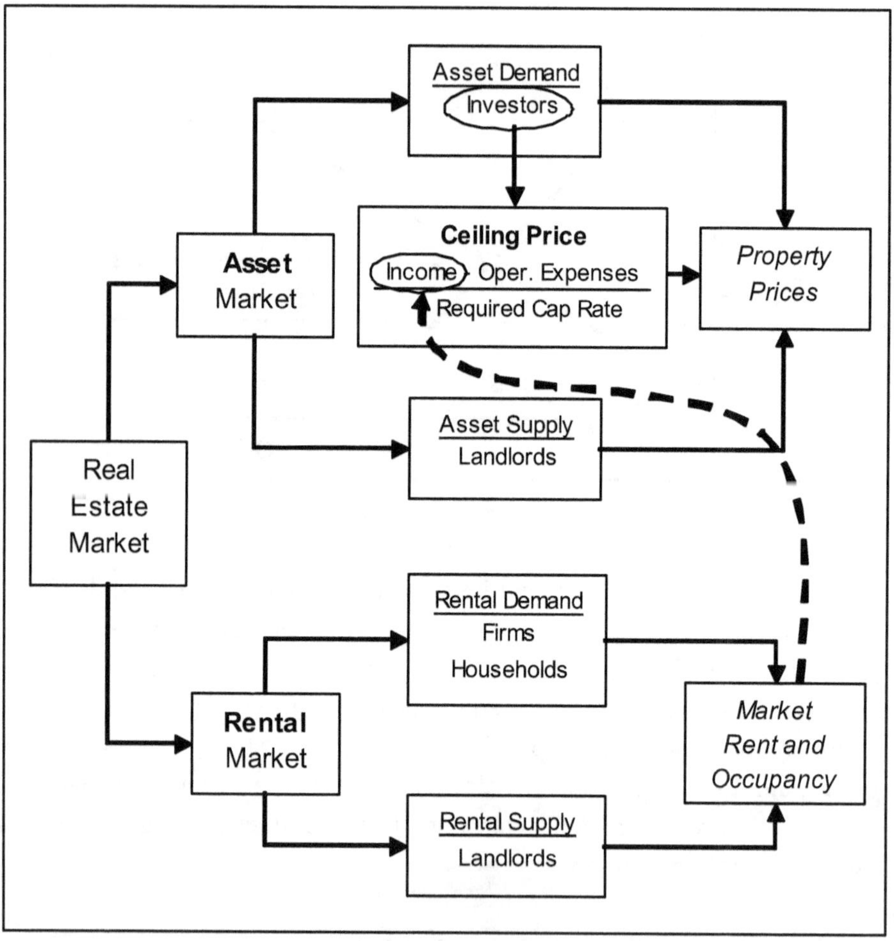

As Goodall (1979) suggests, a transaction will take place as long as one or more potential buyers have ceiling prices above the floor price of a seller. The market price/rent will be higher the stronger the seller's bargaining position is. For example, when the market is under-supplied, sellers have a greater negotiating power, compared to periods during which the market is oversupplied. If there are many buyers with ceiling prices above the floor prices of the sellers, property prices and rents will be determined through competitive bidding. In a perfectly competitive real estate market, the price of land, developed properties, and rental space will stabilize at the level for which the amount of space offered by the sellers equals the amount demanded by the buyers. This price level is what the economists refer to as the *equilibrium price*.

To better understand how market rents are determined, and how rent/price increases may occur, assume for a moment that the amount of space demanded by companies is greater than the amount of space offered for leasing in the office market. In such a case, landlords with vacant space experiencing high demand will raise asking rents. This increase in asking rents will trigger changes, in both demand and supply. On one hand, some additional landlords will enter the market, offering additional space for lease as market rents move above the minimum (floor) rent they require in order to lease space. On the other hand, some renters will "drop out" of the market, as asking rents move above the maximum (ceiling) rent they are willing to pay. These adjustments will continue until the amount of space available for lease equals the amount of space demanded by renters. At that point, no renter will have any incentive to further bid up rents.

In case the amount of space demanded is smaller than the amount of space supplied, landlords will start reducing asking prices in order to attract renters, and eventually, rents will fall enough so that the amount of space demanded becomes equal to the amount of space supplied. Is there any evidence that the real estate market operates in such a way? The answer is yes. Rosen and Smith (1986) and Wheaton (1988) presented evidence from the housing market and the office market, respectively, which demonstrates that rents/prices have been decreasing in response to excess supply.

WHAT MAY CAUSE MARKET RENTS AND PRICES TO INCREASE?

The important thing to keep in mind when thinking about how a free market works is that when the demand-supply balance is disturbed, market rents and prices start *moving* accordingly in order to bring the market back into balance.

If we assume the market begins from a point at which space demanded is equal to the space supplied, prices should be stable. Economists describe this situation as the market being *at equilibrium*. If this balance is disturbed, either in favor of demand or in favor of supply, prices should start moving. In particular, if demand becomes greater than supply (due to non-rent/price factors) then rents/prices *have to rise* in order to force enough buyers/renters to drop out of the market and enough suppliers to enter the market so that the amount of space demanded equals the amount of space supplied.[10] Similarly, if supply decreases while demand remains constant, there will be excess demand, which will again force prices/rents to *rise*. However, because of the durability of real estate, sudden decreases of an area's property inventory cannot occur in the normal course of events. An area's inventory of properties, however, may decline gradually *if the amount of space build is smaller than the amount of space that "drops out" of the market* due to physical deterioration and functional obsolescence.

If supply increases while demand remains constant, or if demand decreases while supply remains constant, there will be excess supply, which will force prices to *fall* in order to induce enough suppliers to drop out of the market and enough buyers/renters to enter the market.

Based on this discussion, we can identify two broad principles of rent and value increases, with the condition that the market is neither oversupplied nor undersupplied:

1) An increase in the demand for space or properties while supply remains constant

2) A decrease in the supply of space or properties while demand remains constant

---

[10] In the real estate economics literature, it is widely accepted that for the real estate market to be truly in balance, the quantity of space supplied should not exactly equal the amount of space demanded. Many analysts have argued that there must be some vacant space, or in other words, supply should be greater than demand, in order to allow normal search operations for renters looking for space and buyers looking for properties. The percentage of stock that needs to be vacant in order to facilitate such normal market operations is referred to as the *normal* or *structural vacancy rate*.

To better understand the first principle of property-income and value increases, consider a nice residential community, called Paradise, with few vacant housing units and limited development under way, due to zoning controls. If, for some reason, demand for housing suddenly increases considerably so that the existing vacant units are far from adequate to cover it, housing rents and prices in Paradise will register strong increases.

Demand for housing in Paradise may increase considerably, due to a number of reasons, such as intensive office development in a nearby community, which brings a great number of new white-collar employees to the area. Since there is a tendency for people to seek housing close to their workplace, it is logical to assume that many of these new employees will seek housing in Paradise too.

An important characteristic of the supply of real estate, which explains why short-run increases in prices/rents can be very strong in response to a strong increase in demand, is the *construction lag*, that is, the lag between the time a real estate project is perceived and the time it comes out in the market. This lag, which is due to the time needed to complete necessary studies, design, secure financing, get permits, and build a project, ranges from one to many years, depending on the size and nature of the development. This characteristic is *very important*, because if demand suddenly increases considerably, supply will not be able to respond immediately, unless lots of new buildings are about to be completed and enter the market. This is not very likely, however, if the demand increase is sudden or considerably greater than usual.

As a result of the supply's inability to respond quickly to changing market conditions, a strong increase in demand will originally create supply shortages, which will force prices to start rising, at least in the short-run. Because of the inertia/rigidity of supply, strong demand increases can trigger strong rent/price increases *as long as the market is not oversupplied*. However, as new supply starts to come out gradually, rent and price growth should decelerate, unless demand keeps rising faster than supply. As we have seen in the discussion of the cyclical behavior of the real estate market, property prices (and rents) seem to rise for a few years at an accelerating rate when the market comes out of the downturn, but after that, rent and price growth decelerates and turns negative eventually, due to a combination of strong supply growth and a slowdown in demand growth.

THE SUPPLY OF REAL ESTATE

It is clear from the discussion so far that both demand and supply have to behave in a particular way in order to make rent and property value increases happen. In particular, strong demand increases will produce *strong rent and property value increases* only if:

a) the market is not oversupplied at the time a strong demand increase occurs, and

b) supply remains stagnant, or grows at a very slow rate after the increase in demand takes place

The aggregate supply of a particular property type at any given point in time comprises all existing buildings of the type considered that are used or are available for use. For example, the aggregate supply of housing includes all buildings that are used or are available for use as residences. The total aggregate supply for a given property type is often referred to as *total stock* or *total inventory*. According to the US Census Bureau, the nation's aggregate housing supply in 2003 was about 120 million units. The majority of these units—62 percent—were single-family, detached houses. The rest of the units were distributed, with percentages ranging between 3.3% and 8.3%, in structures with different numbers of units (see Figure 15). Manufactured/mobile homes or trailers represented about 3.3% of the US total housing supply in 2003.

Figure 15 – Distribution of US Total Housing Supply by Type of Structure in 2003

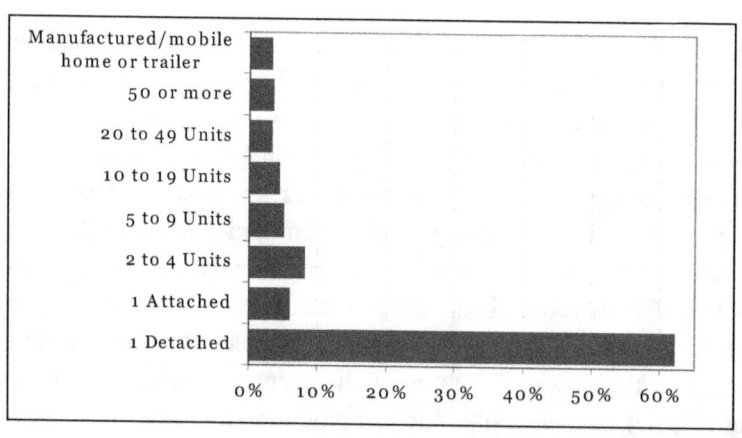

Source: US Census Bureau

Real Estate Investing for Double-Digit Returns

In terms of market activity, an important concept is *available supply*. Available supply refers to the number of units or amount of space available for rent or purchase to firms and households looking for space or houses. For example, the available supply of rental housing includes all vacant housing units offered by their owners for leasing. In the owner-occupied housing market, available supply includes all new houses and existing houses up for sale. In substance, the amount of space or units represented by the available supply is the amount that interacts with increases in demand, jointly *determining changes in market rents and prices*. Within this context, available supply is an extremely important notion from the perspective of property value increases.

To better convey these concepts let's review the latest numbers from the US Census Bureau regarding the mode of occupancy and number of vacant units in the housing market. According to the 2003 numbers, 61.6% of total housing units (excluding mobile homes or trailers) were owner-occupied, 28.7% were renter-occupied, while 9.7%—representing about 11.4 million units—were vacant (see Figure 16). However, notice that of the 11.4 million units that were vacant in 2003, only 3.6 million units (representing 31.6% of total vacant units) were available for renting, 1.3 million units were available for sale, and 0.9 million units were available for sale or renting (see Figure 17). Thus, the total available supply of rental housing available in 2003 equaled about 4.5 million units.

Figure 16 – Distribution of US Total Housing Stock by Type of Tenancy

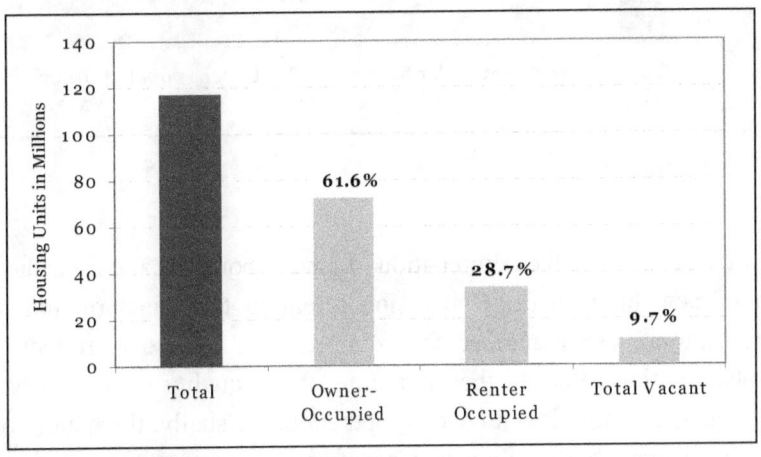

Source: US Census Bureau

From a value-growth perspective, the important question is how an area's available supply can grow, and *what factors may restrain such growth*. A market's available supply of rental space in a specific use can grow through the addition of the following components:

a) newly completed buildings offered for leasing (new construction)
b) previously occupied space that becomes vacant and re-enters the market
c) buildings converted to the use under consideration and offered for leasing
d) rehabilitated buildings that were out of the market due to dysfunctionality

Figure 17 – Vacancy and Availability of US Housing Units in 2003

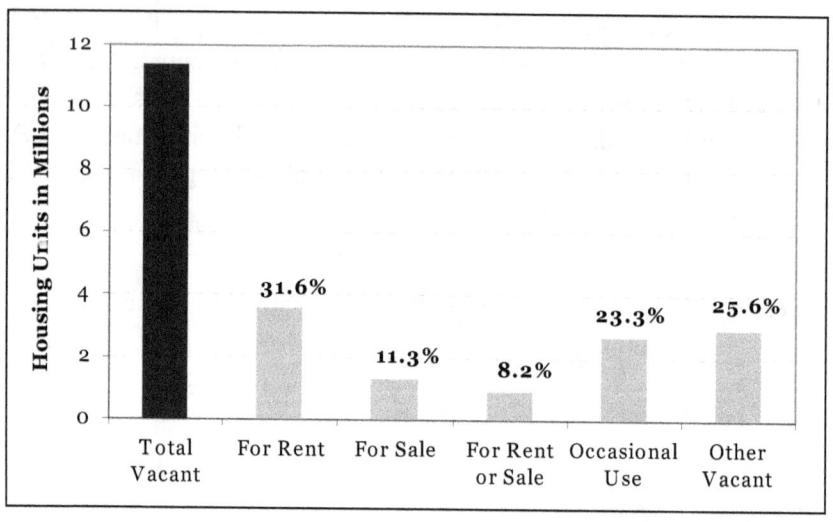

Source: US Census Bureau

New construction is the combination of land, labor and capital for the production of new built space. Conversion refers to the transformation of a structure from one use to another (for example, from hotel to apartments). Finally, rehabilitation refers to the upgrading of the quality of a deteriorated, unused structure so that it can become operational. Usually, the major source of increases in available supply is new construction.

The construction of a new building is an investment, and as such, is driven by *profitability factors*. Profitability is determined by costs and expected revenues. Because of the long time that intervenes between project conception and project completion, expectations play a crucial role in investment decisions regarding new construction. Within this context, new construction activity depends on:

a) Expected demand, property sales prices, and rents
b) Construction costs, which include cost of materials and labor
c) Land costs
d) The cost of borrowed funds (interest rates)
e) Profitability of investments in alternative investment vehicles

When the market vacancy rate is low and *new construction activity is restrained*, strong demand increases will result in greater property rent and value gains. For this reason, it is very important to understand how the aforementioned factors contribute to the reduction of development and new construction activity in a real estate market. The following changes in these factors are likely to result in *reduced levels* of new construction (assuming all other factors that affect new construction remain constant):

a) *Worsening of expectations* regarding future demand, rents, and property rents/prices will result in less optimistic revenue projections and lower profitability estimates, which will induce developers and investors to supply a lower amount of new space in the market.

b) *Land and development cost increases* will increase project costs and, for a given level of expected property revenues, will reduce profitability, thereby discouraging some developers and investors from proceeding with planned projects. Therefore, new construction activity should decrease as a result of such developments. Rosen and Smith (1986) detected a strong statistical relationship between increases in construction costs and decreases in housing additions and alteration expenditures.

c) *Interest rate hikes* will increase the cost of borrowed funds and make several large projects infeasible or too risky to finance with borrowed funds. Therefore, such events should result in a deceleration of new construction activity.

d) *Reduction in the relative profitability of real estate* investments will induce large financial institutions to reduce the percentage of their investment portfolios in real estate. This will result in a decrease in the flow of equity capital in real estate development projects, which in turn should contribute to a decline in new construction activity.

Beyond the aforementioned influences, the response of the supply of real estate to unpredicted demand increases will depend on the length of the development process and local growth controls, which may limit the amount of new space that can be built within a jurisdiction. The development process can be divided into four stages:

a) Idea conception, planning, design, and feasibility assessment
b) Application for and approval of building permit
c) Start of construction
d) Completion

Notice that the length of the development process will increase, and supply growth will be slower (all else being equal), if there are difficulties in obtaining building permits. Such difficulties may be due to lengthy regulatory processes and growth restrictions imposed by local governments in an effort to limit growth within the boundaries of their jurisdiction. The length of the design and construction phases is usually greater in large, complex projects. The length of the construction stage may also increase due to bad weather and delays in the delivery of construction materials (Charles, 1977). Charles presents evidence indicating that construction time increases during periods of economic decline and shortens during periods of economic growth. This supports my argument that the best time for investment is when the market comes out of a recession because at that point supply grows at the slowest rate while demand grows at the fastest rate.

When assessing an area's supply prospects, it is important to have in mind that not all projects in the planning stage move to the permit stage, and not all projects for which a building permit application is filed get a permit. Furthermore, some projects that do get a building permit may not reach the next stage—the start of construction. Finally, although most of the projects that break ground are completed, there may be a small number of projects that do not get completed. In any case, building permits should provide a good approximation of the new supply entering the market a year or two ahead.

A study carried out by the US Census Bureau over the period 1999-2004, regarding the housing market, verifies the close relationship between levels of permits and completions. This relationship is especially strong in the case of single-family houses, which constitute the overwhelming majority of new housing construction. However, in the case of multi-family housing, the study found a significant deviation between the number of units authorized by building permits and the number of units completed. According to the study, the major contributing factor to this difference was the re-classification of units to single-family homes after the permit was issued.

The findings of this study, which also examined the relationship between permits and starts, are presented in Table 1. As this table shows, during the period of the study, the total housing units started were 97.5% of housing units authorized by building permits, while 96% of units started were completed. Based on these percentages, it can be inferred that the total housing units completed were 93.6% of the total housing units authorized by building permits.

Table 1 — Starts vs. Permits and Completions vs. Starts

	Starts as Percent of Permits	Completions as Percent of Starts	Completions as Percent of Permits
Total Units	97.5%	96.0%	93.6%
Single-Family Un	102.5%	96.5%	98.9%
Multi-Family Uni	77.5%	92.5%	71.7%

Source: US Census Bureau and author.

In the case of single-family houses, starts were 102.5% of permits, due to reclassification of units from multi-family to single-family after the permits were issued, while completions were 96.5% of starts. Based on these percentages, it can be inferred that single-family housing units completed were 98.9% of units authorized by building permits. Finally, in the case of multi-family buildings, starts were 77.5% of permits issued, due to reclassification of units from multi-family to single-family, while completions were 92.5% of starts. Based on these percentages, it can be inferred that multi-family housing units completed were 71.7% of units authorized by building permits.

In terms of overall building activity in the nation's housing market, it is interesting to note that according to the US Census Bureau, in 2005, local governments issued building permits for a total of 2.147 million housing units. This represents an increase of 3.7%, compared to the number of housing units permitted in 2004, which reached 2.07 million. In both years, the overwhelming majority (about 80%) of new units permitted represented single-family units, while 18% of the units permitted were in structures with five or more units (see Figure 18).

Figure 18 – Distribution of Housing Units Permitted by Type of Structure

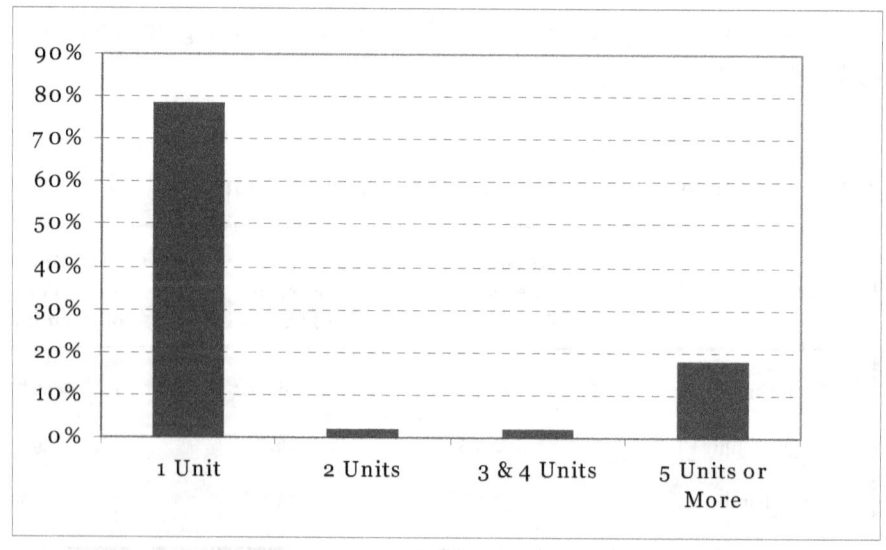

Source: US Census Bureau

Monitoring whether the number of units represented by permits issued is increasing or decreasing is important because it provides an understanding of the momentum developing in the market. However, it is even more important to understand what these new units represent in terms of housing *stock growth rates*. According to data provided by the US Census Bureau and calculations performed by the author, the number of units authorized by building permits in 2004 and 2005 represent stock growth rates of 1.7% and 1.6%, respectively.[11]

GROWTH CONTROLS AND RESTRICTIVE ZONING

Given the importance of restrained supply in triggering robust property rent and price increases when strong increases in demand for real estate take place, growth controls and restrictive zoning deserve special attention. During the recent decades, many communities in the United States, especially the West Coast, registered significant housing price increases largely due to zoning controls and growth regulations, which restrained the supply side of the housing market. By the early 1970s, growth management and control efforts had slowed down and even stopped growth in many suburban communities. Some of the reasons that cultivated such anti-growth attitudes include the overcrowding of local schools, the potential overloading of the local sewage treatment system, and the inadequacy of water reserves to cope with peak demand days (Frieden, 1979).

Local governments use two types of measures to limit further development: 1) growth management measures, and 2) stop-growth measures. The growth management measures are based on federal and state legislation regarding environmental protection. Some examples of such legislation include the National Environmental Policy Act of 1969, the Coastal Management Zone Act, which affects land use regulation in 34 states, the Clean Air Amendment Act of 1970, and the Water Pollution Amendments of 1972 (Shenkel, 1980).

---

[11] Total housing stock data is available from the Census Bureau as of 2003. The total housing stock for 2004 and 2005 was calculated by adding to the previous year's total housing stock 95% of the number of units authorized by building permits during the respective years. With estimates of the housing stock for 2003, 2004, and 2005, it was possible to calculate the 2004 and 2005 stock growth rates as the percent change in the stock during each year.

Another interesting example of supply constraints is the Williamson Act, which authorized cities and counties to set up agricultural preserves. Within these areas, property owners enter into an agreement with the local government to maintain their land for agricultural use, in exchange for preferential tax assessment of the property. This is not possible if the constitution does not allow properties to be assessed at below market values, in which case voter approval of a constitutional amendment is required. The purpose of such legislation was the protection of agricultural land and open spaces (Frieden, 1979).

In California, significant growth control measures have been established based on the Water Quality Act, the Environmental Quality Act, and Proposition 20. The Water Quality Act gave to the State Water Resources Control Board the power to stop development of projects that violated water quality standards. The Environmental Quality Act introduced the requirement for environmental impact reports for any project proposed by private development firms and local or state government agencies. Finally, Proposition 20 established six coastal zone commissions with the authority to block development projects, which they have done on numerous occasions (Frieden, 1979).

Stop-growth measures that can limit new development activity include moratoria on residential building permits, high development fees, such as construction taxes and city/county water fees, and limitations in the expansion of utility systems. Such development moratoria are usually justified by local governments with the rationale of preserving public health and the community's quality-of-life standards (Frieden, 1979).

Development moratoria and other growth control measures greatly reduce the amount of vacant land available for development, making the land market tighter and inflating land and property prices. In addition, they make review procedures for new developments more complicated, time-consuming, and uncertain, thereby delaying the development process and increasing the risk involved in investing in new projects.

In a study of the San Jose housing market, carried out by the Urban Land Institute, it was estimated that 20% to 30% of the increase in housing prices resulted directly from San Jose's growth management measures. The new growth controls not only *increased housing prices*, but also reduced the variety of housing types available in the market. The empirical evidence presented by Frieden suggests that growth controls affect *the spatial distribution of new supply*, and, therefore, locational rents and prices. For example, the evidence suggests that growth controls in Marin County deflected development to other parts of the San Francisco area.

Evidence presented by Elliott (1981) suggests that strict growth controls do not necessarily result in strong price increases in the communities that adopt such controls. In particular, the evidence presented by this analyst suggests that growth controls will result in strong price increases *only if they are present in most of the communities in the metropolitan area*. The impact on housing prices was found to be considerably lower in metropolitan areas where growth controls were not widespread.

THE DEMAND/SUPPLY INTERACTION IN THE REAL ESTATE MARKET

Demand and supply in the real estate market are rarely balanced because of the slow adjustments of supply and prices/rents in response to changes in economic and demographic factors that trigger changes in demand. Supply responds slowly because of the time it takes to plan and develop a property, while market rents adjust slowly because of multi-year leases that fix rents at certain levels. Since the real estate market is rarely in balance, it would be useful if investors could use an indicator to gauge whether there is excess demand or excess supply, since each situation implies different things in *terms of the direction rents or prices may be moving in the future*.

The most commonly used indicator of the *mismatch* between demand and supply in the real estate market is the vacancy rate. This represents the percentage of rentable space that is vacant. For example, a market with 1 million square feet of total rentable space, 100,000 square feet of which is vacant, has a vacancy rate of 10%. Obviously, as demand and supply conditions change through time, the vacancy rate changes too. For example, according to US Census Bureau data, over the period 1970-2004, the vacancy rate for rental housing units in structures with five or more units has fluctuated between 6.4% and 11.5% (see Figure 19).

Vacancy rates differ not only across the major property types (residential, office, retail, and industrial) but also across sub-types within the same property type. For example, over the period 1970-1998, the vacancy rate for rental housing units in one-unit structures (single-family houses) was consistently *lower* (by at least three percentage points) than the vacancy rate for units in residential buildings with five or more units (see Figure 19). The greatest difference (7.8 percentage points) between the vacancy rates of these two rental housing segments was registered in 1988, when the vacancy rate for single-family houses dropped to 3.6%, while the vacancy rate for units in multi-family structures with five or more units climbed to 11.4%.

Figure 19 – Vacancy Rates for Different Types of Rental Housing Units: 1970-2004

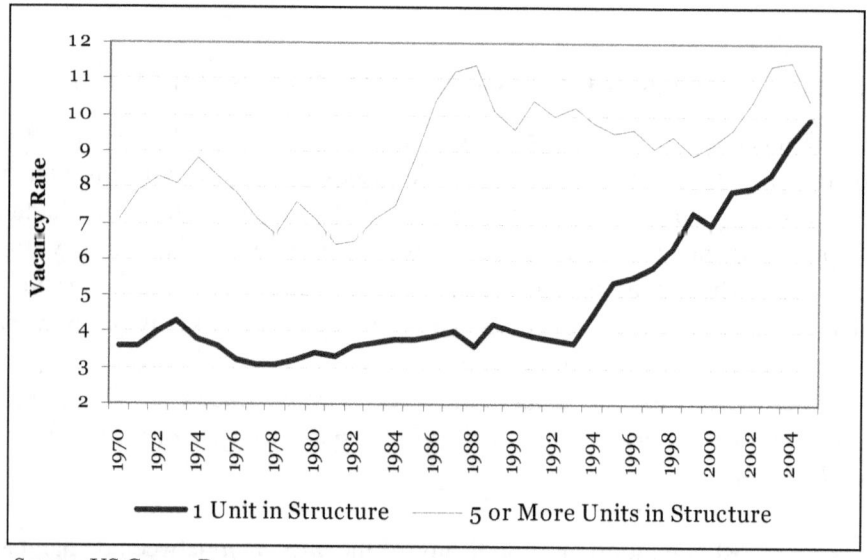

Source: US Census Bureau

It is important to note that the vacancy rate for units in multi-family structures with five or more units has registered a cyclical pattern with clearly greater fluctuations than the vacancy rate for single-family rental units. In fact, as Figure 19 indicates, the latter has not registered any cyclical pattern, since during the 24-year period 1970-1993, it fluctuated minimally between the 3% and 4% mark, while since 1994 it has been mostly on a steady upward path that brought it up to 9.9% by 2004. The important conclusion from these numbers is that vacancy rate levels and trends differ significantly across market and property type segments. For this reason, when evaluating a specific property, investors need to make sure that they are looking at the vacancy rate measure that best represents *the geographic market and type segment within which the property under consideration truly competes.*

It has been argued in the real estate literature that the true amount of excess supply is not represented by the market vacancy rate, but by its difference from a structural or normal vacancy rate (Rosen and Smith, 1983). Rosen and Smith define the structural vacancy rate as the amount of vacant space required for the normal operation of the rental market. For example, the argument often cited is that for renters to make a reasonable search effort there must be a minimum amount of vacant space. Another definition based on the optimal-inventory theory defines the structural vacancy rate as the inventory that landlords keep vacant to be able to take advantage of anticipated increases in market rents (Shilling, Sirmans, and Corgel, 1987; Sivitanides, 1997).

If we accept that the structural vacancy rate represents the vacancy rate level at which market demand equals market supply, it follows that when the market vacancy is below this rate, there is excess demand, and rents (and prices) should be rising. On the contrary, when the market vacancy rate is above the structural vacancy rate, there is excess supply, and rents (and prices) should be declining. Figure 20 demonstrates these dynamics.

Research on the topic (Sivitanides, 1997) suggests that the structural vacancy rate should vary through time and across metropolitan areas, depending on whether the market is hot or cool. In particular, it should be higher when absorption is strong and rents are rising because landlords will be induced to reserve more space for future leasing in order to take advantage of higher rents later, as they expect rents to continue to rise.

Figure 20 – Nominal Vacancy Rate, Structural Vacancy Rate, and Rent Change

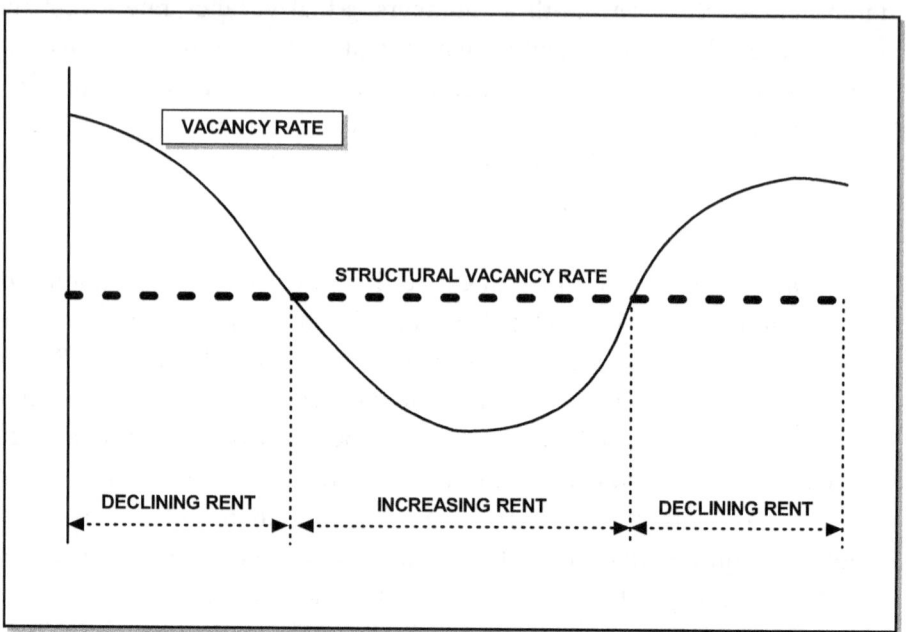

The concept of the structural vacancy rate is relevant, when comparing markets, in the sense that areas with higher vacancy rates may not necessarily have a greater oversupply. It is hard, however, to apply this concept in practice because of the difficulty in quantifying each market's structural vacancy rate. So, is there a magic vacancy rate number that investors can use to evaluate whether there is excess demand or supply? In practice, in the office market, vacancy rates below 10% are looked upon favorably, while in the retail and warehouse market, vacancy rates below 7% or 8% are considered good. These figures, however, should be used with flexibility, depending on the demand and supply growth prospects of the specific market under consideration.

To sum up, as of now we have determined that rents and property values will increase, at least in the short run, if a demand increase (not due to falling prices) occurs without a corresponding increase in supply. Such an increase would be sustainable in the longer term if there were no response from supply. However, under normal conditions, supply will not remain constant after strong rent and price increases take place. Increases in market prices will induce property owners to put more properties up for sale or lease and motivate developers to build new buildings. As supply increases to satisfy excess demand, price and rent growth will decelerate, and eventually rents may start declining. If supply does not overreact, the market should stabilize at a rent/price level higher than the level that prevailed before the demand increase took place. If supply does overreact, the market will go through a cyclical movement, during which rents and prices may decline below their original level. Evidence both from the housing and commercial real estate market has shown that developers do overreact to increases in property prices (Wheaton, 1987).

Based on the discussion so far, one could argue that the greatest price increases should occur in the first one to two years after an unexpected demand increase takes place. This suggests that holding the property for more than two to three years, after a strong demand shock has taken place, may reduce profits and investment returns significantly.

How Much Will Rents/Prices Increase in Response to a Surge in Demand?

A crucial question that comes to mind when thinking about real estate demand increases and their effect on property rents/prices is how much higher the new price will be after the market stabilizes, or by how much rents/prices will increase after supply responds. According to conventional economic theory, the magnitude of the price increase will depend first on the magnitude of the demand increase. For example, all else equal, an influx of thousands of new buyers/renters in the market should result in greater price/rent increases than the entry of only a few hundred new buyers/renters. Thus, *greater increases in the quantity demanded* should result in greater rent/price increases.

Two more factors determine the magnitude of the price increase that may take place in response to a surge in demand. These include the *sensitivities* of buyers and sellers to price increases—that is, to what extent buyers and sellers drop out or enter the market, respectively, in response to price increases. The smaller the sensitivity of buyers/renters to price/rent increases, the higher the increase in property prices/rents after a demand increase takes place. For example, if housing buyers are not very sensitive to price increases, market prices must rise a lot before excess buyers drop out of the market. Similarly, less sensitivity to price increases on the part of supply will also induce higher increases in property prices after a demand increase takes place. The reason is that only considerably higher prices will induce suppliers to provide the additional amount of space needed to cover the excess demand.

Economists refer to the sensitivity of buyers/renters to price/rent increases as the *price elasticity of demand*; it is measured as the ratio of the percentage change in quantity demanded over the percentage change in price. When the percentage decrease in demand (or the quantity demanded) is greater than the percentage increase in price (in which case the absolute value of this ratio is greater than one) then demand is considered as price elastic. On the contrary, if the percentage decrease in demand is smaller than the percentage increase in price (in which case the absolute value of this ratio is less than one) then demand is considered as *price inelastic*.

Notice that demand increases will result in greater price increases, both in the short- and the long-term, if the *demand is price inelastic*. Therefore, investors pursuing high returns and big profits should be looking for property types and markets with price inelastic demand behavior.

According to conventional economic theory, demand for necessity goods should be less elastic than demand for luxury goods. Based on this rationale, housing demand should be price inelastic, to the extent used to cover a household's need for shelter, not a desire for a vacation home. The sensitivity of buyers/renters to price increases should be associated with affordability (relationship of property prices, or corresponding required mortgage payment, to income). The more affordable prevailing prices are, the greater the ability of buyers to withstand price increases without dropping out of the market.

Unfortunately, scientific estimates of price elasticities of demand for the different property types are difficult to find. Gerking and Boyes (1980) presented estimates of the price elasticity of demand for owner-occupied and rental housing for 37 metropolitan markets. Their estimates indicate that the demand for *owner-occupied housing was price inelastic* in all 37 markets covered by their study! This provides a strong indication that robust demand increases for owner-occupied housing will result in strong value increases, at least in the short-run, as long as the market is not oversupplied. The estimates of this study also show that the demand for rental housing was price inelastic in several markets and price elastic in other markets.[12]

Kau, Lee, and Sirmans (1987) have estimated the price elasticity of demand for residential land for 31 major cities in the country for the period 1967 to 1987. Their estimates provide strong evidence that the demand for *residential land is price inelastic*, since all 31 estimates ranged between 0.65 and 0.85.

On the supply side, studies of the office market by Wheaton (1987) and the housing market by Harter-Dreiman (2003) suggest that supply of both property types is quite *elastic*. In particular, according to the latter study, estimates of the price elasticity of housing supply range between 1.4 and 2.7 for large metropolitan markets (the 20 MSAs with the largest population density in 1990) and between 0.9 and 2.1 for small metropolitan markets (the 20 MSAs with the smallest population density). Harter-Dreiman estimated also the price elasticity of housing supply for two types of markets: constrained and unconstrained. This distinction was based on a regulatory index constructed by Malpezzi (1996) using several criteria, such as approval time, permit issuance time, zoning regulations, and adequacy of infrastructure.

Harter-Dreiman's estimates of the price elasticity of housing supply range between 1 and 2.1 for constrained markets and between 2.6 and 4.3 for unconstrained markets. These estimates indicate that housing supply is price elastic in both types of markets, *even the constrained ones* (since it has values greater than one). They also indicate that housing supply is much more elastic in unconstrained markets, compared to constrained ones. Overall, these estimates suggest that the supply risk of residential investments is lower *in small and constrained metropolitan markets*.

---

[12] In particular, the price elasticity estimates for owner-occupied housing ranged from -0.26 in the San Francisco-Oakland area to -0.62 in Baltimore, with most estimates being below -0.50. The estimates of the price elasticity of demand for rental housing ranged from -0.17 in San Francisco Oakland to -1.36 in Baton Rouge. Notice that the price elasticity of demand is a negative number, since price increases result in decreases in demand.

Since constrained supply is critical in triggering strong rent/price gains when demand increases, it is interesting to look at the specific residential markets that have been classified as constrained in Harter-Dreiman's study. As Table 2 indicates, this list includes several large, popular markets, such as Atlanta, Boston, Fort Lauderdale, Los Angeles, Miami, New York, Orlando, Philadelphia, San Diego, and San Francisco.

The important points to remember from this section is that the magnitude of price/rent increases, as a result of a surge in demand, will depend on the magnitude of demand increase—how much more space will be demanded—and on the sensitivity of buyers/renters and sellers/developers/landlords to price/rent increases. Empirical studies have shown that the demand for housing is not very sensitive to price increases, while supply seems to be sensitive to such increases. This means that a surge in housing demand in a non-oversupplied market is likely to result in strong price increases, but supply is likely to overreact. This point provides further support to the *short-term hold strategy*, since initial real estate rent/price increases may be cancelled by rent/price declines later, due to the overreaction of supply.

The strategic conclusion is that investors should be looking for property types, markets, and locations that:

1) Are about to experience strong increases in demand for real estate

2) Are characterized by price inelastic, or price-insensitive property or space demands, perhaps due to greater affordability, as determined by current prices/rent levels and household incomes or firm profits.

3) Are characterized by inelastic, or price-insensitive, supply—either due to the scarcity of development inputs such as land, labor, or capital, or restrictive government regulations, growth controls, and time-consuming government processes.

Table 2 – Markets where Housing Supply was Most and Least Constrained in 2003 (According to Harter-Dreiman Study)[13]

"Constrained" Residential Markets	"Unconstrained" Residential Markets
Akron	Buffalo
Allentown	Chicago
Atlanta	Dallas
Baltimore	Dayton
Birmingham	Denver
Boston	Detroit
Charlotte	Gary
Cincinnati	Grand Rapids
Cleveland	Greensboro
Columbus	Greenville
Fort Lauderdale	Hartford
Honolulu	Kansas
Indianapolis	Minneapolis
Los Angeles	New Orleans
Miami	Oklahoma City
New York	Phoenix
Newark	Portland
Orlando	Richmond
Philadelphia	Salt Lake City
Pittsburgh	St. Louis
Providence	Tampa
Rochester	
Sacramento	
San Diego	
San Francisco	
San Jose	
Syracuse	
Toledo	

Source: Harter-Dreiman, M. 2003. "Drawing Inferences about Housing Supply Elasticity from House Price Responses to Income Shocks." OFHEO Working Paper 03-2

---

[13] Based on Malpezzi's (1996) definition of a regulatory index.

SUMMARY

- Properties with market-driven value-increase potential are properties with prospects for robust rent/income increases due to strong economic and/or population growth expected to take place in the market within which they are located.

- Property rents are determined in the rental market through the interaction of landlords, who supply space for leasing, and households and firms that demand space.

- Property prices are determined, in the asset market, through the interaction of investors looking for assets to buy, and landlords who offer properties for sale. However, there is a vital link between the asset and the rental market, as the prices investors are willing to pay in the former depend on property rents and occupancies, which are determined in the latter.

- Big increases in property rents and prices can be triggered if demand for space increases considerably while supply remains constant. An important requirement for this to occur is that the market *is not oversupplied* when the strong increase in demand takes place.

- In theory, increases in property rents and values can also be triggered by significant decreases in supply while demand remains constant; however, this cannot occur in the normal course of events because real estate is durable, and the existing inventory (supply) can only decrease gradually, due to aging and obsolescence.

- A very important characteristic of the supply of real estate is that it reacts slowly to unexpected increases in demand because of the long time it takes to plan and complete a real estate project.

- Demand and supply in the real estate market are rarely balanced, due to the slow adjustments of supply and rents/prices in response to changes in economic and demographic factors that trigger changes in demand.

- The most commonly used indicator for assessing the extent to which a real estate market is balanced is the vacancy rate. Although determining the exact rate at which a real estate market is balanced is not an easy task, in general, a vacancy rate below 10% in the office market,

7-8% in the retail market, and 5% in the housing market may be viewed favorably. These vacancy numbers, however, should be used with great flexibility depending on the demand and supply growth prospects of the market under consideration.

- ➢ Increases in property rents and prices will be greater, the greater the magnitude of demand increase and the smaller the sensitivity (price elasticity) of demand and supply to rent/price increases.

Chapter 5

Real Estate Demand and Value Increases

Components of Demand for Real Estate

By now, it should be clear that demand increases in the face of constrained supply constitute the major force that triggers big property rent and value gains. Within this context, it is important to understand the different dimensions of real estate demand (see Figure 21).

First, demand for real estate is *multi-dimensional*, as it encompasses size, quality, functionality, layout, and other characteristics of the property. Equally important, perhaps even more so, are the characteristics of the immediate and broader location of the property, since real estate is fixed at a given location.

Second, demand for real estate is *segmented*, not only along major property types, such as residential, office, retail, and industrial, but also along *sub-types* within each type and *quality subcategories* within each sub-type. For example, we can distinguish several distinct sub-types of residential properties, such as single-family detached houses, townhouses, and apartments. Furthermore, within each of these housing sub-types, we can distinguish high-quality, medium-quality and low-quality units. Notice that demand is segmented along these housing sub-types and qualities. For example, households looking for a single-family house are unlikely to end up buying an apartment. Furthermore, households looking for a high-quality single-family house are unlikely to end up buying a medium-quality house.

Figure 21 – Major Dimensions of Real Estate Demand

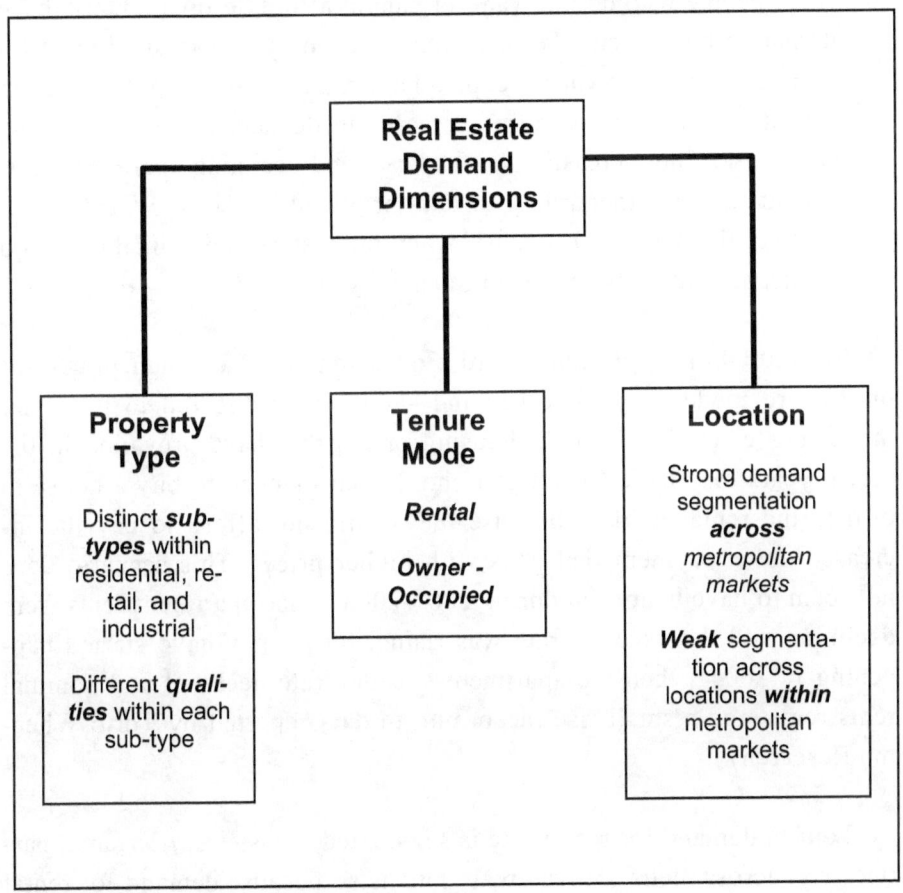

Third, demand for real estate is segmented along *tenure mode*, since the economics of renting and owner-occupancy are quite different. While the dominant mode in housing is owner-occupancy, office and retail real estate markets are primarily rental markets. For example, almost 80% of the office space in the US office market is rented, not owner-occupied (Wheaton, 1987). The distinction of demand by tenure mode is important in understanding the dynamics of the various property markets.

Demand for owner-occupied property and demand for rental property are connected because they are substitutes. For example, when the demand for owner-occupied housing decreases, the demand for rental housing should increase (if the total number of households in the market remains constant). People who do not want, or cannot afford, to own a house have no alternative but to rent. Thus, factors that tend to cause significant increases in demand for owner-occupied housing, such as sharp decreases in interest rates, will tend to cause decreases in demand for rental housing and vice versa. The increasing vacancy rate and declining apartment rents in the United States (according to data provided by Torto Wheaton Research) over the period 2001-2003, when interest rates declined to record low levels, are probably the result of such dynamics.[14]

Substitutability between tenure modes implies that when prices for one tenure mode rise, some demand should be redirected to the other mode. For example, the high housing prices that have prevailed in the recent years may have forced households that planned to buy a house to turn to the rental market, because they could not afford to pay the increased down payment that goes with higher prices. This scenario does not seem to have happened during 2001-2003, since apartment rents were declining and the vacancy rate was rising, but it may have started happening in 2004, when the apartment vacancy rate declined and nominal rents registered a small rise (according to data reported by Torto Wheaton Research).

Fourth, demand for real estate is segmented across *locations* and, particularly, across metropolitan areas. This is so because demand for rental and owner-occupied property in one metropolitan area can rarely be satisfied by properties in another metropolitan area, due to distance considerations, unless two metropolitan markets are separated by a small distance. For example, a person working in Boston, Massachusetts is unlikely to look for housing in Stamford, Connecticut. Similarly, a firm serving clients in the Los Angeles area is unlikely to seek space in San Diego when its lease in a Los Angeles office building expires. Demand is only weakly segmented across locations within a metropolitan area, since household and firm demand for properties or space can be satisfied in many alternative locations within an urban area. In other words, there is

---

[14] Torto Wheaton Research, 200 High Street, 3rd Floor, Boston, MA 02110-3036, Tel: 617-912-5200, Fax: 617-912-5240

considerable substitutability across locations within the same metropolitan area.

Finally, in thinking about demand for any type or subtype of real estate, we need to distinguish between *aggregate* demand at the market level and *demand at a specific location* within that market (locational demand). Although there is considerable substitutability across locations within the same metropolitan area, increases in aggregate market demand for a specific property type will not be equally distributed to all locations within that market because of the uneven distribution of locational advantages.

Within this context, it appears that the best-case scenario for getting the strongest value gains is to invest in the most attractive locations within markets expected to experience strong increases in aggregate market demand. The investor needs to assess carefully the spatial dynamics of the urban area in which he/she is investing, and confirm that the locations that appear to be the most attractive at the time of investment are expected to remain so in the years ahead. In other words, the investor needs to evaluate whether the attractiveness and competitiveness of such locations is threatened, in the medium term, by future developments in the area. Furthermore, the investor needs to ensure that these attractive locations are not oversupplied, nor are expected to become oversupplied in the years ahead.

THE CONCEPT OF UTILITY AND DEMAND

The fundamental concept that underlies demand for any property is what economists refer to as *utility*. Thus, understanding the factors that influence the utility of a property can provide clues for identifying factors that can trigger changes in demand. Real estate buyers and renters demand properties and rental space, respectively, because they can derive some utility by using them. Utility refers to the overall satisfaction that an individual, household, or firm receives by utilizing the specific property. Developers and investors use properties primarily as a means of generating profits. Apartment renters utilize the rented space as a means of satisfying their shelter needs. Homeowners utilize properties as a means of satisfying their need for shelter, as well as long-term financial security. Firms utilize rented space to offer their services or goods to their clients.

Overall, utility can be thought of as the overall usefulness or package of benefits a property provides to a specific user. Obviously, the usefulness of a property to a specific user group (a household or a firm) depends on its characteristics, such as permissible use, size, functional layout, and equipment. Most importantly, because real estate is fixed in terms of location, the utility a property offers to a specific user is greatly influenced by its location, and particularly, by its locational advantages and disadvantages, as determined by the nature and quality of its immediate environment, and the kind of services, employment centers, and consumers (in the case of commercial properties) that are easily accessible from it. For example, the components of the utility of a residence may include a convenient, functional, air-conditioned interior, a safe and well-landscaped neighborhood, convenient commuting to work, and easy access to a neighborhood shopping center.

The utility of location and other attributes of a property may be different for different types of population groups. For example, proximity to a train station may be of higher utility to a low-income household than to a high-income household because the former often has no alternative means of transportation. We will review in more detail what locational attributes are valued by the different users of real estate in the next chapter, which focuses on the forces that trigger demand increases for different property types.

The concept of utility is the foundation in understanding the sources of demand and identifying circumstances that may trigger demand and property income or price increases. Higher utility usually means higher willingness to pay on the part of the buyer or the renter, which, in a non-oversupplied market, should translate to an increased income-earning capacity for the property. Possibilities for increasing considerably a property's utility to its current users or other users can result in considerable value gains. Thus, in evaluating the potential of a property for significant value increases, the investor should examine whether it offers such possibilities.

In thinking about how the utility of a property can change, and what developments may trigger such changes, it is important to distinguish two basic sources of utility for a property user: *use/quality* and *location*. The extremely important point that investors striving for high returns should keep in mind is that significant improvements in the use/quality of a property and its location may create circumstances and opportunities for big profits. Such improvements translate to increases in utility, which in a non-oversupplied market should translate to value increases. Investors who can foresee such favorable utility shifts will gain a significant advantage in identifying opportunities and properties with big profit potential. With the term "favorable" I am obviously referring to shifts that result to an upgrade of a location and/or property and can trigger value gains, as opposed to unfavorable shifts that can lead to a downgrade of a location and/or property and to value losses.

CHANGES IN DEMAND AND THE PRINCIPLE OF OUTBIDDING

Changes that increase the utility of a property should lead to favorable changes in its demand status and value. We can identify three types of favorable changes in the demand status of a property:

1) Change from a non-demand status to demand status
2) Strengthening of demand for current use
3) Strengthening of demand by another use or user who is willing to pay more to occupy the space

The change of non-demand status to a demand status refers to vacant sites and properties that, due to a change in their immediate and broader environment, become attractive to developers, firms, or households for development or use. Examples of such properties are vacant sites that are not accessible or difficult to be served by utility lines, and as such are inappropriate for development. However, if utility companies extend utility lines and the property becomes appropriate for development, its demand status will change, as some developers or investors may become interested.

The second type of demand change, that is, the strengthening of the demand for current use, occurs when the productivity of the property in its current use increases. For example, consider a convenient store whose sales increase, due to the development of a nearby high-rise residential development. In such a case, the tenant of the store would be willing to pay a higher rent to continue using the space.

The third type of demand change occurs when an increase in the utility of the property makes it more attractive to groups that can afford to pay more than the current user. In this case, a change of the current use of the property may be warranted, in order to take advantage of the increased utility it can provide to a different user. If that is the case, developers will act as agents of the group willing to pay a higher rent by acquiring and redeveloping, or renovating, the property so that it can be used by this group. The essence of the phenomenon described here is that current uses are taken over by higher-paying uses. I will refer to this phenomenon as *outbidding*. Outbidding is a very important process in triggering value increases and as such, it deserves special attention.

The principle of outbidding is a useful thinking framework, in terms of identifying circumstances that may trigger property value increases, since every time a group or use outbids the current tenants or current uses, an increase in property prices and rents must occur. Such increases occur because the only way the new group can displace current uses or tenants is by paying higher prices or rents. At this point, I need to emphatically clarify that outbidding refers to involuntary displacement of existing users that do not want to relocate, but cannot avoid it because they are not willing or able to pay the levels of rents and prices the newcomers pay.

Theoretically, low and/or middle-income neighborhoods that become attractive to higher income groups after extensive investments are made, as is the case with inner-city revitalization, have prospects for significant value increases, since outbidding is about to occur. However, before committing money to a property in such a neighborhood, it is important to assess the strength of the area, as well as how attractive it is becoming to higher income groups. Planned developments should be examined to make sure that the critical size and quality of amenities, as well as the overall environment needed to make the area attractive to such groups will be there.

Besides income and affordability, three other factors may play important roles in determining what persons or firms are going to occupy a specific location—the combination of rent, density, and quality of space demanded. For example, consider a site that can be developed as either a multi-story apartment building or single-family housing. It is possible that the site will be developed with a multi-story apartment building eventually rather than single-family houses, because it may be more profitable, given the number of units that can be developed in each use, the respective development costs, and market prices.

The outbidding principle applies to all components of the land use market, that is, residential, office, retail, recreational, and industrial. Within this framework, commercial sites will be occupied by the type of firms that are willing to pay the highest rent. These are the firms that expect to extract the highest profit by operating at a given location. For example, a cluster of low-quality commercial, recreational, and office uses, close to a neighborhood that has recently experienced a massive inflow of high-income households should eventually be replaced by high-quality commercial spaces, occupied by firms offering high-quality, high-income goods and services. Such uses will become much more profitable than existing ones after the transition of the nearby neighborhood has taken place. Thus, buying a commercial property in such a cluster before it transitions to a more prestigious, higher-quality cluster could prove highly profitable.

According to Wheaton (1984), outbidding of a current use, earning reasonable return by another higher-quality use through significant redevelopment, is only feasible under two conditions:

1) the outbidding use is in very high demand, and
2) it can be developed at a much higher density or can command much higher rent

These two conditions are necessary because the developer who buys the property and redevelops or converts it has to overcome the cost of demolition or conversion, in addition to the cost of land and existing improvements. This suggests that, in looking for sites and properties that are good candidates to be converted to a more profitable use, it is important to carefully assess required conversion costs.

With the costs of conversion/demolition in mind, it can be argued that vacant sites may have an advantage over sites with an existing structure, which is very unsuitable to accommodate the overtaking use. If we go back to our example of the middle-quality commercial cluster transforming into high-quality space offering high- income services, vacant sites in that cluster may offer more profitable opportunities for covering the emerging need for high-quality space than would buying and converting existing structures.

The case of the transitioning commercial cluster falls within the boundaries of the outbidding principle. However, in terms of forming a thinking framework, it is useful to distinguish it as a *repercussion* of the original outbidding that took place in the residential uses. This distinction may help identify the spatial pattern and locations where such phenomena will take place, using as a guide the location and the nature of the *original outbidding*. Notice that it may be more difficult to anticipate correctly the spatial pattern and agents of the original outbidding than the location and agents of the repercussion outbidding. The reason is that during the early stages of the original outbidding, there is a great uncertainty as to whether the on-going developments will eventually lead to a massive transition of the neighborhood. However, once this transition reaches a critical size, the repercussion outbidding will follow at the most accessible locations (if there are no limiting factors, such as zoning restrictions or development moratoria).

Another repercussion caused by outbidding is displacement and relocation of the original uses. In this case the displaced users will be in demand for new locations. Displaced households will be looking for new locations with housing and accessibility characteristics comparable to the ones they had before. Displaced firms will be looking for new locations with comparable office space and accessibility characteristics that will burden their clients the least, but will also be at a reasonable distance from the residences of key members of the firm. If the spatial distribution of relocating uses can be predicted, it may lead to the identification of locations and properties with value-increase potential. However, it is difficult to identify the exact locations and sites to which these uses will be relocated. An analytical framework that may help investors get a sense of the possible destinations of such relocated uses is

Sweeny's (1974) framework of a bi-hierarchical structure of housing markets, discussed in more detail in the section that follows.

Closing the topic, I would advise caution in trying to identify whether outbidding is occurring in a neighborhood or not. The investor needs to avoid the mistake of investing in a neighborhood where *filtering* is taking place instead of outbidding. Filtering is the reverse phenomenon during which a use is overtaken by a *lower-quality use*, and values fall instead of rising. An example of filtering is when low-income households move into a moderate-income neighborhood with decreasing rents due to aging structures, deferral of maintenance, and increased vacancies. Investments in a neighborhood that is about to experience filtering are bound to be damaging, since property values will fall considerably.

LOCATIONAL DYNAMICS, LOCATIONAL DEMAND, AND VALUE INCREASES

Within the context of spotting locations with prospects for significant value increases, three aspects of locational dynamics are important: understanding the *path of urban growth* and identifying sites that are likely to be found on such a path, understanding the *spatial distribution of aggregate market demand* and identifying locations that will benefit the most from such increases, and understanding where demand from displaced uses will be transferred.

In the normal course of the urban development process, the utility of a property and location, and therefore its value, changes through time as the area's development proceeds gradually from its initial stages to its final stages, through a multi-year and multi-stage process. Investors that can identify, early in the development process, sites that will be demanded in the future as the development of the area matures, will be able to achieve high profits, since at this early stage, prices will be considerably lower than the final stages when the identification of such sites will be much easier. For this reason, getting a sense of whether and when the development status of a site may come to maturity as the urban development process evolves can help identify investments with big profit potential. Within this context, it is important to understand the dynamics and evolutionary path of the urban and the suburban development process.

Patterns of Urban and Suburban Growth

Understanding how cities and urban areas grow can provide a powerful framework of reference in terms of spotting locations and properties that are likely to experience developments that will increase their values. There are four basic models describing urban structure and the way cities grow:

a. The *Axial-Central theory*, introduced by Hurd (1924), postulates that cities grow in an axial mode, along a transportation axis due to the accessibility advantages offered by sites on this axis, or in a central mode, around a point of attraction based on proximity. Hurd suggests that in the course of urban development, axial and central growth compete with each other, as the city grows in an axial mode away from the center, and central growth follows constantly around the new axial expansions of the city. Thus, urban growth is the result of the combination of these two growth patterns, as the city grows first along the main transportation axes, radiating from the center of the city, with the parts between being filled in at a later stage.

b. The *Concentric Circle theory*, introduced by Burgess (1925), postulates that the city consists of several *concentric rings* of various uses extending around the city's core area—the central business district (CBD). This core area is the most densely developed section of the city and typically represents the prime business, commercial, administrative, and cultural center of the urban area; it contains large office buildings, government agencies, prestigious shopping areas, cultural centers, and entertainment facilities.

The first ring around the circle designating the city's CBD is the transition zone, containing low-income housing, lower-quality commercial activities, and light manufacturing uses. The second ring, moving away from the CBD, contains residential neighborhoods, housing workers employed at the CBD or at the light manufacturing facilities in the first concentric ring. The third concentric ring contains single-family and multifamily residential uses, housing mostly middle-income households. The fourth and final concentric ring is the commuter zone, with low housing density, populated by high-income groups that have chosen life in a less urbanized environment over shorter commuting times. This urban settlement model is based on the dynamic process of filtering, during which the wealthiest households move to new, better, and larger homes in the outer rings, while lower-income households move into the lower-quality, older neighborhoods abandoned by these wealthy households.

c. The *Sector theory*, introduced by Hoyt (1939), combines the axial and concentric ring theories to suggest that a city develops *partially in sectors and partially in concentric ring zones*. Sectors extend along the main transportation arteries, beginning from the center of the city, and represent different uses—wholesale trade, light manufacturing, and low-income housing. Partial ring zones develop further away from the center of the city with uses, such as middle- and high-income housing.

d. The *Multiple Nuclei theory*, introduced by Harris and Ullman (1959), postulates that a city grows in *multiple clusters of complementary uses*. These clusters consist of homogeneous residential areas housing households with similar incomes, and commercial areas serving the specialized needs of these household groups. Although new suburban commercial clusters are no match in terms of size and concentration to the CBD, they do challenge its prominence in the urban fabric. Clusters of special-purpose buildings often found in urban areas, such as the concentration of retail uses in downtowns, the concentration of manufacturing and distribution firms in industrial parks, and clusters of medical offices and facilities around hospitals fall within the scope of the multiple nuclei theory, as they represent groupings of complementary uses around a central use.

Hartshorn and Muller (1992) argue that the new wave of urban growth that will prevail in the 21st century is the *urbanization of the suburbs* and further development of the suburban downtowns in the nation's largest metropolitan areas. These suburban downtowns are often found at suburban nodes of high accessibility, such as key intersections of radial arteries and circumferential highways. According to these authors, these suburban downtowns have further growth potential in the future with the addition of uses that will make them *more comprehensive and/or specialized*. They also foresee that the retail landscape will become more differentiated in terms of market niches because of increasing purchasing power and differentiation in consumer preferences. Hartshorn and Muller describe a five-stage model of suburban development:

1) *Bedroom community*, which refers to the development of residential communities in the suburbs, motivated by the availability of cheap land and financing, as well as the location independence brought by the car and high-speed highways

2) The stage of *independence*, which refers to the development of suburban regional malls, as well as office and industrial parks, which brought jobs close to suburban communities, reducing or eliminating the dependence of suburban residents on central city employment

3) The stage of *catalytic growth*, during which housing and commercial development intensifies and becomes more diversified in terms of quality and price

4) The *high-rise/high-technology* stage, which was marked by the emergence of high-rise office towers housing the growing middle and upper-middle management functions and corporate headquarters, as well as the emergence of high-tech research and development activities, located in selected suburban corridors.

5) The *mature town center* stage, during which cultural, social, and recreational facilities are developed, completing the full spectrum of land uses found in mature urban areas.

These theories can provide a very useful framework for interpreting spatial developments and projecting the path of urban growth, which can lead to the identification of properties and land sites with significant value-increase potential. For example, according to the axial-central theory, the beginning of an axial development along a circumferential freeway is a hint that at some point in time, central growth will follow around that point. This suggests that sites around that axial development have significant appreciation potential.

The multiple nuclei theory suggests that new developments of large residential communities will attract demand for close by services and, therefore, demand for close by commercial space. This suggests that commercial sites most conveniently located with respect to rapidly developing residential communities are likely to have a significant value-increase potential.

Hartshorne and Muller's five stages of suburban development suggest that identifying suburban development patterns that are at the beginning of the independence stage can provide clues to identify residential and commercial sites most qualified to attract the next stage of development—catalytic growth, which should boost property values significantly. Suburban areas that are at the independence stage can be identified using as reference regional and super-regional malls under construction, as well as office and industrial parks under construction. Residential and commercial sites *most qualified to accommodate the upcoming expansion of housing and commercial development, within the area of influence* of these shopping malls and employment centers, should have significant value-increase potential.

Finally, Hartshorne and Muller's prediction that suburban downtowns will be the focus of considerable growth in the coming decades suggests that commercial properties in these downtowns may have a significant value-increase potential.

In sum, the aforementioned theories of urban and suburban structure and growth provide very valuable insights to an investor trying to identify the future path of growth and development in a specific market. In doing so, these theories can be used, in isolation or in combination, to identify which dynamics describe best the situation observed in the area examined.

Patterns of Distribution of New Spatial Demand

Theories of urban growth can help investors understand and anticipate the path of urban growth and the spatial distribution of new demand in the longer-term. Such theories, however, are inadequate in answering the question of how strong increases in market demand due to economic growth will be distributed to existing structures at different locations within the urban area *at a given point in time*. An analytical framework that may help identify which locations may benefit the most from strong economic growth within an urban area is based on the notion of the *hierarchical structure of the market*, introduced by Sweeny (1974). Although Sweeny's model refers to the housing market, it is applicable to other real estate markets as well.

For the purpose of a meaningful dynamic analysis, an area's real estate market should be perceived as consisting of a *bi-hierarchical structure*. This bi-hierarchical structure consists of a *quality hierarchy* within each use and a *spatial hierarchy* for each quality. Within this framework, the residential real estate market of a city consists of submarkets of different qualities, such as the submarket for high-income houses, the submarket for middle-income houses, and the submarket for low-income houses. Furthermore, we can describe the spatial structure of each submarket as consisting of different neighborhoods/communities that can be ranked in terms of their locational strength and attractiveness to best location, second best, etc.

In classifying locations, one needs to take into account another important dichotomy of locational preferences—the dichotomy of suburban versus downtown, or central city. Thus, it may be more helpful to classify the locations of different clusters as downtown and suburban first, and then rank them by strength and attractiveness. The ranking of the different clusters, neighborhoods, or communities should be based on an evaluation of how well they satisfy the different locational requirements for the specific use considered.

The dual strategy I have been suggesting so far is to select first metropolitan markets with the strongest employment, income, and/or population growth prospects, and within these markets, select the locations best positioned to attract the new demand from firms and households. Sweeny's framework can help identify the locations where new demand for commercial and residential real estate will be distributed within a metropolitan market. It is logical to assume that the locations that best satisfy the quality and locational requirements of the *types of households and firms that will be the source of new demand* will be the ones to reap the greatest benefits from metrowide economic growth. For example, if there is an increase in demand for class A suburban office space, it is very likely that that the strongest and most advantageous suburban clusters with class A office space will be the ones to benefit the most from such a surge in demand.

In using Sweeny's framework to identify destinations of displaced uses, the basic hypothesis is that demand displaced from best location will be distributed to the second best, displacing the tenants at that location to the third best location, and so on. This hypothesis is based on the rationale that displaced users will seek locations of similar quality and characteristics with the location they are displaced from. If this hypothesis is true, the displaced uses will turn to locations that rank closest to the location they are displaced from, *as long as the residence-work commuting time remains within acceptable bounds.*

When classifying locations in terms of quality and strength, it is not necessary that every location be better than one location and worse than another. The classification should reflect reality. If two locations have similar locational strength and quality, they should be classified in the same category. If the superiority or inferiority of one location is not clear, one can include it in the closest category and try to keep in mind how it differs from superior or inferior classes. Not all locational differences can be translated into a plus or minus. Some locational attributes are multi-dimensional, and their contribution to the strength of a location is conditional on the nature of locational requirements of the groups that may demand that location.

SUMMARY

- ➢ Demand for property is multi-dimensional and segmented across property types, tenure mode, and location; furthermore, a distinction needs to be made between aggregate market demand and demand at a specific location (locational demand).

- ➢ The fundamental concept underlying demand is utility. An increase in the utility of a property should trigger an increase in willingness to pay on the part of consumers.

- ➢ The utility of a property has two dimensions: use/quality and location. Upgrades in use/quality of a property will result in property-income and value gains, if there is effective demand for the new use/quality and restrained supply.

- ➢ Improvement of the utility of a location, via improvement of accessibility, services offered, and quality of environment, should trigger increases in locational demand, as long as such improvements increase the competitive status of the location.

- ➢ In the normal course of the development process, the utility of a property and location changes as the area's development proceeds.

- ➢ Investors that can identify sites that are likely to be found on the path of future growth will be able to achieve significant profits if they acquire those sites well before development arrives.

- Theories of city growth and urban structure, such as the axial-central theory, the multiple-nuclei theory, the concentric ring theory, and the sector theory, as well as the five-stage model of suburban development, can help property investors better understand observed growth patterns and anticipate the path of urban growth.
- Some analysts believe that the next wave of growth and development will be the urbanization of the suburbs in the nation's largest metropolitan areas, with a focus on suburban downtowns
- Outbidding is an important concept in the realm of property value increases, since for such a phenomenon to take place rents and prices need to rise.
- Outbidding occurs when an increase of the utility of a property make it more attractive to groups that can afford and are willing to pay a higher price than the current user.
- In thinking about locational dynamics and locational demand, it is helpful to map the area's property market into a bi-hierarchical structure of qualities and locations. Such a framework may help understand where new metrowide demand for real estate will be distributed and where uses and users displaced through outbidding may be relocated.

CHAPTER 6

FORCES THAT TRIGGER INCREASES IN DEMAND FOR HOUSING

Residential real estate represents a significant sector, from an investment point of view. Overall, residential investments can range from the acquisition of a single housing unit to the development of new residential communities or high-rise apartment complexes. Most institutional investors focus on the acquisition of high-quality, well-located and well-managed apartment buildings. The purpose of this chapter is to trace the forces driving demand for residential real estate, in order to identify the mechanisms and dynamics that can trigger increases in demand for residential properties and eventually value increases (depending always on supply conditions).

FORCES THAT TRIGGER INCREASES IN DEMAND FOR HOUSING

Housing demand is, on the aggregate, a simple concept, since it refers to the total number of housing units needed to house an area's population. The concept becomes more complex if we try to think of it in more specific terms, such as tenure mode (owner-occupied and rental units), sub-type of housing (single-family detached, single-family attached, apartment, etc.), amenities, and locational characteristics. In this section, I will attempt to shed some light on these issues.

In thinking about drivers of housing demand, we need to distinguish what factors cause increases in aggregate market demand and what factors cause increases in demand for a specific location or locational demand. Since a property is fixed at a given location, it is extremely important to understand from the outset these two mechanisms by which demand for a specific location may increase. Although I referred to these two mechanisms earlier, their repetition here is warranted given the importance of this issue in understanding the forces that can trigger property-value increases:

1) Increases in aggregate market demand, due to economic and population growth, will contribute to increases in demand at many locations within a market. The strongest and most advantageous locations—as perceived by the types of households that represent the increase in demand—are likely to reap *the highest benefits from such increases*. This is where properties with market-driven value increase potential can be found. I refer to this locational demand increase as a *market-driven* increase.

2) Demand for a specific location may also increase due to changes in a property's environment as a result of significant developments in surrounding areas or elsewhere within the urban area. These are the locations where properties with development-driven value increase potential can be found. I refer to this type of locational demand increase as a *development-driven* increase.

Figuring out demand increases at specific locations within an urban area requires an understanding of how aggregate demand for specific types of real estate is distributed across competing locations. The most important principle regarding the distribution of demand for space at different locations within an urban area is the *comparative advantage*. This is a very important concept that real estate investors should always have in mind in their search for properties with significant profit potential.

I suggested earlier using Sweeny's framework of bi-hierarchical structure in classifying locations in terms of their comparative advantages. Investors looking for profitable opportunities should be constantly monitoring developments and prospects in the urban fabric, evaluating and assessing how comparative advantages are likely to change. Changes in comparative locational advantages shift demand for real estate from one location to another, *raising property values and rents in the latter* and depressing property values and rents in the former. This is true not only as far as intra-urban demand shifts are concerned (shifts among locations within the same urban area), but also as inter-urban demand shifts (demand shifts from one urban area to another).

WHAT MAY CAUSE INCREASES IN AGGREGATE MARKET DEMAND FOR HOUSING

The basic unit of housing demand is the household. The link between housing demand and the number of households is set by definition since, according to the US Census Bureau, the term household refers to one or more individuals living together in a family or non-family setting in a separate housing unit. Thus, increases in aggregate demand for all housing types are equivalent with increases in the area's number of households. Within this context, the following forces (see Figure 22) can trigger increases in housing demand:

1) *Household Growth* (increases in total market demand for housing)

2) *Income increases* (increases in demand for both rental and owner-occupied housing)

3) *Decreases in mortgage rates* (increases in demand for owner-occupied housing)

4) *Expectations of rising prices* (increases in demand for owner-occupied housing and investor demand for apartments)

Household Growth

The number of households that live in an area can increase through household formation.[15] Household formation can occur through:

- Internal growth in the number of households, determined by

    Demographics

    Social factors, such as divorce rates or marriage rates

- Net migration

Demographics determine household formation to a significant extent, as new households are formed at different rates within the various age and income groups. Thus, an increase in the number of an area's households can occur by simple aging of the existing population, *if age groups with higher*

---

[15] In academic language, the change in an area's number of households from period to period is referred to as net household formation. When the number of an area's households increases, net household formation is a positive number, while when the number of an area's households decreases, net household formation is a negative number.

household-formation rates increase their percentage contribution to the area's total population (assuming no loss of households due to deaths).

Figure 22 – Forces that Trigger Increases in Aggregate Housing Demand

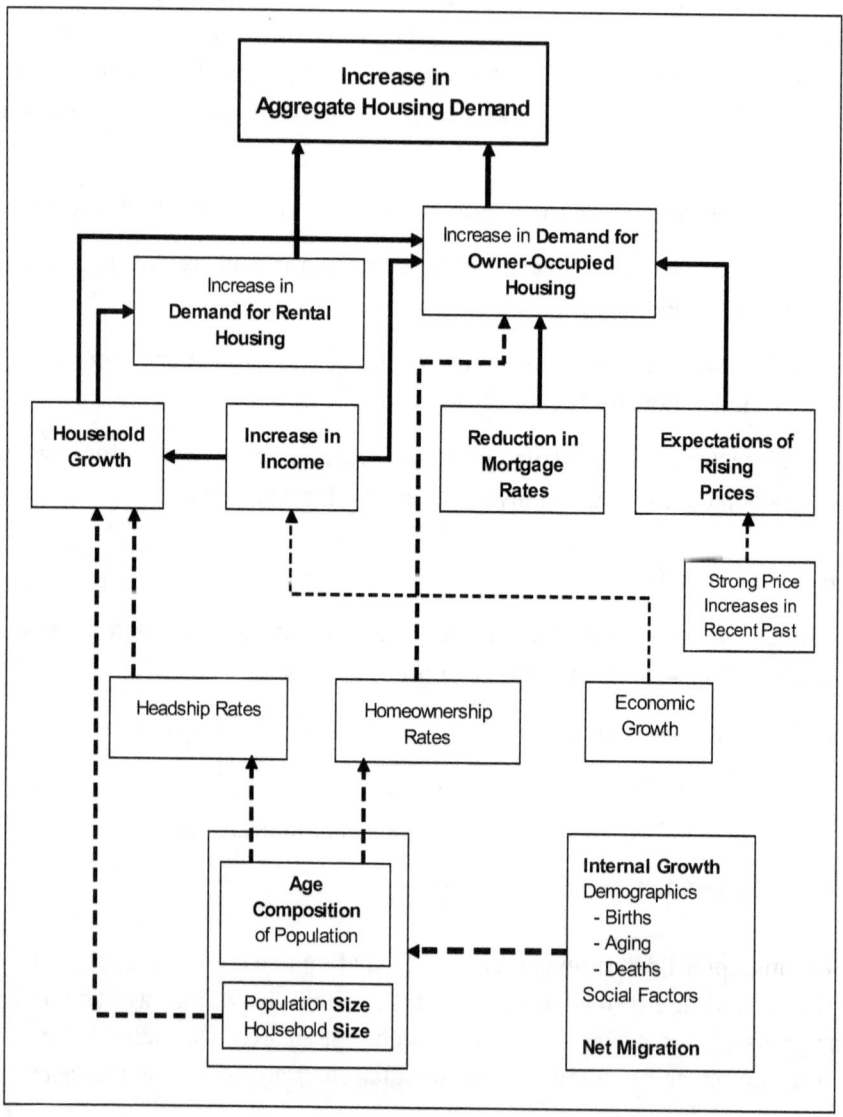

Data from the 2000 Census indicates that household formation (as measured by the percent of household heads in each age group) rises sharply from 20% at age 21 to about 50% by age 30. Household formation rates continue rising slowly to 55% by the age of 45, and reach 60% at the age of 65. Obviously, if by the dynamics of deaths, aging, and migration, the number of persons over 30 years old living in an area increases significantly, then, all else being equal, the number of households and demand for housing in that market must increase significantly.

With these in mind, it should be noted that significant fluctuations in historical birth rates could generate considerable variations in new household formation in the years ahead as baby boom or baby bust generations age and enter household-forming age groups.

When thinking about the impact of demographic structures and changes in housing demand, it is important to watch trends with respect to three critical age groups, which tend to represent the three major stages of a household's life cycle:

a) 25-34—includes mostly young, married households, with no children, demanding mostly rental housing and smaller, lower-priced, single-family units or apartments (this is referred to as the *pre-nest* stage of the life cycle)

b) 35-54—encompasses launching and maturing (move-up) families, demanding mostly owner-occupied housing and larger, higher-quality, single-family units, depending on income (this is referred to as the *full-nest* stage)

c) 55 and older—includes older households, demanding mostly owner-occupied housing and smaller, single-family units, condominiums, or apartments, depending on income (this is referred to as the *empty-nest* stage)

Notice that, based on the above idiosyncrasies of these three groups, we can infer the following dynamics and prospects:

a) Increases in the age group of 25-34 will trigger *increases in demand for smaller rental housing units and smaller low-priced single-family units.*

b) Increases in the age group of 35-54 will trigger *increases in demand for larger, higher-quality, owner-occupied, single-family housing units*, and

c) Increases in the number of people over 55 should trigger *increases in demand for smaller, owner-occupied, single-family units, condominiums, and apartments.*

Data from the US Census Bureau, which describe how homeownership rates change with the age of the household head, strongly suggest that increases in the number of persons over 39 years old *will boost demand for owner-occupied housing.* In particular, as of the fourth quarter of 2005, data collected through the Current Population Survey (CPS)/Housing Vacancy Survey (HVS) and published quarterly by the US Bureau of the Census, shows that homeownership rates rise sharply as the age of household head increases (see Figure 23). In particular, homeownership rates start at 25% for household heads below 25 years old and rise sharply to 67% as the age of the household head reaches the 35-39 group. From that point on, homeownership rates rise at a considerably slower rate, stabilizing at 80% as the age of household head reaches 55.

The 2000 age-specific homeownership rates, reported by the same survey, are similar to those registered in the fourth quarter of 2005. The only visible difference is that younger age groups (up to 39 years old) show a *higher* homeownership rate by 2 to 4 percentage points in 2005. This may be due to the considerably lower interest (and mortgage) rates that prevailed in 2005, compared to 2000, which made housing more affordable. Assuming that homeownership rates will not change significantly in the years ahead, it can be argued that a strong increase in the number of households headed by persons over 40 years old will contribute to significant increases in the demand *for owner-occupied housing.* Given the substitutability that exists between renting and owning a house, a significant increase in the number of households headed by persons younger than 30 years old should trigger strong increases in the demand *for rental housing.*

Figure 23 – Age-Specific Homeownership Rates, as of the Fourth Quarter of 2005

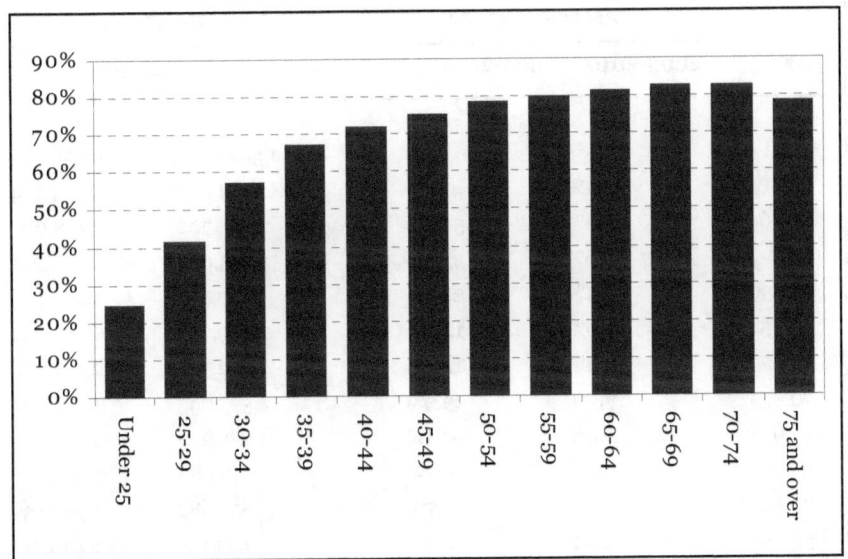

Source: US Census Bureau

In order to place the above discussion in context, it is useful to review the population projections by age group released by the US Census Bureau in 2004. Table 3 presents the expected growth for the different age groups over a five-year horizon (2005-2010) and a ten-year horizon (2005-2015), based on these projections. As this table indicates, age groups *within the 55-69 range* are expected to register the strongest percent gains, at rates exceeding 10% during the first period and 20% during the second period.

The age group of 60-64 is expected to be the fastest growing age group, increasing at a rate of 28% over the period 2005-2010, and at a rate of 44% over the period 2005-2015. In absolute terms, *about 3.6 million people are expected to be added* to this group over the period 2005-2010 and about *5.7 million* people are expected to be added over the period 2005-2015. The age group of 85 and older ranks also among the first three fastest growing age groups in percentage terms, but in terms of number of people it ranks somewhere in the middle. It is interesting to note that over the period 2005-2015, the largest decreases (amounting to about 4 million people) are expected to occur within the age groups of 40-44 and 45-49.

Table 3 – US Census Bureau Population Projections by Age Group

Age	Percent Change 2005-2010	Percent Change 2005-2015	Absolute Change 2005-2010	Absolute Change 2005-2015
Total	4.5%	9.1%	13,428,447	26,858,653
60 - 64	28.1%	44.1%	3,661,895	5,743,904
65 - 69	20.2%	54.3%	2,048,702	5,498,090
85+	19.6%	33.2%	1,003,064	1,701,272
55 - 59	12.4%	24.7%	2,147,743	4,290,273
50 - 54	11.0%	12.0%	2,189,387	2,392,424
25 - 29	8.2%	12.4%	1,622,546	2,442,120
70 - 74	7.0%	29.3%	597,047	2,486,482
5 - 9	6.4%	11.1%	1,239,310	2,156,273
0 - 4	4.5%	9.1%	930,683	1,862,878
20 - 24	4.1%	4.7%	852,987	986,659
30 - 34	2.1%	10.1%	424,157	2,010,712
80 - 84	1.6%	0.4%	88,852	24,205
45 - 49	0.9%	-6.8%	200,977	-1,527,544
15 - 19	0.8%	-4.4%	164,414	-928,938
75 - 79	-2.6%	5.2%	-189,856	384,774
35 - 39	-3.5%	1.6%	-732,602	-326,079
10 - 14	-5.1%	0.7%	-1,070,416	146,001
40 - 44	-7.7%	-10.9%	-1,750,443	-2,484,853

Table 3 highlights two important points. The first is that, according to these projections, the total population of the US is expected to increase by about 13 million over the period 2005-2010, and by 26 million over the period 2005-2015. The second point is that this net population gain will include mostly people in the age group of 50- 69, which, as discussed earlier, have *high headship and homeownership rates*. These observations suggest that, all else being equal, this population growth will translate to household growth and increases in housing demand. Furthermore, given the age structure of the additional population, it should translate to increases in demand for *smaller*, owner-occupied, single-family units, condominiums, and apartments.

Death rates, in combination with birth rates, affect the size of the total population. When death rates are lower than birth rates, then the area's total population increases. Population increases due to new births that outnumber deaths, however, will have minimal, if any, effect on household increases, since most couples represent already separate household units by the time a baby is born. Deaths, though, can contribute to household losses, especially if the deceased represents a person living alone.

Social factors, such as *marriage rates* and *divorce rates*, also affect the rate of household formation and household size. Higher marriage rates can have a negative effect on household formation if two separate households merge. Higher divorce rates may have a positive effect on household formation, since in most cases one household splits into two separate households, thus contributing to smaller household size. Besides divorce rates, household size is also affected by the prevailing culture regarding marriage and family with notions of late marriage and smaller families contributing to smaller household sizes. As will be discussed below, employment and income growth also plays a role, as it allows young adults living in family and non-family settings to move out and form their own household.

Household size is a critical variable for household growth, because if it gets smaller through time (as it has been the case for the last 45 years, according to data available from the US Census Bureau), an area's total number of households will increase, even if the population remains constant. Table 4 presents population and household trends since 1960. This data confirms the long-term trend towards smaller households in the United States. Furthermore, it demonstrates how declining household size can *accelerate considerably household growth*. Notice how stronger household growth is compared to population growth from 1965 to 1980, when household size was declining at rates ranging between 5.4% and 6.4%. For example, during the period 1970-1975, when household size declined by 6.4%, the number of total households grew by 12.2%, although population only grew by 5%. During the 1990s, household size remained practically stagnant, but it has shown signs of further decline in the first three years of this decade (see Table 4).

Table 4 – Household Size Trends in the United States: 1960-2003

Year	Population in Households	All Households	Household Size	Change in Household Size	Population Growth	Household Growth
1960	176.877	52.799	3,35			
1965	190.688	57.436	3,32	-0,9%	7,8%	8,8%
1970	199.079	63.401	3,14	-5,4%	4,4%	10,4%
1975	209.093	71.120	2,94	-6,4%	5,0%	12,2%
1980	222.942	80.776	2,76	-6,1%	6,6%	13,6%
1985	233.462	86.789	2,69	-2,5%	4,7%	7,4%
1990	245.503	93.347	2,63	-2,2%	5,2%	7,6%
1995	262.324	98.990	2,65	0,8%	6,9%	6,0%
2000	274.327	104.705	2,62	-1,1%	4,6%	5,8%
2003	285.984	111.278	2,57	-1,9%	4,2%	6,3%

Source: US Census Bureau

Finally, *net migration* can also contribute to increases in the number of households living in an area. Net migration is actually the difference between immigration and outmigration. If immigration is greater than outmigration, then the area's population and number of households should increase. Net migration flows (domestic or international) play an increasing role in triggering population increases when natural population growth is slow. According to the Census Bureau (2003) during 1995-2000, over 22 million Americans changed their state of residence, with approximately half relocating to a state in a different region.

Inflows and outflows of domestic migrants vary widely across states, with both winners and losers in terms of net migration flows. As Figure 24 indicates, the state that benefited the most from domestic migration flows during the period 1995-2000 was Florida, with a net migration gain of over 600,000 people, followed by Georgia, North Carolina, Arizona, and Nevada, with net migration gains ranging between 230,000 and 350,000 people. Such population increases must have contributed to significant increases in the number of households in these states and, therefore, in housing demand.

Figure 24 – Top Ten States with the Largest Domestic Net Migration Flows in the US during 1995-2000

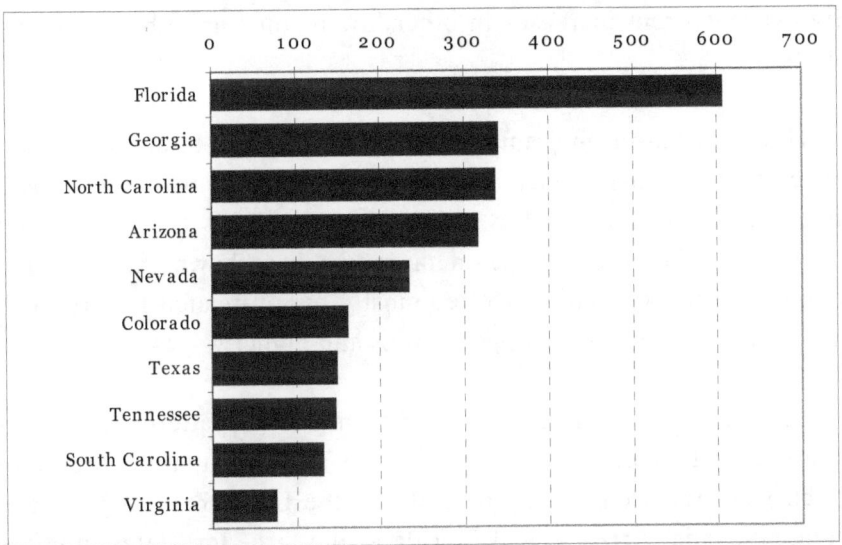

Source: US Census Bureau

The three states that registered the largest net domestic migration losses were California, New York, and Chicago. In fact, California registered the largest net domestic migration loss, exceeding 800,000 people, which seems surprising, given that this state is considered one of the country's most attractive areas. However, this number is especially misleading for California, which is the recipient of large international migration flows. An estimate of net migration flows by California's Department of Finance (CDF), which takes into account international migration, found that from year-end 1995 to year-end 2000, the state registered net migration gains of about 870,000 persons. CDF also estimated that from 2000 to 2004, the state added more than 1.2 million people, due to domestic and international migration.

Saiz (2001) reports results that link migration flows to housing demand and prices. In particular, this analyst found a strong relationship *between immigration in 1990 and increases in moderate-quality housing rents* during 1990-1992. Such a finding provides evidence of increases in housing demand due to immigration, which in turn triggered increases in housing rents. Saiz also found that immigration in the Miami area expanded the renter population by 9% in 1980, and that housing rent increases in low-income, Spanish-speaking areas of the city exceeded rent increases in other low-income units by 6 percentage points.

The main reason migrants move from one place to another is to improve their status either in terms of employment and earning opportunities or in terms of overall living conditions, including amenities and climate. Empirical work on migration has shown that movements across labor markets are motivated mostly by job-related factors, such as expectations for better job opportunities and higher wages.

Having in mind the inter-state net migration patterns presented in Figure 24, it is not surprising that the state population projections, which were released in July of 2005 by the US Bureau of the Census, feature Nevada, Arizona, and Florida as the three top states in terms of population growth by 2010 and 2015 (see Table 5). In particular, the US Bureau of the Census predicts that the population of Nevada will grow by 14% over the period 2005-2010 and by 30% over the period 2005-2015. Population in Arizona and Florida is expected to grow by 13% and 10%, respectively, over the period 2005-2010 and by 27% and 21%, respectively, over the period 2005-2015. It is interesting to note that the nation's most populated state, California, ranks eleventh, as it is expected to register population increases of 6% and 11% during the two periods.

The strong population growth rates in the three top states (Nevada, Arizona, and Florida) translate to average annual growth rates, ranging between 2% and 3%. If these population growth rates materialize, they should contribute to considerable increases in the demand for housing in these states, assuming no adverse economic, demographic, or interest rate conditions will counterbalance their effect on the housing market. The extent to which such demand increases will translate to increases in housing prices will depend on the *housing supply conditions* in the cities that will be the beneficiaries of this population growth.

Table 5 – US Census Bureau Population Projections, July 2005: 20 Top States in Terms of Population Growth

State	2005-2010	2005-2015
Nevada	14,4%	30,0%
Arizona	13,1%	27,7%
Florida	9,9%	21,1%
Texas	8,2%	16,7%
Idaho	7,8%	15,8%
Georgia	7,4%	14,6%
North Carolina	7,4%	15,0%
Utah	7,3%	15,1%
Virginia	6,1%	12,1%
Delaware	5,7%	10,8%
California	5,6%	11,3%
Washington	5,4%	12,0%
Maryland	5,4%	10,9%
Oregon	5,4%	11,6%
New Hampshire	5,4%	10,8%
Hawai	5,0%	8,6%
Alaska	5,0%	10,8%
South Carolina	4,9%	9,5%
Minnesota	4,8%	9,5%
Colorado	4,6%	9,3%

Increases in Income

Increases in income can contribute to increases in demand for housing in several ways. First, income increases are likely to contribute to new household formation, as they may allow many individuals living in a family or non-family setting to form their own household. For example, young adults living with their parents are likely to form their own households as soon as their financial situation allows it. A study of the household-formation behavior of young adults by Di and Liu (2003) presents evidence that supports this proposition. Burns and Grebler (1986) also assert the positive effect of income growth on household formation and housing demand. Increases in the number of an area's households are more likely to occur when increases in an area's total income are the result of employment growth as opposed to increases in average household income without job growth.

Second, increases in the average income of an area's households, especially those headed by persons in the prime renting age group of 25-35, may contribute to increases in the demand for owner-occupied housing and to decreases in the demand for rental-housing in the area. Keeping housing prices constant, higher incomes will make housing more affordable to several renters and enable them to enter the market for owner-occupied housing. Notice that the shift of existing households from the rental market to the owner-occupied market *may not necessarily result in a decrease in total demand for rental housing*, due to the phenomenon described in the previous paragraph. For example, if the number of new households that are formed and enter the rental market because of income increases is greater than the number of existing renters that shift to homeownership, the total rental demand in the area will actually increase.

Finally, increases in the income of households in the full-nest stage will allow them to upgrade their housing situation, thereby triggering increases in demand for larger and higher-quality houses.

Reduction in Mortgage Rates

Mortgage rate reductions make the financing of housing purchases cheaper, thereby allowing more households to buy a housing unit. Decreases in mortgage rates to 40-year historical low levels, which took place in the early 2000s, triggered significant increases in demand for owner-occupied housing, which in turn generated big value gains for those who were lucky to enter at the beginning of the steep rise in housing prices that followed. Mortgage rates have started rising slowly from their forty-year, record-low levels, and most economists expect them to rise further in the medium-term future. If mortgage rates continue rising in the future, they will have a negative effect on housing demand (all else being equal). The magnitude of the effect will depend on the speed by which interest rates rise. For example, a slow, gradual increase is more likely to have a smoother effect than a steep ascent.

Expectations of Rising Prices

Homeowners are both users and investors, although some households may view the purchase of their house more as a means for satisfying a need rather than as an investment. Most households realize that buying a house represents a significant commitment of capital and understand the investment nature of their decision. Furthermore, many first-time homebuyers know they will eventually resell their first home in order to upgrade to a better and larger house when their income allows it. In addition, homeowners know their house is the only collateral they can use to borrow large sums of money. As the value of their home increases, the amount of money they can borrow increases, too. In this sense, it represents a major means of financial security. For these reasons, homebuyers are strongly interested in the appreciation potential of the properties they buy and the prospects for capital gains from their resale.

The investment nature of owner-occupancy and the importance of appreciation expectations in the home-buying decision have created a paradox in the housing market. In particular, it has been observed and verified that during periods of rising prices, housing demand rises! This seemingly violates that fundamental law of demand, which postulates that when the price of a good increases, demand for that good decreases. This interpretation, however, is not accurate, because demand increases for owner-occupied housing are not triggered by the higher price levels but by the expectations of price increases in the future. These expectations are triggered by the rising prices at the time of purchase, as buyers extrapolate continuation of these trends in the future.

Closing, let me point out that I didn't mention housing prices as a potential factor for contributing to household formation and, therefore, to housing demand, on purpose. Remember that this book focuses on increases in demand that can potentially trigger price increases, which means the discussion needs to focus on the non-price factors that trigger increases in housing demand.

WHAT MAY CAUSE INCREASES IN LOCATIONAL DEMAND FOR HOUSING

Based on the broader framework developed in terms of how demand for a specific location may increase, we can distinguish two types of housing demand increases that can occur at a specific location: 1) market-driven increases, and 2) development-driven increases.

When thinking about market-driven demand increases, the question is—which housing locations will benefit the most from an increase in broader demand for housing? My hypothesis is that the most attractive and most advantageous neighborhoods, which *better match the demands and affordability level of new buyers*, as determined by their demographic and income profile, will be the ones that will benefit the most in terms of value gains from increases in aggregate market demand (assuming no increases in supply). What makes a neighborhood attractive to housing buyers or renters? It is widely accepted that housing consumers value the following locational characteristics:

a) Convenient access to jobs and employment centers
b) Nice, quite neighborhood environment
c) Convenient access to a good school
d) Convenient access to services
e) Convenient access to shopping and recreational destinations
f) High level of public services
g) Proximity to a public park or greenbelt
h) Proximity to the beach (if the city is a coastal city)
i) Low property tax rates

In thinking about increases in housing demand, as well as how this demand may be distributed across locations, we need to distinguish between demand for *new* housing units and demand for *existing* housing units; the former will be distributed to *new residential developments*, while the latter to *relatively mature neighborhoods*. Within this framework, it can be agued that investments in the most advantageous neighborhoods (developing or relatively mature) in markets where owner-occupied or rental housing demand is predicted to increase considerably and supply is expected to remain stagnant or grow slowly, are likely to allow significant profits (see Box 2).

In searching for locations with strong potential for development-driven increases in demand for housing, investors need to consider what kind of developments can increase the attractiveness of a residential area. Based on the discussion so far, we can argue that the following developments can improve the attractiveness of a residential neighborhood and trigger increases in location demand for housing (see Figure 25):

BOX 2

Pinellas County's Most Attractive Communities Register Strongest Value Increases

On June 1, 2005, St. Petersburg Times reported that while property values in Pinellas County increased by an average of 13.2% from last year, property values at beach communities, such as Redington Shores, NorthRedington Beach, Madeira Beach, and Treasure Island registered the highest year-to-year increases, exceeding 20%. The very strong value increases at these locations were the result of the increased demand for housing in the area, due to the low interest rates and the dominance of these communities in terms of attractiveness. This is an example of the potential effectiveness of the double-focus strategy suggested in this book—investing in the most attractive locations in markets expected to register strong increases in demand for housing.

---

a) *Considerable improvement of access to jobs and employment centers*—such improvement can occur due to construction of new subway station in neighborhood, development of large office and industrial parks at short driving distance from the location under consideration, and completion of new freeway or major transportation artery passing outside but near the borders of the community

b) *Considerable improvement of neighborhood environment*, through sidewalk and road improvements, tree planting, landscaping, and street lighting

c) *Relocation or opening of a good school* at a conveniently close location

d) *Development of shops, services, and/or recreation facilities* close enough to provide convenient access to residents, but far enough to spare residents from any nuisance from increased traffic

e) *Significant upgrading of the level of public services* provided (police and fire protection), without significant increases in property tax rates

f) *Development of a large park or greenbelt* very close to the location under consideration

Figure 25 – Forces that Trigger Increases in Location Demand for Housing

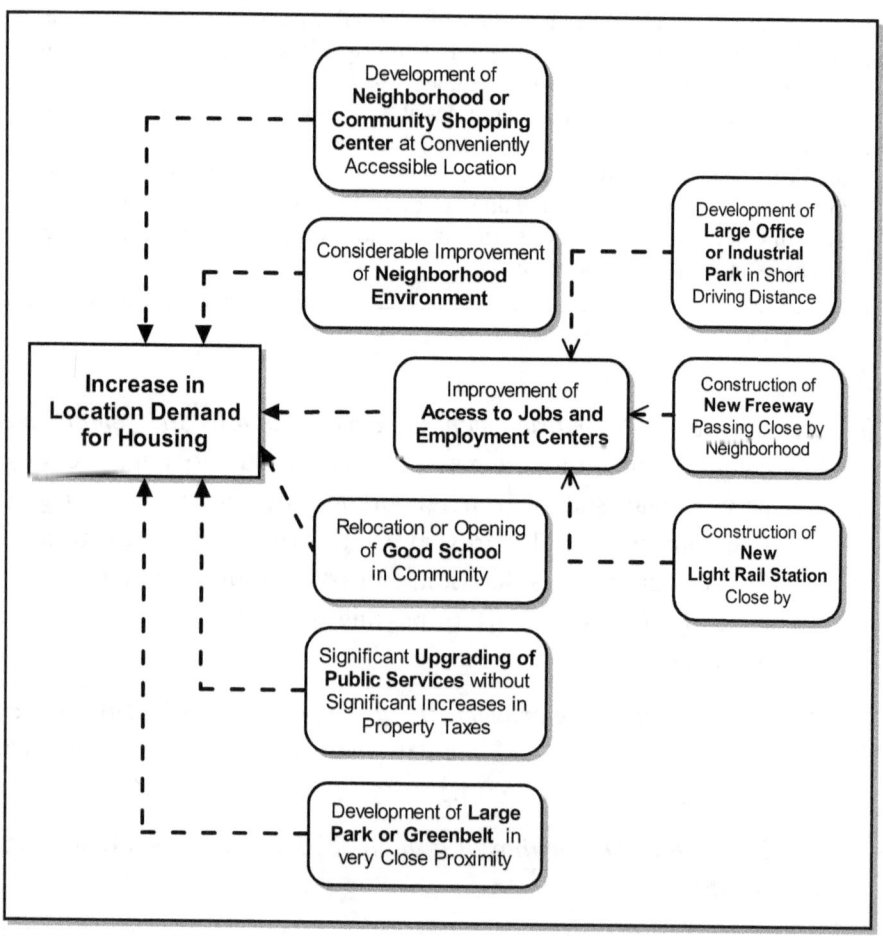

To understand the value that consumers place on residential amenities, consider that a study conducted in 1995 by American Lives, Inc.

reported that 77.7% of the study participants rated natural open space as "essential" or "very important" in planned communities. A number of studies have verified the higher value of properties adjacent to large tracts of open public space. For example, a study by Correll, Lillydahl, and Singell in 1978 estimated that the average value of a property adjacent to the greenbelt would be 32% higher than that of a similar property 3,200 feet away. In addition, a study of the effect of proximity to a park in Columbus, Ohio on residential values found that homes that faced the park sold at a price 7% to 23% higher than the price at which similar residential properties just one block away were sold (Weicher and Zerbst, 1973).

Finally, a study carried out in 2005, by the Economic Research Associates, on behalf of the Illinois Association of Park Districts, concluded that neighborhood and community parks can have a significant effect on the values of nearby properties.[16] In particular, based on the review of relevant studies, analysts indicate that homes facing neighborhood parks may get an up to a 20% boost in value, while homes facing community parks may get an up to a 33% boost in value. Property-value benefits seem to extend 600 feet, in the case of neighborhood parks, and 2,000 feet, in the case of community parks.

If we reverse these findings, it can be argued that properties that are nowhere near a greenbelt or a park could appreciate significantly if large public open space was developed very close to them. Therefore, the development of a new large park in a relatively densely developed area would contribute to significant increases in the values of adjacent properties. If the area is not densely developed when the park is constructed, increases in values of adjacent properties may not be very strong. There is little doubt, however, that such properties will *appreciate considerably faster* than properties that are not in close proximity to the park as the area becomes more densely developed.

In sum, properties in neighborhoods that are expected to improve significantly in terms of amenities and accessibility to services and the broader urban area should appreciate considerably in value as the developments that

---

[16] Economic Research Associates, 20 E. Jackson Boulevard Suite 1200, Chicago IL 60604,Tel. 312.427.3855, FAX 312.427.3660, www.econres.com

will trigger such improvements materialize. However, it is important that these neighborhoods are located in housing markets that are not about to become oversupplied.

SUMMARY

> ➢ In thinking about forces that can trigger increases in demand for different property types, we need to distinguish between increases in aggregate demand within an urban area and increases in locational demand.

> ➢ Increases in aggregate market demand for all types of housing or a particular type of housing (such as owner-occupied, rental, high-income, low-income, etc.) can be triggered by increases in the number of an area's households, increases in income (total income or average household income), increases in the population over 40, decreases in interest rates and mortgage rates, and expectations of rising prices.

> ➢ Increases in locational demand for housing can be triggered by significant improvements of accessibility to jobs and employment centers, relocation or opening of good schools at nearby locations, improvement of access to services, upgrading of the level of public services provided, significant improvement of neighborhood environment, and nearby developments of large parks or greenbelts.

Chapter 7

Forces that Trigger Increases in Demand for Office Space

In contrast to residential properties that are used by households, commercial properties include mainly office, retail, and industrial buildings that are used by firms. Office properties rank high in the preferences of institutional real estate investors.

As was the case for residential real estate, when thinking about forces that may trigger increases in demand for office buildings and office space, we need to distinguish between the macroeconomic factors that trigger increases in broader market demand and physical developments in the urban fabric that can trigger increases in demand at specific locations.

What May Cause Increases in Aggregate Market Demand for Office Space

The demand for office space is a derived demand because firms rent space as an input to the production of services or goods they provide to businesses and households in the local, regional, or national economy. According to office building surveys, the major tenants of office space are firms providing finance, insurance, real estate (FIRE), and other services, including primarily professional, business, and government services (Wheaton 1987). Within the service sector, DiPasquale and Wheaton (1996) consider the following types of firms as office space users: advertising, computer and data processing, credit reporting, mailing and reproduction, legal and social services, membership organizations, and engineering and management services. Thus, if market demand for such services increases, demand for office space will also increase (to the extent that the additional demand for services cannot be satisfied by existing firms without using any additional space).

The aggregate demand for office space at the broader market level refers to the total amount of square feet of office space demanded by all firms interested in operating within that market. This is actually the sum of the individual office space demands of each of these firms. The demand of an individual firm for office space depends on the size of the firm, that is, the number of its employees and the amount of office space used per employee.

Within this context, the total amount of office space demanded at the broader market level is determined by the *number of firms* utilizing office space (I refer to these firms as office firms), the *size of each firm* in terms of number of employees, and the amount of *office space per employee* demanded by each firm. Actually, aggregate demand for office space in a market is the product of these three factors (number of firms x average number of employees per firm x square feet per employee). Also notice that the product of the number of office firms times the average number of employees per firm gives the *total office employment* in the market under consideration.

Obviously, the greater the number of firms, the greater the average number of employees per firm, and the greater the amount of square feet per employee required by each firm, the greater the total amount of office space demanded within a market. Within this context, increases in aggregate market demand for office space can be triggered by (see Figure 26):

1) *Increases in the number of office firms* operating in the market
2) *Increases in the average number of workers employed* by each office firm, and
3) *Increases in the amount of office space per employee* demanded by each firm.

Figure 26 – Forces that Trigger Increases in Aggregate Demand for Office Space

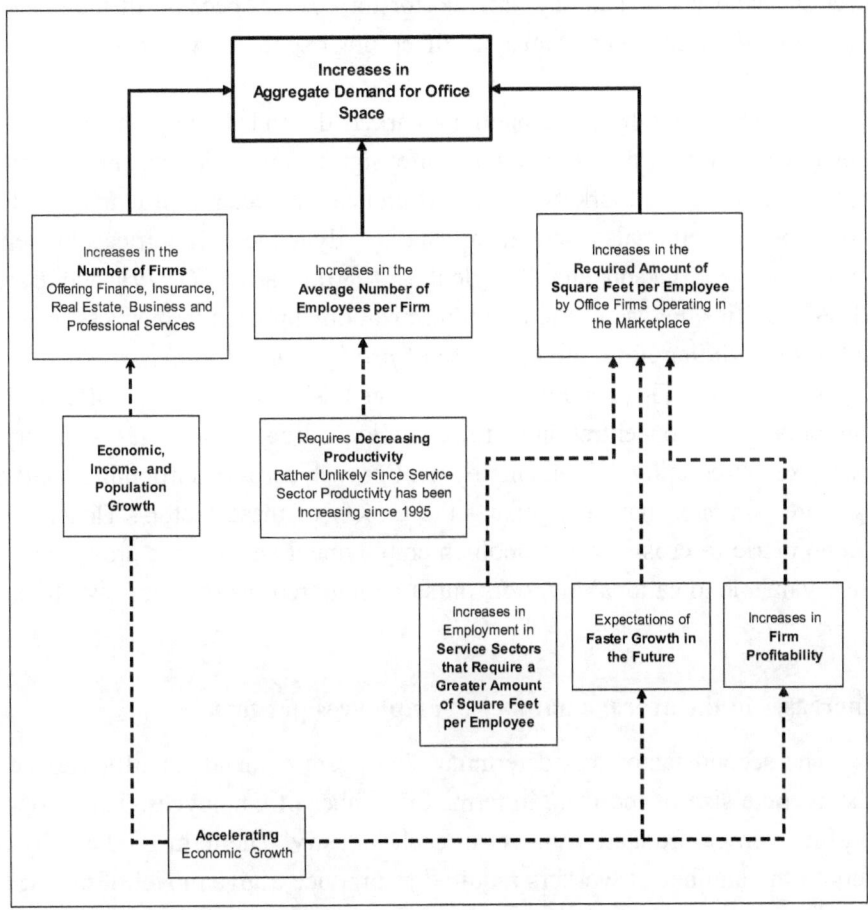

Notice that aggregate office space demand will increase if one or more of these factors increase, as long as no counterbalancing decreases in the other factors take place. Also, notice that the stronger the increases in these factors, the stronger the increases in market demand for office space (all else being equal).

Increases in the number of office firms operating in the market

Increases in the number of office firms operating in the market can be triggered by economic, population, and/or income growth (see Figure 26). Such growth will trigger increases in demand for services, which in turn will stimulate the birth of new firms and/or expansion of existing ones. It should be noted that the service sector, which includes most of the office-space-using firms, has been growing faster than any other sector for decades because of the ongoing transition of the economy from a manufacturing one to a service one.

Economic growth of metropolitan markets depends largely on how the national economy is doing, but there are significant variations in economic growth rates across markets due to differences in sectoral structure, production cost differentials, and local market dynamics. Empirical evidence presented by Erickson and Wasylenko (1980), Carlton (1979), and Bartik (1984) verifies the use of the cost minimization approach in business location selection and, therefore, the influence of *production cost differentials* in driving job growth. These studies suggest that business location is affected by agglomeration (concentration of firms), unionization rates, wages, and corporate taxes. Predicting though employment growth across metropolitan markets is more complex than recognizing the effects of these factors. That is why econometric forecasts of metropolitan employment and income growth can be very valuable to national investors pursuing high returns in office investments.

Increases in the average number of employees per firm

The second factor that determines aggregate demand for office space is the average size of the firm, in terms of number of employees. This depends on the average productivity level in each industry. The term productivity refers to the number of workers required to produce a given level of output (or number of workers needed per unit of output). If firms in service industries find themselves in a position where they will need to use more workers to produce the same level of output, the average number of employees per firm will increase and demand for office space will increase, too (all else being equal). Such a development would represent a decline in productivity though.

The outlook for productivity declines and increases in the average number of workers employed by office firms is highly questionable, given a long-term trend of *rising productivity*. Normally, automation and technological advancements make each employee more efficient and more productive, increasing the output produced per worker and reducing the total number of employees needed to produce a given amount of output. Economists and real estate analysts have expressed fears that rapidly rising productivity (output per worker), due to advancements in technology and information processing, may limit office employment growth in the future. An alternate view is that most possibilities for dramatic improvements in office worker productivity have been exhausted. Nevertheless, productivity losses, which are needed to push the average number of employees per firm up, are not very likely in the foreseeable future.

Increases in the space per employee demanded by office firms

Non-price factors that influence office space requirements per employee include the *type of services* provided by the firm, the *growth prospects* of the firm, and the *profitability* of the firm. Within this context, increases in the square-feet-per-employee requirements of office firms can be triggered by:

a) Employment growth in service activities that *require a greater amount of space per employee*

b) Expectations for faster growth in the future

c) Increases in office firm profitability

Increases in service activities that require a greater amount of space per employee- Space requirements per office worker vary by industry. It is often agued that space requirements are greater in the case of firms that are active in the prestigious finance, insurance, and real estate sectors. Carn et al. (1988) suggest that space-per-worker requirements *vary by occupation*, with managers and professionals occupying more square feet than clerks and secretaries. Therefore, the average square feet per employee should vary across markets, depending on the *composition of their service industries* and their *occupational structures*. Thus, employment growth in service sectors that *use managerial and professional labor in greater proportions* should contribute to an increase in the average square feet per employee.

Daniels (1975) suggests that the amount of space occupied by each office worker has increased steadily throughout the years, for a number of reasons. These include the growth of administrative and professional occupations, which tend to utilize more space per worker, the increasing scale of office machines and equipment, and the increase of ancillary space in office buildings, such as staff lounges and reception rooms. Daniels argued that future changes in the demand for office space per worker would depend on the degree to which elite office activities that demand a greater amount of space per employee continue to increase their share in the nation's total economic activity.

Expectations for faster growth in the future-Expectations regarding future growth prospects affect a firm's demand for office space, because commercial leases are usually multi-year, making the leasing of space a long-term commitment on the part of the firm. For example, if a firm evaluates that it will be growing faster in the immediate and mid-term future, it will demand a greater amount of space per employee in order to accommodate future expansion needs. If, however, the company expects deceleration of its growth rate, it will demand less space per employee. Firms tend to be more optimistic when the economy is growing, as opposed to when it is declining. Therefore, it is more likely that firms will expect faster growth in the future, when economic growth is accelerating. This suggests that during periods of accelerating employment growth, office space demand gets a double boost This double boost is likely to come from increases in office employment and increases in required office space per employee. Therefore, short-term investments in office buildings, in markets where economic growth is about to accelerate, is likely to provide big profits, if the market vacancy rate is low and completions of new office space are expected to be low.

Increases in office firm profitability-The amount of space per employee demanded by a firm should also be influenced by its profitability. For example, increases in company profitability should reduce pressure to restrict office space use, as less profitable firms might need to do. Sivitanides (1990), in an unpublished study of 19 major office markets in the US, found that areas in which office employment represented a smaller share of total employment, the amount of occupied office space per employee was greater. This can be explained based on the profitability argument, if we assume that each of the office-space-using firms in these areas enjoys a greater market share (since the total pie is divided among a smaller number of firms) and is, therefore, more profitable.

Based on the above discussion, we can trace the characteristics of markets and circumstances likely to create the *dynamics that will generate high returns*, in the short-term, for investments in office buildings:

- The major office space using sectors—FIRE, business, professional, and government services, are predicted to grow rapidly in the near future
- The local economy is predicted to grow at accelerating rates
- The local market vacancy rate for office space is relatively and sufficiently low
- Supply of new office space is expected to remain stagnant or grow slowly (based on building permits issued in the last 12 months and buildings under construction that may have obtained a building permit earlier)

PROSPECTS FOR INCREASES IN OFFICE EMPLOYMENT AND OFFICE SPACE DEMAND

The long-term trend of increases in service employment, which has fueled increases in demand for office space in the past, is likely to continue in the future, but at a slower pace compared to the past, as indicated by projections of employment in major service sectors, prepared by the Bureau of Labor Statistics for the period 2004-2014. These projections, as well as historical statistics, for the period 1990-2004 are presented in Table 6.

Table 6 – Bureau of Labor Statistics Projections of Employment in Major Service Sectors

Industry sector	Thousands of jobs			Numeric change		Average Annual Percent Change	
	1994	2004	2014	1994-2004	2004-14	1994-2004	2004-14
Information	2,739	3,138	3,502	399	364	1.4%	1.1%
Financial activities	6,867	8,052	8,901	1,185	849	1.6%	1.0%
Professional and business services	12,174	16,414	20,980	4,240	4,566	3.0%	2.5%
Other services	5,202	6,210	6,943	1,008	733	1.8%	1.1%
Federal government	3,018	2,728	2,771	-290	43	-1.0%	0.2%
State and local government	16,257	18,891	21,019	2,634	2,128	1.5%	1.1%

As Table 6 indicates, the Bureau of Labor Statistics (BLS) predicted that employment in major office using sectors would continue to rise over the period 2004-2014, but at rates lower than the ones registered in the previous ten years (1994-2004). *Professional and business services* are expected to grow considerably faster than other major service employment sectors. In particular, employment in professional and business services is expected to grow at an average annual rate of 2.5%, while employment in financial activities, information services, and other services, as well as state and local government employment, is expected to grow at rates ranging from 1.0% to 1.1%. All in all, BLS predicted that, between 2004 and 2014, professional and business services will add about 4.6 million new jobs, while state and local government employment will grow by 2.1 million jobs. Financial and other services are expected to add about 1.5 million new jobs over the same period.

The challenge for real estate investors pursuing high returns is to identify which metropolitan markets are about to register the strongest office employment growth and then identify office clusters that are bound to benefit the most (in terms of rent and value gains) from such increases. Econometric forecasts of office employment growth, new supply estimates, and vacancy rate projections are necessary inputs for identifying the markets with the best prospects for strong office rent and value gains.

BASICS OF LOCATIONAL DEMAND FOR OFFICE SPACE

When thinking about locational demand for office space, it is important to remember that there is great location substitutability within a metropolitan area. This substitutability is the result of several factors, including the fact that many office firms have a metrowide or regional clientele, and their revenues are not affected by their specific location within the metropolitan area. Furthermore, significant advances in communication technologies that reduced the need for face to face contacts, and transportation improvements that made most locations within today's metropolitan areas easily accessible within reasonable travel times, have contributed significantly in diminishing locational advantages among office-space clusters within the urban fabric.

Another important location aspect of the office market is the segmentation between *CBD* office locations and *non-CBD* office locations, with the former typically considered more prestigious and dominant in terms of size, concentration, and comprehensiveness of services offered.

Locational demand for office space may also be differentiated along certain dimensions that influence firm locational requirements. In particular, the following distinctions are helpful when thinking about locational demand for office space:

- General-purpose office firms vs. special-purpose firms that have special locational requirements
- Type of operations performed—front or back office functions
- Type of labor used—executive vs. clerical

The distinction between general-purpose firms and special-purpose firms is useful, as the latter may have special locational requirements. For example, medical office buildings tend to cluster around a large health facility. With this in mind, one can anticipate that the construction of a new hospital will result in an increase in demand for medical offices at nearby locations.

The distinction between front-office and back-office operations has also implications in terms of locational requirements. For example, front-office operations require good accessibility to potential clientele and perhaps a prestigious location, whereas back-office operations have neither of these two requirements and can be performed at secondary, low-rent locations. Many of the first firms that moved to cheaper office space in the suburbs were divisions of downtown firms, which realized that they could reduce their rental costs by splitting their operations in this way. This suggests that an increase in the number of firms with significant back-office operations may result in increases in demand for cheaper suburban locations.

The extent to which a firm uses mostly executive or clerical labor is important as far as location access is concerned. For example, firms using mostly executive labor may value more locations with good access to nice, upscale, residential neighborhoods that can house their employees. On the contrary, firms using mostly clerical labor may prefer locations with good broader private and public transportation access.

Given considerable substitutability across office locations within the same metropolitan area, demand for office space at a given location depends on its attractiveness and advantages in satisfying the locational requirements of office firms vis a vis other competing locations in the urban area. Thus, demand for office space at a given location may increase if a location becomes more attractive, relative to competing office clusters, or when the *comparative advantages of an office cluster increase*. Notice that some locations may become attractive because of declining rents. Obviously, since we are interested in demand increases that will cause office rent and value increases such locations should be avoided.

To understand what may make a location more attractive to office firms, we need to understand how office firms choose locations. The primary objective of a typical firm is *profit maximization*. In applying this framework, office firms consider their costs and revenues at alternative locations and choose the one that appears to maximize their profits. The revenues of a firm depend on access to clients, availability of specialized information and contacts, market share, competitiveness of the industry, and the state of the economy. Obviously, for firms that expect to earn about the same revenue at any location within the metropolitan area, profit maximization is equivalent to cost minimization when choosing a location. In such a case firm costs at alternative office clusters will be the primary determinants of location choice. The major costs of an office firm include labor costs, that is, wages paid to employees, office space rents, and transportation and communication costs.

In terms of cost factors, Daniels (1975) argues that transportation costs are of less significance for office firms than manufacturing firms. According to various surveys, proximity to clients, as well as labor availability and cost, play an important role in office location decisions. A survey of 571 offices in Greater London found that proximity to clients was the major factor that determined the location decision of the largest proportion of the survey participants. A *Fortune* market research survey of 61 corporations found that considerable importance was assigned to factors affecting *employee access to work*, and *labor distribution and availability*. Another survey of four major firms providing office location services in Houston concluded that the three most important location factors for office firms were: a) mobility and general access, b) residential location of employees, and c) linkages to other businesses. In addition, three out of four location experts answered that labor distribution was of primary concern in the case of executives and specialized employees, and important in the case of general employees (Rice Center Community Research Development, Corp., 1979).

MARKET-DRIVEN INCREASES IN LOCATIONAL DEMAND FOR OFFICE SPACE

Market-driven increases in locational demand for office space will occur in markets where employment in office sectors is expected to grow rapidly. Which locations will capture such increases in demand? I would argue that the strongest and most advantageous locations are more likely to be the major beneficiaries of such demand increases. Thus, locations that have a comparative advantage in terms of satisfying the locational requirements of office firms are more likely to feel the greatest pressure from new demand and register the strongest price increases (assuming that there is no oversupply). Based on the discussion of the previous subsection, it appears that productivity and cost reduction are the primary concerns of office firms when choosing locations. In particular, office firms value the following locational characteristics:

a) Close access to basic business support activities

Close access to facilities that can provide services typically sought by the firms in support of their business activities, or by employees during working hours, such as banking, basic business services, restaurants, and shopping can help reduce the time costs of accommodating such needs and increase firm productivity.

b) Access to client base

Good access to residential areas is valued especially by firms providing services mostly to households rather than businesses. Also, areas that are poorly served by competitors provide opportunities for capturing untapped market demand and increasing a firm's market share. In this sense, businesses may find commercial space in poorly served areas attractive.

b) Access to business service concentrations

Since linkages play an important role in firm location choice, office firms should value access to business concentrations because it reduces the cost of interpersonal contacts with their clients, business associates, or input providers. The effect of this factor, however, may have been weakening, due to advances in information and telecommunication technologies. In a study of rental rates paid by office firms in the Los Angeles area, Sivitanidou (1997) presents evidence showing that the importance of access to business service centers may have been decreasing through time.

c) Access to labor

Surveys cited earlier indicate that office firms value access to labor because it may reduce the time and cost of their labor searches. Furthermore, it may reduce the cost of wages, since workers living close to their workplace may be willing to accept lower wages. Office firms may seek central-city and CBD locations if specialized labor is dispersed, while suburban locations may be sought if labor skills are clustered in the suburbs.

d) Freeway and airport access

Good freeway access should render firms more productive because it will reduce the time and costs of business trips at any destination within the market they operate. Proximity to freeways and freeway junctions should also be valued by firms, as it provides greater access to labor and potential customers over a larger geographic area. Good airport access is becoming increasingly important, due to the globalization of business activity and the resultant need for increased air travel. Within this context, improvement of a location in terms of these access advantages should contribute to greater firm productivity, potentially greater revenues, and lower costs.

e) Prestige and visibility

Location prestige and visibility are especially important for high profile firms and corporate headquarters. Usually, downtown locations or prestigious suburban nodes are the preferred locations of these types of firms.

f) Access to amenable residential communities

Firms should value locations with good access to high-quality residential communities, with low crime rates and high levels of amenities and public services, for two reasons. First, they provide access to an upper-income client base. Second, they provide good access to skilled labor, thereby reducing labor search costs. Good access to amenable residential areas becomes more important for firms employing a higher proportion of managerial labor.

Office clusters that have comparative advantages in terms of these characteristics may be the ones to attract the bulk of new office space demand as the area and its economy grows. Within this context, investors should:

- First select metropolitan areas that have low vacancy rates and are expected to register strong growth in office employment, and then
- Within these markets, focus on properties located within the clusters with the greatest comparative advantages in terms of the aforementioned locational attributes

WHAT MAY CAUSE DEVELOPMENT-DRIVEN INCREASES IN LOCATIONAL DEMAND FOR OFFICE SPACE

Development-driven increases in locational demand for office space will occur when nearby or more distant developments in the environment of a given office cluster induce increases in demand for office space at that location. In trying to identify what types of urban development projects may trigger increases in locational demand for office space, we need to think about the kind of developments that will increase the utility of a location to office firms. Obviously, improvements in locational attributes valued by office firms should increase a location's utility to such firms. Therefore, one can argue that the following developments should trigger increases in locational demand for office space (see Figure 27):

a) Improvement of nearby access to basic business support activities
This could happen in the case of significant commercial/retail development in a cluster poorly served by business support activities.

b) Improvement of location access to business concentrations
A location's access to business concentrations could improve due to major transportation projects that make business concentrations within the metropolitan area more easily accessible from the location

under consideration, or due to ongoing developments of new office clusters at a reasonable distance from the location under consideration.

c) Improvement of location access to labor

Significant improvements of a commercial node's accessibility to a large pool of workers should increase considerably its attractiveness to office firms and trigger increases in location demand for office space. These demand increases should in turn translate to rent increases, if there is no excess supply. Significant improvement of the accessibility of an office cluster to labor could occur through the development of a nearby light transit rail station, the construction of new major transportation arteries that improve considerably its general access to the area, or intensive residential developments in areas around the cluster.

Figure 27 – Forces that Trigger Increases in Location Demand for Office Space

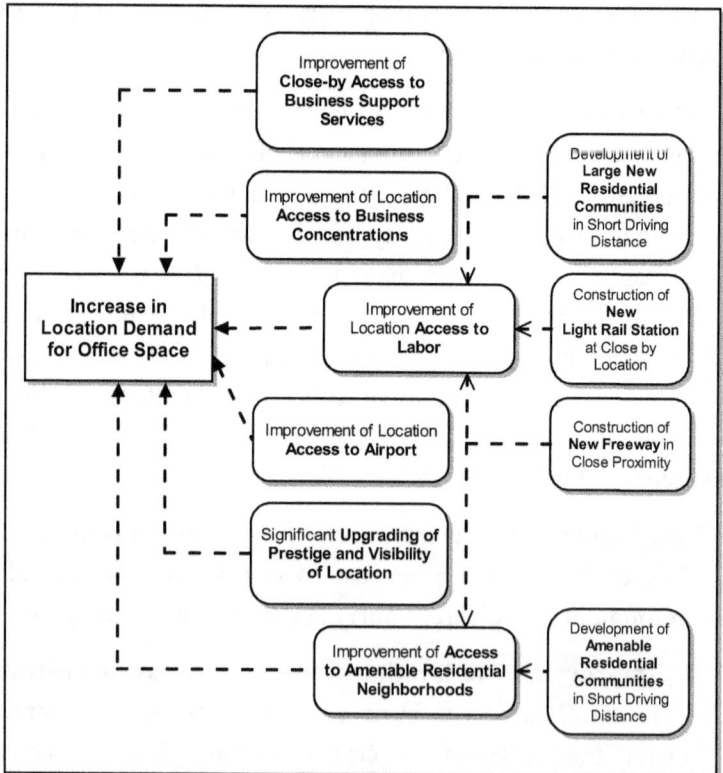

d) Improvement of airport access

A location's access to an airport could improve either due to major transportation projects that will provide easier access to the airport, or due to the construction of an airport at a location easily accessible from the location under consideration by the existing transportation infrastructure. It is obvious that the construction of a new airport could be a big value-increase driver for locations that gain convenient access to it and investors seeking big-profit opportunities should closely monitor any announcements relevant to such developments. However, it should be noted that very close proximity might not be desirable because it may have a negative effect on values due to the noise associated with airport operations.

e) Improvement of prestige and visibility of location

Improvement of the prestige and visibility of an office cluster may occur due to new developments and additions of high quality, high-rise modern office buildings, high-profile professional and commercial firms, and prestigious support facilities.

f) Improvement of access to amenable residential communities

Improvement of the access of an office cluster to amenable residential areas can occur through new major transportation improvements in the area. Also, suburban commercial-space clusters in areas where high-quality residential development is relatively light will gain improved access if new amenable residential communities are developed at a short driving distance.

From this discussion, it is clear that, supply conditions allowing, office locations with potential for big-value increases include existing office-space concentrations about to improve considerably their general access to residential communities and business concentrations within the urban area, as well as expanding clusters about to become more comprehensive and diversified in terms of the range of support services they provide. Finally, office clusters on the verge of transformations that will boost considerably their prestige and visibility are also good candidates for high-return investments.

Notice that improvements in locational advantages need to be strong enough to upgrade the location significantly in terms of its *comparative advantages* vis as vis other competing office concentrations, in order to result in considerable increases in demand for office space. For example, if competing office clusters increase their locational advantages to the same extent, or more, then improvement of locational advantages at a given cluster may not result in increases in location demand. However, it is unlikely that all office clusters in an urban area will benefit equally from major transportation and urban/suburban development projects going on in the area.

Within this context, identifying office space clusters that have potential for strong development-driven demand increases involves the following steps:

    a. Identify major on-going and planned developments in the urban area

    b. Identify office clusters that stand to experience the greatest improvements in their locational attributes from such developments

    c. Evaluate how the landscape of comparative advantages across clusters will change

    d. Evaluate how changes in comparative advantages among the different concentrations within the urban area will affect the flows of new office-space demand across the different locations

    e. Identify emerging new leaders of the urban office landscape, if any

    f. Verify that the clusters identified as the most likely beneficiaries of upcoming strong increases in office-space demand have a low vacancy rate and are expected to add very little new space to their inventory in the next couple of years

SUMMARY

- Increases in aggregate demand for office space can be triggered by increases in the number of firms offering finance, insurance, real estate, and other business and professional services, by increases in the average number of workers employed by office firms, and by increases in the amount of square feet per employee demanded by office firms. Increases in the latter may be triggered by growth expectations, increases in firm profitability, and increases in the number of office firms with higher square-feet-per-employee requirements.

Real Estate Investing for Double-Digit Returns

- Increases in aggregate market demand for office space are likely to induce demand increases at most office space clusters within an urban area because of great locational substitutability across locations. Locations, however, more advantageous in terms of characteristics valued by firms, such as access to support services, client base, business service concentrations, labor, airport, and amenable residential communities may stand to benefit the most from such market-wide demand increases.

- Strong increases in development-driven locational demand for office space can be triggered by considerable improvement in locational characteristics valued by office firms, most of which can occur at all office clusters that will be found on, or close to, the path of major urban transportation projects, such as freeways or mass transit lines.

CHAPTER 8

FORCES THAT TRIGGER INCREASES IN DEMAND FOR RETAIL SPACE

BASICS OF DEMAND FOR RETAIL SPACE

The demand for retail space is a derived demand, since retailers demand space as a means of satisfying household demand for goods and services. In other words, retailers demand store space at a specific market or location when they evaluate that there is consumer demand for the goods or services they sell and that the consumers are inadequately served by the existing competition.

Locational demand for retail space and store locational patterns with respect to consumers depend on the characteristics of the goods/services sold and, specifically, *how homogeneous* (standardized) they are, and *how frequently* consumers need to buy them. Retailers selling goods and services bought in high frequency tend to locate *quite close* to consumer concentrations. Furthermore, retailers selling highly heterogeneous products tend to cluster in order to allow consumers to make the comparisons they need to make before committing to a purchase (comparison shopping).

Goods and services sold by retailers can be classified into four major categories, based on how homogeneous they are and how frequently they are purchased (see Carn et al., 1988):

a) *Convenience goods*, representing standardized goods bought at high frequency from the store located closest to the consumer (food, drugs, etc.)

b) *Shopping goods*, representing less standardized goods that are purchased less frequently and involve some comparison-shopping (furniture, clothing, etc.)

c) *Personal services*, representing services purchased often from the store most conveniently located with respect to the consumer (shoe repair, dry cleaning, etc.)

d) *Specialized services*, representing services that are bought less frequently and involve some comparison shopping (insurance, travel, etc.)

Product heterogeneity and frequency of purchase can help us understand how traditional shopping center formats have arisen and how they locate with respect to the consumers. The most commonly found shopping center formats include:

a) Neighborhood shopping centers, which are usually anchored by a supermarket or a drugstore and include a small collection of other stores selling convenience goods or personal services. Since these stores are selling goods and services purchased with high frequency, they are located close to consumer concentrations and draw the majority of their customers from a small area around their location (within a driving distance of 15 minutes). In other words, their primary trade area is small. The typical size of neighborhood centers ranges between 50,000 and 100,000 square feet.

b) Community shopping centers, which are usually anchored by a discount store, junior department store, or a variety store, and comprise stores that offer mostly convenience goods, personal services, and, perhaps, some shopper's goods (furniture and clothing) or specialized services. Their typical size ranges from 120,000 to 400,000 square feet, and their area of influence extends to about a 30-minute drive from their location.

c) Power centers, which include national tenants advertising heavily on television. Their size ranges from 150,000 to 300,000 square feet, and their area of influence extents up to a 40-minute drive from their location.

d) Regional shopping centers, which are typically anchored by one or two full-line department stores and offer a wide range of shopper goods and specialized services, as well as some convenience goods. They typically include recreational facilities, and their size ranges from 800,000 to 2,000,000 square feet. Their area of influence extends up to a 45-60 minute drive from their location.

e) Super-regional shopping centers, which are typically anchored by three full-line department stores and offer a wider range of shopper goods and specialized services, including recreational facilities. Their size is usually greater than 2,000,000 square feet, and their area of influence extends up to a 60-minute drive from their location.

Power centers represent a somewhat newer retail format, relative to the other four. Although the aforementioned typologies of retail centers are commonly found, retail center formats are often being challenged, as retailers and developers seek strategies and shopping environment settings that will enable them to increase market share. For example, some other retail-center formats include super-neighborhood centers, which are neighborhood centers with larger anchors, off-price centers selling higher-end brand-name products at considerably reduced prices, and outlet centers, which represent a collection of outlet factory stores.

The structure of retail leases, which typically include a percentage of store sales, provides a significant inducement to developers/investors for optimizing a center's design and tenant mix and venturing into new retail formats. Schmitz and Brett (2001) indicate that shopping center types are becoming less distinct as tenants typically found in regional malls venture into other center formats, and vice versa. Furthermore, hybrid formats targeting specific market segments are emerging.

THE DETERMINANTS OF AGGREGATE MARKET DEMAND FOR RETAIL SPACE

Retailers demand space in a market as a means of satisfying household demand for goods and services. Therefore, the aggregate demand for store space within a market depends on *consumption patterns* and retail purchases across the different product lines. Since retail space requirements vary considerably across product lines, the correct way to perceive total demand for store space in a market is to think of it as the sum of differentiated space demands by product line. This framework is especially useful as we move from the abstract concept of aggregate demand for the total market to specific locations and smaller-scale areas.

Aggregate demand for retail space depends on the *volume of sales* by product line and the *square feet per dollar of sales* required by retailers in each product line in order to operate efficiently. The quantity of sales by product line will depend both on market size and household structure, as well as on other economic forces, as indicated in Figure 28 and listed below:

1) Total population and number of households (size factor)
2) Population/household age mix (structure factor)
3) Household income mix (structure factor)
4) Credit conditions (economic-environment factor)
5) Consumer expectations (economic-environment factor)
6) Relative prices (economic-environment factor)
7) Tax and other policies (economic-environment factor)

Before discussing these factors, it is important to understand the overall pattern and path of their influences on an area's retail sales and space demand. The key factors underlying the volumes and types of retail purchases across product lines are total population size and spending patterns. Spending patterns describe how households/ consumers distribute their purchases across different product lines.

Notice the dynamics described in Figure 28. Spending patterns are determined by two major structural characteristics of the area's population and households: a) its age mix, and b) its income mix. The age mix of the population refers to the distribution of population and household heads across different age groups. The income mix refers to the distribution of population/households to different income groups in terms of annual income earned from employment or investments. The amount of household income that is available for retail purchases is influenced by various economic factors, such as consumer expectations, credit conditions, and government tax policies.

Figure 28 – Determinants of Aggregate Market Demand for Retail Space

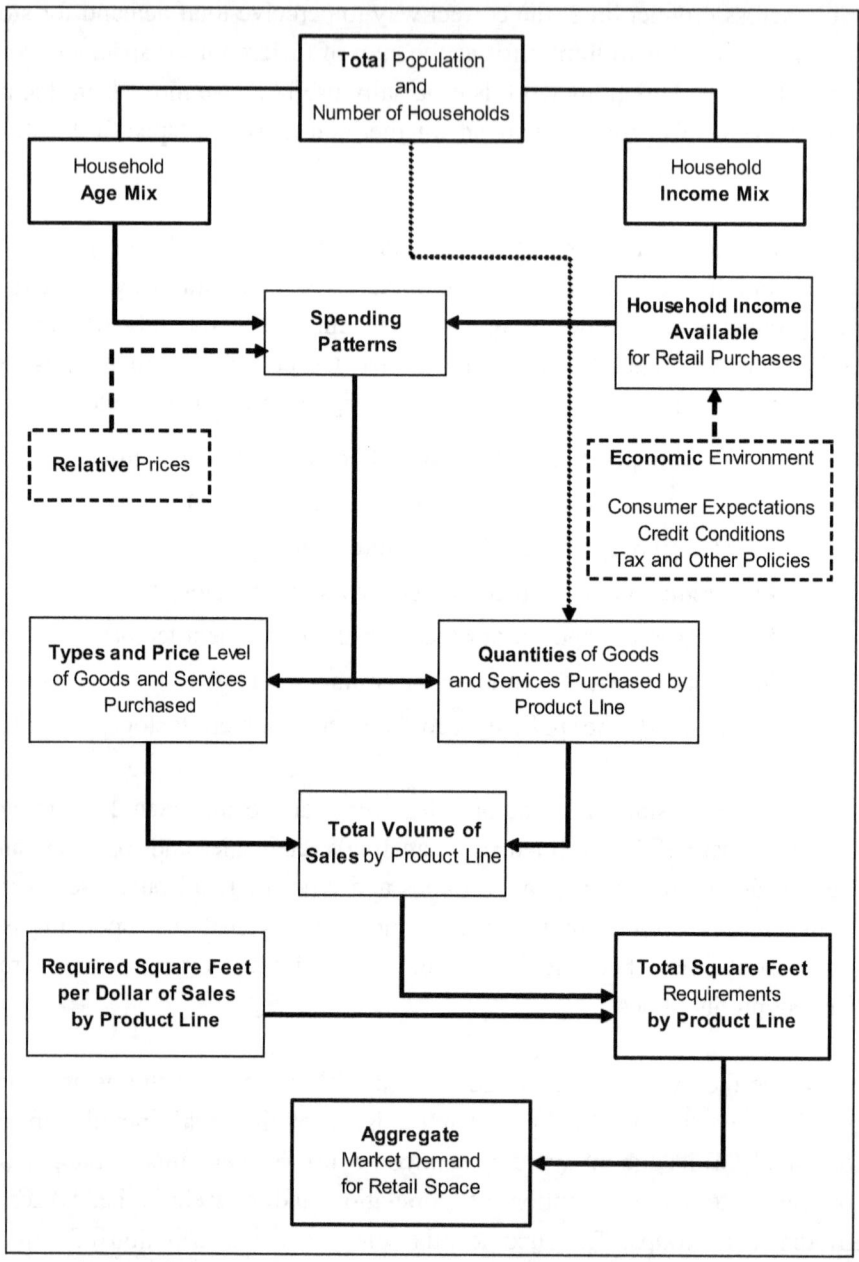

Spending patterns determine the types, price levels, and quantities of goods and services purchased by households. Thus, the *total* quantity of goods and services purchased within each product line are determined by both *spending patterns* and *total population size*. The quantities of goods and services sold, along with respective prices, determine the *total volume of sales* in each product line. Volume of sales and space requirements per dollar of sales determine total space requirements within each product line. The sum of the total retail space requirements by product line represents the aggregate demand for retail space in a market.

The dynamics described indicate that the types and volumes of retail goods likely to be demanded in an area determine the types and amount of space demanded by retailers operating within that market. Understanding how the factors listed above influence consumer expenditures will help form *a frame of reference for identifying circumstances that trigger increases in sales for different product lines and demand for retail space.*

Total Population and Number of Households

Population size does affect the magnitude of consumer expenditures in a given area since each individual has its own consumption needs. The total number of households also affects total consumption expenditures since some are household-related as opposed to individual-related. Compare, for example, the case of ten people forming ten households (each one living on its own), with the case of ten people forming five households. Assuming that each household spends the same amount on furniture and kitchen appliances, expenditures on these items in the case of the ten households will be twice as much, compared to the expenditures of the five households. Total expenditures on clothing, though, will be the same in both cases, if we assume that each individual spends the same amount of money on this item.

Demographic/Age Composition

The demographic/age composition of an area's population in terms of age, sex, household size, etc. influences the types of purchases made in that area. Notice that household characteristics and, therefore, the types of goods purchased, change as a household goes through the different stages of the life cycle. For example, young individuals or couples without children (pre-nest stage) form smaller households and spend less on home-related items and more on food away from home. As couples get married and have children (full-nest stage), household size increases, and expenditures related to kids, housing, and food at home increase significantly. As children grow up and move out of the family home, household size gets smaller (empty-nest stage), expenditures get smaller and shift towards items related to older age. Within this context, the age composition of household heads summarizes this information as it captures the different stages of the life cycle.

To better understand the impact of demographic composition on spending patterns, consider the following extreme and unrealistic example of two communities with very different demographic structure. The two communities are Community A, with a population comprised of only young, married couples who own their houses and have kids, and Community B, with a population comprised of only retirees living in rental housing with no kids. Obviously, retail sales in these two communities will differ in many respects. For example, in Community A, there will be many sales of kid-related goods and services (kids clothing, shoes, toys, school items, and so on), as well as housing-related goods (Home Depot), since all households own their houses. On the contrary, in Community B, there will be minimal sales of kid-related goods (gifts for grandkids, perhaps) and limited sales of housing-related goods, since its residents, being renters, refrain from serious home-improvement activities.

In a study of differences in retail expenditures per capita across 250 MSAs, Ingene (1984) verified the effect of the different life-cycle stages on consumption patterns. For example, he found that the percentage of households/individuals in the full-nest stage had the *greatest positive impact* on retail expenditures.[17] In other words, a one-point percentage increase in these households was associated with the greatest percentage increase in retail expenditures. Such impact is consistent with the theory that predicts large expenditures on food, clothing, and durable goods at this stage of the life cycle.

---

[17] The different age/life-cycle groups used in the econometric analysis were composite variables, generated through an appropriate statistical procedure. This analysis generated (among others) three groups of age/life-cycle related variables out of many demographic characteristics examined in the study. The pre-nest group consists of individuals between 25 and 49 years old and households headed by individuals between 25 and 44 years old. The full-nest group includes children of all ages, middle-aged people, households headed by middle-aged individuals, and large households. Finally, the post-nest group includes older people and households headed by older individuals and refers to the stages of empty nest and solitary survivor.

Increases in the percentage of households/individuals in the pre-nest stage was also found to contribute to increases in retail sales, but to a lesser extent compared to the full-nest stage effect. This is consistent with the theory that predicts purchases of durables, furniture, automobiles, and clothing by individuals and households at this stage. Not surprisingly, the percentage of households/individuals in the post-nest stage (referring to two life-cycle stages, namely empty nest and solitary survivor) was found to have a negative effect on expenditures per household, specifically as they pertain to department, furniture, and variety stores.

The bottom-line conclusion from Ingene's analysis is that increases in the number of households in the full-nest stage of their life cycle should trigger *significant increases in sales of clothing, durables, and food*. Such increases will in turn boost demand for store-space within these product lines. On the contrary, increases in the number of persons and households headed by older individuals in the empty-nest and solitary-survivor stages are likely to result in decreases in sales of department, furniture, and variety stores, and therefore, reduction in demand for store-space in these product lines.

Household Disposable Income

Income influences significantly spending patterns, since it determines the level of a household's retail expenditures and the types of goods purchased. The major source of income for most households is employment earnings, which tend to increase, as a person gets older. Thus, *household income changes as a household goes through the different stages of the life cycle*. For example, single young adults tend to have lower incomes than mature married couples, who are further on the wage scale due to experience and, potentially, earn two incomes, as both husband and wife may have jobs. Furthermore, wages and employment earnings are influenced by economic growth and other economic factors.

Table 7 indicates how the level of a household's *disposable income* for retail expenditures is determined. As this table indicates, the disposable income available to a household for retail purchases is what is left from total income earned after taxes, interest payments, housing expenditures, expenditures on health, education, and public transportation, and savings are taken out. Thus, factors that influence household expenditures *on non-retail items* have an effect on the level of disposable income available for retail expenditures. These factors are discussed below.

Table 7 – Determinants of After Tax Disposable Income Available for Retail Purchases[18]

	After Tax Disposable Income Available for Retail Expenditure.
	Personal Income
minus	Personal Tax and Nontax Payments
equals	Disposable Income
minus	Interest Paid
minus	Personal Transfer Payments to Foreigners
minus	Housing Expenditure
minus	Expenditure on Selected Services (Health, Education, Public Transportation)
minus	Savings
equals	Disposable Income Net of Expenditure on Housing, Selected Services, and Savings
Note:	The above disposable income figure proxies more closely the income available for retail spending

Consumer Expectations, Credit Conditions, Tax Policies, and Relative Prices

Besides income and demographics, retail-spending patterns are influenced by factors such as consumer psychology and expectations, credit conditions, tax policies, and relative prices. For example, a thriving economy shapes *optimistic* consumer expectations, encouraging households to save less and *spend more*. Macroeconomic shocks that raise fears or hopes of potential negative or positive effects on the economy may also affect consumer expectations and sentiment. According to data drawn from the University of Michigan Survey of Consumers, and the Survey of Current Business (published by the US Department of Commerce), both consumer confidence and

---

[18] From the unpublished book draft *Market Analysis for Real Estate* by Rena Mourouzi-Sivitanidou.

real consumption (spending adjusted to take into account increases in the prices of goods and services) registered sharp declines in August 1990, when Iraq invaded Kuwait (Abel and Bernanke, 1995).[19]

Consumer spending patterns are also influenced by the availability of consumer credit and by tax policies. Higher availability of consumer credit is usually reflected in lower interest rates, which stimulate household borrowing either through home-equity financing and re-financing or unsecured loans. This increased borrowing translates to higher disposable income, which leads to increased spending and *larger volume of retail sales*. Tax policies influence the level of a household's disposable income, too. For example, decreases in tax rates reduce tax payments and contribute to increases in disposable income.

Finally, sizable changes in relative prices may also affect the distribution of consumer expenditures across the different retail categories. For example, steep increases in the prices of necessity goods will force many households to devote a considerably higher share of their budget on these items and reduce the share spent on non-necessity goods and services.

Required Square Feet per Dollar of Sales

The required square feet per dollar of sales represent the amount of space needed by a storekeeper within a given product line, in order to operate efficiently. In retail terminology, this indicator is actually measured by sales-per-square-foot norms, which represent the average sales per square foot for stores selling a particular type of good or service. This format of measuring the relationship between sales and required space is more practical for analytical purposes, since typically, the analyst will have an estimate of total potential sales, which needs to be converted into square feet requirements. This can be done easily by simply dividing the expected volume of sales in dollars by the appropriate *sales-per-square-foot norm*. For example, consider a particular line of

---

[19] According to Abel and Bernanke (1995), the survey of consumer sentiment, carried out monthly by the Survey Research Center at the University of Michigan, is one of the two best-known surveys of consumer expectations. The second is the one carried out by the Conference Board.

trade, for which the average sales per square foot is $200 per square foot. Consider also that, according to an analysis of the area's sales potential, total sales in this particular product line are expected to reach $20 million. Therefore, the total store-space needed can be estimated as the ratio of $20 million over $200, which yields 100,000 square feet.

Sales-per-square-foot norms vary considerably, depending on the type of store and the setting in which the store is located. For example, a stand-alone furniture store may have fewer sales per square foot than a furniture store within a regional mall. Data on sales-per-square foot norms are published by the Urban Land Institute for each type of store/product line in different shopping center formats, since such norms vary considerably across these dimensions.[20]

WHAT MAY CAUSE INCREASES IN AGGREGATE MARKET DEMAND FOR RETAIL SPACE

The discussion so far points to a set of specific forces that can trigger increases in demand for store space within a market. To better conceptualize these forces, consider a regional mall serving a large geographic area with several communities. Increases in demand for store-space in such a mall can be triggered by the following developments *within its area of influence* (see Figure 29):

- Increases in population and number of households
- Changes in demographic/age composition of households
- Increases in household disposable income

Increases in demand for store space can also be triggered by developments in the *broader economic and business environment*, and particularly:

- Decreases in interest rates
- Improvement of consumer expectations
- Favorable tax policies

---

[20] Sales-per-square-foot norms for different product lines, in different types of retail centers, can be obtained from *Dollars & Cents of Shopping Centers*, published by the Urban Land Institute.

- Increases in the amount of space needed, per dollar of sales, for the different types of stores (which will be reflected in a decrease in sales per square foot)

Figure 29 – Forces that Trigger Increases in Aggregate Demand for Retail Space

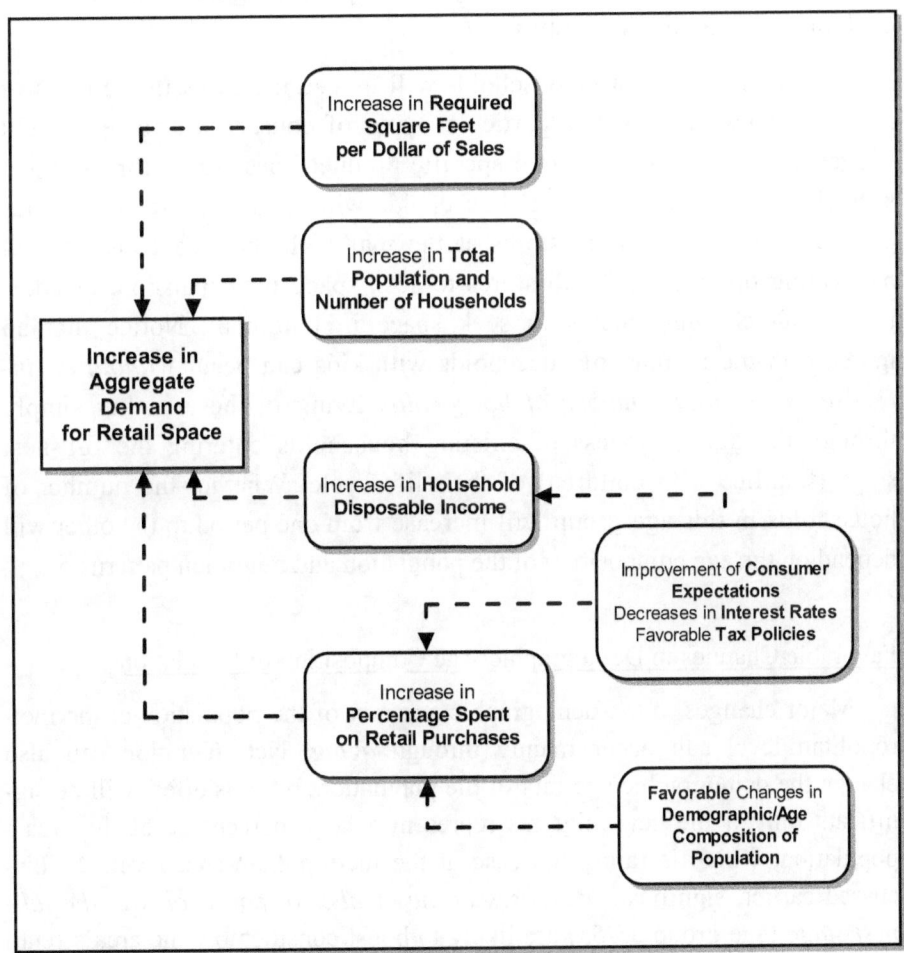

Increases in the Area's Population and Households

All else being equal, increases in the number of households living in the communities served by the regional mall should contribute to increased sales, motivating store operators to expand their store space or new retailers to seek space in the mall. The factors that trigger increases in an area's population and number of households have been discussed in the section on housing demand. As a reminder, these factors include increases in the number of persons in age groups with high headship rates, increases in income that allow young adults to form their own household, increases in divorce rates, net migration, and physical population growth as a result of birth rates outpacing death rates.

Increases in an area's households will induce increases in the sales of *all store types*. Increases in particular types of households, however, will trigger increases in sales within specific product lines. Take, for example, kids clothing. If the number of households with kids increases considerably, sales of kids-clothing stores at the mall will increase considerably, motivating operators of such stores to seek space for expansion, or additional kids-clothing chains to seek space in that mall. Notice that an increase in the number of households with kids can occur *without an increase in the total number of household*s living in the area but simply through the aging process of existing households entering the full-nest stage (families with children) of their life cycle. Whether the number of households in this age group will increase from one period to the other will depend on the age composition of the population and migration patterns.

Favorable Changes in Demographic/Age Composition of Population

Major changes in the demographic/age mix of the population at the metropolitan level can occur mainly through *aging*. Net migration can also change the demographic/age mix of the population, but this effect will be significant only if the new migrants represent a large percentage of the area's population, which is rarely the case at the metropolitan-area level. As discussed earlier, significant *increases in the number of households in the full-nest stage* (age group 35-55) are likely to boost considerably the area's retail sales and demand for retail space. Such increases will in turn trigger *retail rent and value increases if the area's retail vacancy rate and completions of new retail space are low.*

Reliable metropolitan-specific *population projections by age group* can provide very valuable insights regarding upcoming changes in the age structure of the population and metro-wide patterns. In this sense, they can be instrumental in identifying markets about to experience changes in their demographic mix, which will significantly boost the area's retail sales and demand for store space.

Population projections are meaningful for understanding upcoming changes in an area's retail sales only if they refer to a geographic level that secures that there will be *zero or minimal leakages* of purchases to other areas. For example, population projections for a small community provide very little insights with respect to the amount of sales of non-convenience goods at stores within that community, since many purchases of such items are likely to take place at stores outside of the community. Metropolitan population projections, however, are very meaningful since almost all purchases by people residing within this geographic unit are carried out at stores *within its boundaries*.

Increases in Household Disposable Income

Typically, *employment growth and/or increases in wages* are the major forces that trigger increases in the after tax, disposable income available to households. Employment growth contributes to income increases because as more jobs are added to the economy, more people are earning income. Employment growth will generate wage increases if an area's labor supply is not perfectly elastic and there is no oversupply of workers. Labor supply is considered as perfectly elastic if the number of workers in an area can increase without any increases in wages. However, in markets that have no oversupply of labor and some wage increases are necessary in order to attract some additional workers, employment growth *will be accompanied by increases in employment earnings*.

Markets with inelastic labor supply are more likely to experience greater wage increases in the face of increased demand for workers. An area is considered to have an inelastic labor supply *if high wage increases* are needed to attract additional workers in the area. A typical contrast often cited in order to demonstrate this point is that of Boston and Los Angeles. Boston, with its long and heavy winter, scarcity of land for development, and expensive housing, may have greater difficulty in attracting additional workers compared to the greater Los Angeles area, with its mild and warm climate, plenty of land for development, and significant migration flows from Mexico. Within this context, Boston's labor supply could be considered more inelastic compared to Los Angeles. If employment in the two areas grows at the same rate, Boston's wages should increase faster than will those in Los Angeles (all else being equal).[21]

Identifying markets with prospects for strong employment and income increases is not a simple task and requires serious analysis and complex econometric modeling. For this reason, it is important for investors seriously interested in achieving high returns, to review econometric forecasts of employment and income growth from reputable firms that specialize in economic forecasting. Alternatively, investors interested in assessing the prospects of economic and income growth in the market in which they live can inquire at the local planning department, the local Chamber of Commerce, and the economic development division of the local government, to examine whether there are reliable forecasts for the local economy.

Decreases in Interest Rates, Improvement of Consumer Expectations, and Favorable Tax Policies

Decreases in interest rates are triggered by macroeconomic conditions and affect all markets within the country. The record-low interest rates of the early 2000s were supported by the low inflationary environment and slow economic growth. Inflationary trends are considered a key factor in triggering increases in interest rates. Strong oil price increases in 2005 did create fears of inflationary trends, which as of the time of this writing, did not materialize, helping interest rates remain low. Inflation and interest rates tend to rise with strong economic growth.

Strong economic growth increases the likelihood of rising inflation and interest rates, which have a negative effect on consumer purchases. At the same time, however, economic growth *improves consumer expectations*, which have a positive effect on retail sales because consumers tend to save less when they are more optimistic about the future. Finally, *reduction of taxes* paid by households will, by definition, contribute to increases in after-tax disposable income and retail sales. Tax cuts are a matter of government policy.

---

[21] For wages to increase in any of the two markets, the unemployment rate needs to be close to what is considered as equilibrium in the labor market, which is around 5%. If the unemployment rate is much higher it is doubtful whether new jobs will be taken at higher than previously wages.

Increases in the Square Feet Needed per Dollar of Sales

Increases in the square feet needed per dollar of sales will also trigger increases in demand for retail space. Such increases may occur due to changing sales and marketing practices adopted by retailers in their struggle to attract customers and maximize their market share. An example of such a practice is the McDonalds' store format, which incorporates a kid's playroom, a trend that has been followed by other fast-food chains.

Conclusion

In sum, real estate investors, pursuing big profits in the retail arena, are more likely to achieve their objective if they invest in markets that:
- are about to experience strong employment, income and/or population increases, or strong increases in the number of households headed by persons in the 35-50 age group.
- have low retail vacancy rates and limited new construction of retail space

Investments in such markets are likely to be even more profitable if they take place during periods of decreasing interest rates and tax rates.

WHAT MAY CAUSE INCREASES IN LOCATIONAL DEMAND FOR RETAIL SPACE

Based on what it has been discussed so far, one can argue that the following developments can trigger increases demand for retail space at a given location (see Figure 30):

1) **Development of new residential communities, high-rise apartment or office complexes in close proximity**

    The rapid development of new residential communities will generate additional demand for retail space at easily accessible shopping centers or store clusters that can *conveniently serve the needs of the newly created communities*. However, such demand will not necessarily trigger retail space rent increases if too much new retail space comes out in the market at the same time that such new residential communities are created. The story in Box 3 emphasizes the importance of choosing locations that *not only are expected to experience strong retail demand increases, but also have a restrained supply of new space.* High-rise apartment and office developments at nearby locations should also help increase a shopping cluster's sales and locational advantages.

Figure 30 – Forces that Trigger Increases in Locational Demand for Retail Space

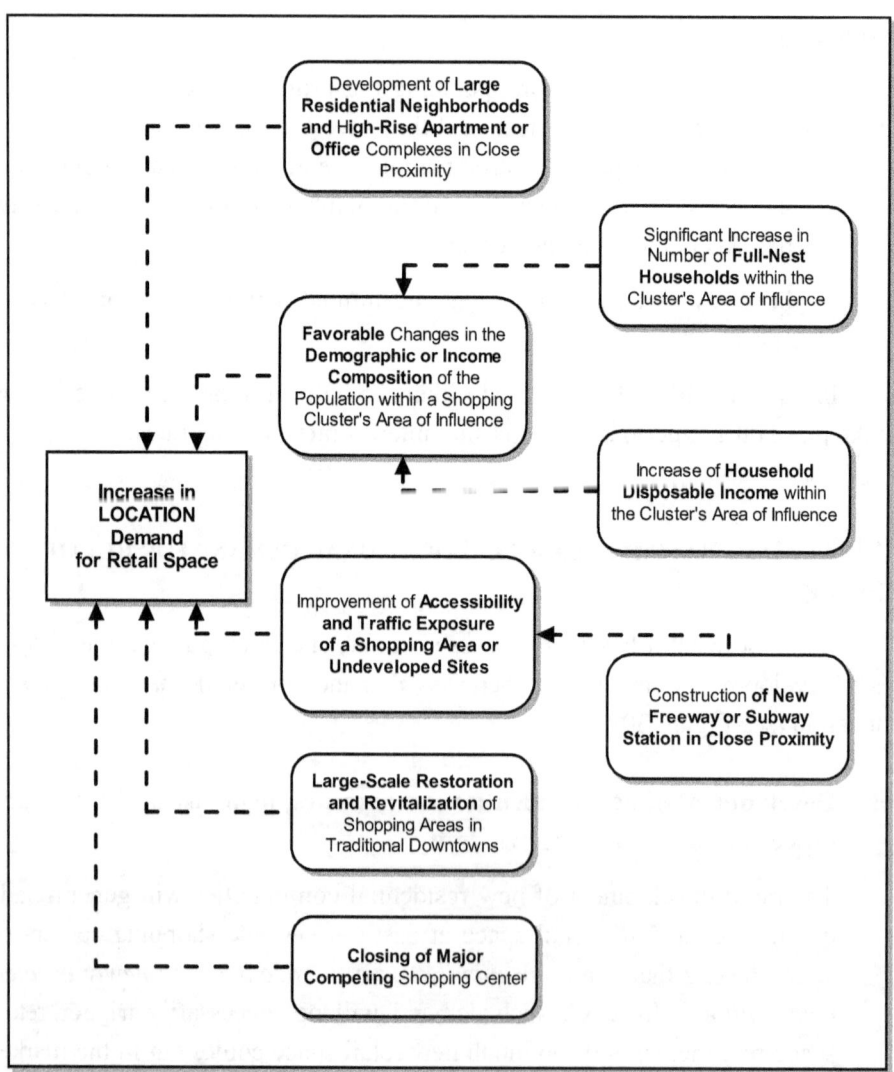

> **Box 3. Retail Space Demand Up by 58% in the Dallas Fort/Worth Market in 1999**
>
> In 1999, www.realpage.com reported that total demand for retail space in the Dallas/Fort Worth market increased by 58%, due to a rapid increase in the area's base population and the retailers' response to favorable market fundamentals. Most of this new demand was registered in newly constructed retail properties serving growing neighborhoods. It is important to note that the areas in which retail space demand increased the most were the fast growing residential pockets of southern Collin County, southern Denton County, and northeastern Tarrant County. However, rent growth was moderate (only 2.7%), because too much new retail space entered the market at the same time.
>
> This case demonstrates the two points I am trying to emphasize. First, large developments of new residential neighborhoods generate increases in demand for store space by retailers. Second, such increases, as strong as they may be, will not result in strong rent and price increases if a massive supply is entering the market at the same time.

2) **Favorable changes in the demographic/income composition of population within a shopping cluster's area of influence**

Significant changes in the demographic profile of the population living in the primary trade area of a retail cluster can create demand for *new types of stores with greater income-earning capacity* than existing ones. For example, the transition of a middle-income neighborhood to a high-income one will benefit the most conveniently accessible store cluster, as the purchasing power in the retail center's trade area will increase and translate to more sales and greater income-earning capacity for the stores. This kind of transition, though, is not typical in the normal course of city growth and maturity. What is typical is the opposite, that is, high-income neighborhoods transitioning to middle- or low-income neighborhoods as houses age and wealthy people move to new, trendy, well-landscaped neighborhoods in the suburbs. This kind of transition will have a negative effect on the rents that neighboring retail space will command, and on retail property values. Most cases of transition of low-income to high-income neighborhoods have to do with *central city revitalization projects*, during which deteriorated neighborhoods are overtaken by high-income professionals working in the CBD, after extensive upgrading.

Another development that could increase the sales, and therefore the locational advantages of a shopping cluster, is a significant *increase in the number of full-nest households within its area of influence*. This would contribute to significant sales increases because full-nest households are big spenders on a wide range of retail items.

3) **Improvement of accessibility and traffic exposure of a shopping cluster**

The construction of major transportation arteries, the redirection of traffic flows due to major transportation improvements, or development of large facilities with regional attraction may result in significant increases in passing-by traffic and exposure of retail properties or undeveloped commercial sites that will be found on the path of these developments. Such improvements in accessibility and traffic exposure will improve considerably the earning capacity of these properties and will trigger significant value increases.

4) **Large-scale restoration and revitalization of shopping areas in traditional downtowns**

Such improvements, which are often carried out through a partnership between the private and public sector, when substantial in quality and scale, can result in significant upgrading of the area, strong increases in consumer visitations, and eventually, store sales. Increased sales will result in increased demand for space, and if supply remains restrained, retail rents and property values should register significant gains.

5) **Closing of major competing shopping center**

The closing of a major shopping center should increase the locational advantages of *other competing locations*. At the regional mall level, the benefit from the closing of a center and the increase in locational advantages of competing centers will be greater, the fewer the competing centers are. At the neighborhood and community center level most of benefit will go to the centers that are direct competitors of the center that goes out of business.

SUMMARY

- Increases in aggregate demand for retail space for all product lines can be triggered by increases in income, population and households, greater availability of credit, tax cuts, and improvement of consumer expectations regarding the economy. Increases in aggregate demand for store space within a particular line of trade can be triggered by these factors, as well as by changes in the demographic composition of the area that result in increases in age groups that demand such a product.

- Market-driven increases in demand for retail space should benefit most retail locations within a metropolitan area.

- Increases in development-driven demand for retail space at a retail cluster can be triggered by the development of nearby large residential communities and high-rise apartment or office buildings, by favorable changes in the demographics and income of residential communities located within its area of influence, by considerable improvement of its broader accessibility, by a significant increase in its visibility and exposure, and by large-scale restoration and revitalization, if it needs one.

CHAPTER 9

SPECIFIC SUB-CATEGORIES OF PROPERTIES WITH SIGNIFICANT VALUE-INCREASE POTENTIAL

Based on the detailed discussion of what may cause increases in demand for different property types, we proceed to the identification of specific circumstances and categories of properties with significant value/price increase potential. The list of sub-categories presented here is not exhaustive and includes specific types of properties that fall under the first two of the four broader categories of properties with big profit potential. In particular, the sub-categories below fall under the categories of properties with market-driven value-increase potential or development-driven value-increase potential:

1) Properties located in municipalities with strong population and/or employment growth prospects and restrained supply
2) High-income housing in communities with increasing income, restrained supply, and low vacancy rate
3) Residential properties in neighborhoods that are about to experience significant upgrading of their environment
4) Residential and commercial properties in inner city neighborhoods that are about to experience significant upgrading
5) Properties with compatibility recovery potential
6) Properties with complementarity improvement potential
7) Properties with potential for significant improvement of their accessibility, visibility, and traffic exposure
8) Vacant lots with potential for becoming more suitable for development
9) Properties with potential for an upgrading zoning change

10) Owner-occupied housing during periods of sharp decreases in interest rates
11) Monopoly properties

1) PROPERTIES LOCATED IN MUNICIPALITIES WITH STRONG POPULATION AND/OR EMPLOYMENT GROWTH PROSPECTS AND RESTRAINED SUPPLY

Strong increases in the population and/or employment of an area characterized by low vacancy rates and limited new construction should trigger rent and value increases for almost all property types. Population and employment growth is associated with increases in the number of households and total income. As a result of such growth, more households will be looking to buy or rent housing, more people will be shopping in all types of stores, and more money will be spent on goods and services in the local market. Therefore, demand for housing and other types of real estate that provide shopping, entertainment, and other services should increase. If the local real estate market is not oversupplied (it has a low vacancy rate) at the time this rapid population and/or employment growth takes place, these increases in demand should trigger strong increases in rents and sales prices for all property types, at least in the short-run. This will happen because of the construction lag, which delays the delivery of new space needed to cover the sudden increase in demand.

If rapid growth in the area considered continues, and supply keeps rising at a relatively slow pace, rents and prices should continue to rise. However, it is likely that the strong price and rent increases triggered by the initial demand shock will motivate an excessive response on the part of real estate developers and investors, unless the area has inherent supply constraints, such as land shortages or strict development and growth controls. If supply overreacts, prices and rents will take a downturn after a few years, as the additional space coming out in the market is greater than the amount required by the additional households and firms. For this reason, it is safer to buy just before or just after rents and prices start rising, and *sell as they are still rising* (see discussion on how to best take advantage of cyclical movements in property prices in Chapter 2).

For investors seeking high returns and big profits, just choosing metropolitan markets that are expected to register strong employment and/or population growth is not enough. They need to go a step further and identify, within the selected metropolitan markets, the locations where property values will get the greatest boost; these locations are the communities/municipalities expected to grow the fastest, and have not only a relatively low vacancy rate, but also limited space that is under construction.

Notice that population growth and employment growth may not occur within the same municipalities and communities of the selected metropolitan market. For example, population growth may be manifested in some communities, which are exclusively residential and do not include commercial structures within their boundaries, while employment growth may be realized in municipalities with a significant amount of commercial space and potential for expansion of such commercial clusters.

Residential communities expected to benefit the most in terms of population growth may present highly profitable housing development opportunities, if land can be bought at reasonable prices and supply is under control. Notice, that reasonable land prices for the investor who seeks high returns are those that do not incorporate large premiums for future increases in housing demand in the area, because this is exactly the force that will trigger strong appreciation gains. If most of these gains are already incorporated into the purchase price, the investor's return will not be high.

The discussion so far suggests that population and economic growth in markets with low vacancy and restrained supply are very likely to lead to rapid increases in property prices and rents in the short run, which may not be sustainable in the long run. In fact, Lourgant (1989) found a negative relationship between apartment earnings and employment growth in Phoenix, AZ. More specifically, apartment earnings were declining as employment was growing rapidly after 1984. On the contrary, in Denver, where employment growth was considerably slower, apartment earnings were more stable. The explanation of the negative long-term impact of rapid employment growth on apartment earnings in Phoenix is that developers overreacted to the rapid growth in the area by building more apartment units than needed, thus creating an oversupplied market with declining rents. Again, these findings support the *strategy of short-term holding periods* for investments in rapidly growing communities and markets.

The bottom-line conclusion is the *dual emphasis* that real estate investors need to place in selecting locations with strong prospects for population and employment growth:

(a) Select metropolitan markets that are expected to grow rapidly in terms of employment/population and have low vacancy and restrained supply

(b) Within these metropolitan markets

　　i. for investments in housing, select residential communities that are expected to register the strongest population growth

　　ii. for investments in commercial properties, select commercial clusters/municipalities most likely to absorb the rising demand for goods and services from rapidly expanding residential areas, as well as from broader metropolitan growth

Spotting Locations About to Experience Population and/or Employment Growth

The basic component of the strategy discussed in this section is identifying markets/communities with very good prospects for rapid population, employment, and/or income growth in the immediate and medium-term future. Notice that a municipality or community within a metropolitan area may be growing faster than the whole market since population and new jobs are not distributed uniformly across the different communities. For example, if a metropolitan area is predicted to grow rapidly in terms of population, most of this population growth will be distributed, by necessity, to suburban communities, since the central city is already densely developed and there are few possibilities for development of additional housing units.

The best way to go about identifying metropolitan markets with strong prospects for employment, population, and/or income growth, is to obtain metropolitan-area forecasts of employment and population from competent economic forecasting companies. These forecasts are produced with the help of complex macroeconomic and area-specific models, using the best knowledge and technology available to predict the path of national and local economies. Purchasing forecasts for a few metropolitan markets is relatively cheap. It gets expensive, however, if the investor wants to buy forecasts for many metropolitan markets, in order to identify those with the strongest employment/population growth prospects.

If, for some reason, the purchase of competent economic growth forecasts for several metropolitan areas is not possible, one technique for identifying markets with prospects for strong employment growth is to examine current employment growth rates for a large number of markets and sort out those that are growing at the fastest pace. Then, the investor, or his/her consultant, needs to get employment and population growth forecasts from metropolitan-wide agencies or county governments to *verify that the selected markets are likely to stay on the path of rapid growth*. Getting employment and population forecasts from local governments is advisable, even if econometric forecasts from vendors are available, because local government agencies are in a position to know very well the peculiarities, strengths, and weaknesses of the local economy. Although such forecasts are unlikely to be based on complex econometric models, they will provide a good crosscheck for forecasts produced by national firms.

Caution is needed when using recent employment and population growth rates to select markets for real estate investments. First, it must be verified that current rapid growth is not masking a long historical path of slow growth. Furthermore, extra caution is needed, since past and current performance is not a guarantee for future performance. Despite consistent rapid growth in the recent past, the local economy may be approaching a turning point that will result in slow employment and population growth in the future. It is also possible that the local real estate market is very close to taking a downturn, even if rapid employment and income growth appears very likely in the future. This may happen because the high employment growth rates of the recent past may have triggered an excessive development activity. That is why reliable projections of expected developments in the local economy and the *local real estate market* can prove invaluable.

Recent employment/population growth rates can be used to identify communities/municipalities with strong growth prospects within metropolitan markets targeted for investments; the caveats just mentioned though still apply. A riskier and harder to apply strategy is to identify communities and municipalities that have not been growing rapidly recently, but are expected to grow rapidly in the immediate future, due to significant gains in their comparative advantages and recent favorable economic developments. This strategy is harder to apply, since one needs to obtain employment/population forecasts by municipality, which are difficult to find because they are not produced by national forecasting firms. Furthermore, this strategy may be riskier, since the investor will be entering a submarket that has not shown yet any signs of rapid growth.

Whichever selection technique/strategy is used, a *serious supply analysis* is absolutely necessary before making any investment. It is important to assess very carefully the amount of new space planned and under construction, to make sure the market is not about to be flooded by an excessive amount of new space. Such development will dampen the positive price effects of the anticipated employment/population growth, making that area a poor investment choice.

Information on upcoming developments and the number of recent building permits issued can be obtained from the local planning department. A critical question that needs to be answered is whether the number of building permits issued in the last couple of years was unusually high. Another relatively easy-to-get source of information on building activity is the *Current Construction Reports*, published monthly by the Bureau of the Census. These reports contain information about the number of residential building permits approved each month, and the total for the whole year, for every county and major city in the United States. A thorough supply analysis of the area under consideration should also take into account information about projects currently under construction as well as projects that have been authorized by building permits but haven't started yet.

Although the cornerstone of the strategy advised here is the identification of communities/municipalities with strong employment/population growth prospects, there is a special case of communities that may suitable for profitable property investments, although they may be predicted to grow at a slow pace. I am referring to *communities/municipalities that are highly desirable, but are growing at a very slow pace*, not because of lack of demand, but because of severe zoning and growth constraints that restrict development, thereby preventing the local population and employment base to rise rapidly. In theory, these communities should be characterized by a long-term imbalance in favor of demand, which should keep prices on an upward path for long time. In fact, prices in these markets are likely to *rise faster* than the metropolitan average, in the case of strong demand increases due to their high desirability and the restrained supply. Of course, at some point in time, high prices will erode demand and make them less desirable.

In my opinion, properties in highly attractive communities with severe zoning constraints that maintain the attractiveness of these communities represent good investments with probably low risk. Many urban researchers have presented evidence indicating that zoning restrictions and growth controls have been very effective in raising housing prices in local residential markets (Frieden, 1981; Elliot, 1983)

Closing this section, I would strongly suggest that real estate investors refrain from using intuition or other simplistic thought processes to predict whether an area will grow slowly or rapidly, because economic and spatial dynamics are complex. However, it may be possible to successfully locate communities about to experience population and employment growth within the market one lives, if she/he follows closely what happens in the local economy and all development projects that are in the planning or construction stage. However, the economic growth prospects of the market as a whole are still quite relevant because it is unlikely that property values within a community will rise a lot if the metro-wide economy and real estate market is performing poorly.

In summary, the possibility of two strategies emerges, one short-term (two-three year holding period), and one long-term, where the property is held for a longer period. In applying the short-term strategy, it is important that expected completions of buildings in the targeted property type in the next two years are very low compared to the expected increase in demand. In applying a long-term strategy, investors should turn their attention to highly desirable residential communities that have severe zoning constraints and growth controls. When buying properties in such communities, investors need to make sure that prices are not extremely high when compared to other communities in the metropolitan area, offering the same quality of houses and neighborhood environment.

Restrained supply is a crucial component of the recommended strategy. Land use regulations can play an important role in restraining real estate supply. The major instruments that local governments use to regulate the uses of land are zoning ordinances, the general plan, various housing and building codes, and subdivision controls. Most local controls regulate the use of land by determining land-use districts and by imposing height and density restrictions. The land-use districts determine the mix of allowable land uses within specific geographic areas. Major land-use district classifications include agricultural, single-family residential, multifamily residential, commercial, and industrial.

Density regulations include floor-area-ratio (FAR) restrictions, height restrictions, and open space ratio limits. The floor-area ratio is defined as the total floor area divided by the lot area. For example, a 5,000 square-foot lot with an allowable floor-area ratio of 3.0 cannot be developed with more than 15,000 square feet of build space. Height restrictions include maximum allowable heights. The open-space ratio is the open space of the lot as a percentage of the floor area.

Frieden (1981), who has studied the impact of growth controls and zoning regulations on housing prices in California, points out that the following types of growth control techniques have been responsible for housing shortages and subsequent price increases:

- Agricultural preserves, which were used for the protection of farmland and created shortages of land for development
- Large-lot regulations, which increased the size of the minimum allowable residential site and restricted suburban growth

- Moratoria on new connections to public utility systems, which delay necessary utility extensions and slow down construction
- Staged extension of water and sewer lines and establishment of public service boundaries for these extensions
- Development charges, which increase the cost of new development and discourage developers from launching new projects
- Explicit quotas (limits) for the number of building permits issued every year, which slow down the pace of new construction
- Environmental impact reviews, which create delays and give opportunities to challenge developments in zoning hearings or courts

Most of the studies on the impact of growth controls have focused on communities located in the West Coast, where there is an increasing wave of favoritism towards no-growth policies (Frieden, 1981; Elliott, 1983). In searching for communities with strict zoning and growth controls, investors should inquire at local planning departments as to whether there are shortages of land zoned for the various uses and what kind of growth restrictions are in place. Also, understanding whether there is a widespread no-growth attitude in the community may give clues as to whether the controls that are in place will be maintained, become stricter, or be replaced by growth-friendly regulations.

2) HIGH-INCOME HOUSING IN COMMUNITIES WITH INCREASING INCOME, RESTRAINED SUPPLY, AND LOW VACANCY RATE

As households move through the life cycle and their income increases, they usually upgrade their housing situation and move to a higher-quality home with more space and a backyard, especially if there are kids in the family. If supply in the area is constrained by zoning restrictions and growth controls, demand increases for better and larger homes, triggered by income increases, will push prices of high-income housing upwards. Therefore, attractive, high-income residential communities with low vacancy rates located within markets with strong income growth prospects and effective growth controls should provide opportunities for big profits. Such communities should be located within metropolitan markets expected to register a strong increase in the number of high-income households. As discussed in a previous section, increases in the number of high-income households can be triggered by strong economic growth or by the changing demographic structure, which may result in an increase in the number of households headed by middle-aged persons, which tend to have higher incomes.

The question, of course, is how one can identify markets with prospects of strong income increases. For national investors, the most reliable methodology of doing that is to first obtain income growth forecasts for many metropolitan markets from reputable forecasting firms and sort out those expected to experience the highest growth. Among the markets expected to grow the fastest, investors need to sort out those that have relatively low vacancy rate and are not expected to become oversupplied in the years ahead. Finally, investors need to locate properties in the most attractive high-income neighborhoods located within the selected metropolitan markets. Local investors that limit their activity within the metropolitan area they live should focus on similar properties and locations, if strong income growth is expected, and the market is not about to become oversupplied.

3) **RESIDENTIAL PROPERTIES IN NEIGHBORHOODS ABOUT TO EXPERIENCE SIGNIFICANT UPGRADING OF THEIR ENVIRONMENT**

Improvements in a neighborhood's environment may include creation, expansion, and upgrading of urban parks, street widening, road and sidewalk improvements, parking space improvements, and revitalization of old commercial areas. The latter includes street, sidewalk, parking and façade improvements, and sometimes re-arrangements of land use patterns. If such developments are of such scale so that they improve substantially neighborhood environment they will result in significant increases in property values.

To identify properties in neighborhoods with prospects for significant improvements, one needs to collect information about the nature, location, and timing of improvements scheduled or planned by local government agencies. Such information can be obtained by visiting the local planning department and inquiring about relevant projects that have been approved, as well as those still in the planning stage.

Usually, the planning department of the local government has separate Parks and Recreation Department and Transportation Department. From the former, investors or their consultants can collect information about the location, size, amenities, and construction schedule of new parks, playgrounds, open and recreational spaces, and expansion and upgrading of existing ones. From the latter, one can obtain information regarding street widening, surface upgrading, and sidewalk improvements. From the redevelopment subdivision of the planning department, one can obtain information regarding scheduled improvements in commercial areas.

Investors with a short-term horizon should focus their attention on projects scheduled to start and finish relatively soon (still, large projects that have significant positive impact on the value of surrounding properties should take one-two years to be completed). They should also focus on projects that have not started yet, as the appreciation potential after the project's completion will be greater. Many owners of properties that benefit from large public improvement projects usually know about these projects and either refuse to put their properties in the market until the project is completed, or they require a price premium, if they decide to sell. However, when acquiring such properties before the public improvement projects begin, the investor can claim uncertainty regarding the realization of the project and any subsequent appreciation potential in negotiating a lower price. Furthermore, despite any speculative increases in property prices before the beginning of construction, usually, property prices in the vicinity of large public improvement projects tend to rise further after their completion.

In order to minimize risk, investors need to focus on projects that are highly likely to break ground soon. These projects need to be examined carefully in terms of the nature and boundaries of the planned improvements, in order to spot nearby properties that will benefit the most and will no be affected *negatively*. Caution is needed because, usually, the creation of new open spaces, or the expansion of existing ones, and street widening in mature urban neighborhoods requires that some properties or parts of them be taken over (with some compensation) by the public, in order to secure the additional space needed. Properties affected in this way should be carefully analyzed to examine whether expected value gains outweigh potential losses.

4) Residential and Commercial Properties in Inner-City Neighborhoods About to Experience Significant Upgrading

In the last two decades a phenomenon has been taking place in most of the major cities in the nation. This phenomenon has been called *urban renewal*, and it actually refers to the rehabilitation of relatively low-quality, inner-city neighborhoods, and their transformation to high quality, fashionable neighborhoods, occupied by high-income professionals working in the central city.

From the point of view of an investor seeking properties with big profit potential, this case is very interesting, since properties located in neighborhoods that are about to experience the urban renewal transition have a *substantial appreciation potential*. Zeitz (1979), who studied the process of private urban renewal in Georgetown (Washington, DC), found that property values increased dramatically as a result of neighborhood upgrading.

There are two types of renewal: 1) public urban renewal, which is primarily originated and encouraged by the local government, and 2) private urban renewal, which is primarily originated and carried out by private population and business groups. Public urban-renewal activity was stimulated by the creation of a federal program (UDAG) providing funds to cities to rehabilitate their aging neighborhoods. The funds available for these programs, however, have long ago been reduced by the Reagan administration.

For investors seeking big-profit opportunities the important question is how one can figure out whether urban renewal will take place in inner-city neighborhoods. Zeitz (1979) provides many clues as to the elements required to make private urban renewal happen:

1) A significant amount of *solid housing stock* that is not severely deteriorated and can be upgraded at reasonable cost. This means extensively deteriorated neighborhoods are not candidates for such a transition.

2) The economy of the city must have the capacity to provide professional and/or managerial jobs for the high-income population that is ultimately going to occupy the rehabilitated inner-city neighborhoods. Therefore, a *solid employment base in professional/ managerial services* is necessary.

3) Most of the properties in the inner-city neighborhoods must be owned by *absentee landlords*. Therefore, the housing units in these neighborhoods will be either vacant or occupied by tenants. This is necessary because private urban renewal can take place only in neighborhoods where the existing population can be displaced. It is much easier to displace a renter or an absentee landlord than a homeowner. This requirement takes off the list neighborhoods inhabited mostly by homeowners.

4) *Scarcity of housing* in surrounding areas. In light of housing shortages in the broader area, it is more likely that inner city neighborhoods will become desirable after reasonable upgrading, which will enable them to absorb the excess demand.

If a city has all four elements, private urban renewal is possible, but the following additional conditions must also be met in order to make it happen:

1) *Arrival of pioneers* is the first element required to trigger the neighborhood upgrading process. As Zeitz suggests, these pioneers are low or moderate-income groups that themselves do most of the upgrading of their houses

2) *Advertisement and promotion* of the neighborhood by realtors. This is the only way that additional population will start moving in.

3) Intensive *involvement of speculators and builders*. These are the agents that will expand upgrading and make higher-quality housing available to high-income groups who, usually, will not undertake any property improvements on their own. Investors seeking high profits should enter the process as speculators at this stage.

4) *Lending institutions* must be willing to invest in these neighborhoods; speculators, builders, and prospective homebuyers will be able to participate and move the upgrading process only if financial institutions are willing to lend them the required capital. Financial institutions will

do so only after substantial private capital has been invested so that the risks are minimized.

5) There must be a *population determined to live in the city*. The population originally settling in inner-city neighborhoods faces adversarial living conditions, such as noise, litter, and lack of safety as they move into low-quality and high-crime areas. So in order to stay there and make the rehabilitation process happen they have to be determined and able to temporarily live with these adversarial conditions.

6) Gaining *local zoning control* is a critical element for the acceleration of the neighborhood-upgrading process, since some zoning changes will need to take place in order to improve the neighborhood's overall quality and environment.

7) *Affluent population* is also needed in order to occupy the significantly upgraded housing units. At this final stage, prices rise even more, and living conditions improve dramatically. The neighborhood becomes very attractive to higher-income groups, who finally outbid the pioneers that originated the process.

These are the major stages and ingredients of the urban renewal process. It is important for investors to enter at the right time (stage 3 or 4 above), in order to achieve high profits. Zeitz suggests that preliminary identification of upgrading neighborhoods may be possible by evaluating two pieces of information, which are readily available in most cities. The first is the sales activity, that is, the number of sales, and the second is housing prices. Zeitz suggests that increased sales activity, without price increases, may indicate speculative buying *in anticipation* of incoming transition. If sales are increasing while prices are increasing considerably faster than in other neighborhoods in the city, it may be an indication that the neighborhood is at the final stages of the upgrading process.

5) PROPERTIES WITH COMPATIBILITY RECOVERY POTENTIAL

This category includes properties adjacent to incompatible uses that undermine their value. Such properties have appreciation potential merely by the removal or *relocation of the incompatible uses*. For example, residential or commercial properties adjacent to air polluting and noise producing industries or other environmentally obnoxious activities that are about to relocate represent properties with compatibility recovery potential. According to empirical studies, properties located close to incompatible uses are indeed undervalued. Ferguson, Goldberg, and Mark (1988) found that housing units in municipalities with air polluting industries were valued at $5,000-$6,000 less, compared to municipalities without air polluting industries. The localized effect (the effect on properties adjacent to the sites these non-compatible uses occupy) of such uses should be considerably greater; this means the appreciation potential from the relocation of the incompatible use should also be greater. Usually, the values of these properties are further reduced because of under-maintenance or abandonment. Therefore, in cases where there is potential for removing the source of incompatibility, at no or low cost, there is significant profit potential. The following represent examples of properties with compatibility recovery potential:

a) <u>Properties adjacent to air-polluting industries and other obnoxious industrial uses that are about to relocate</u>

The local planning department and other government agencies could be of use in identifying such properties, as they can point out plans to force incompatible uses to relocate out of the community. If such plans do exist, investors need to inquire about the nature and existing location of these uses, and the expected timing and stages of the planned relocation process.

b) <u>Residential properties on significantly congested streets that are about to become decongested because of significant improvements in the area's overall transportation network</u>

It is generally believed that residential properties on heavily congested streets are discounted to a considerable extent because of the noise and air pollution caused by heavy traffic, as well as safety issues that arise for families with kids. This is, again, a compatibility problem. Therefore, if a very busy street going through a residential neighborhood suddenly becomes decongested, residential properties on both sides of the street will gain value. Such decongestion may result from the construction of a new major transportation artery, radial or circumferential, that changes the overall traffic patterns and redirects traffic flows to different streets.

Residential properties about to benefit from the redirection of traffic flows can be identified by talking to the transportation experts at the local planning or transportation department. Transportation departments do a good job in projecting how traffic flows will change in light of major transportation improvements.

6) PROPERTIES WITH COMPLEMENTARITY UPGRADING POTENTIAL

This category includes properties that can be converted to more profitable uses as the spatial demand patterns change due to *changing land-use patterns in nearby areas*. Transitioning residential neighborhoods from low- or middle-income to high-income create new demands in terms of the commercial real estate that serves their needs. Furthermore, large office and commercial developments benefit nearby areas, as they bring more people and purchasing power into the area and shape new patterns of spatial demand. In both cases, properties located reasonably close to the points/neighborhoods where these developments occur have appreciation potential, as long as they can be converted easily to a use that better complements/serves the new land use patterns being shaped. I need not emphasize that, to have a value gain, *the conversion needs to represent upgrading* of the property, not downgrading. Bear in mind that improvement of complementarity of one property with another does not necessarily mean upgrading. We can distinguish two sub-categories of properties under this category:

a) Properties located within a commercial cluster, serving a community that is about to transition to higher-income status

A commercial cluster serving a middle-income community comprises firms and retail outlets offering services and goods appealing to middle-income households. If the community transitions to one of higher-income status, commercial space at such a cluster can now be upgraded to offer services and goods appealing to higher-income households. If we assume that high-income goods and services allow for higher profits than middle-income goods and services, stores and office firms at this cluster should be able to earn higher income. If vendors can earn higher income they will also be willing pay higher rent for occupying space in the cluster. This, in turn, will boost property values. Therefore, after the transition of the community to a higher income status is over, property values at commercial clusters serving the community should register value increases. Value increases will be proportional to the increase in average household income in the community. *Strong increases in average household income should result to strong increases in values* of properties in commercial clusters serving the community.

b) <u>Properties that are about to become more attractive and valuable because of large, nearby developments of complementary uses</u>

In this category, we can distinguish the following specific cases:

b.1) <u>Residential properties located close to a large new office or industrial park being developed in the suburbs</u>
Properties that can benefit from the development of new employment centers in the suburbs include middle-income housing units (rental or owner-occupied) located reasonably close (5-20 minutes driving distance) to the sites these centers are being developed. After the employment center is completed, a number of people working there (especially renters) will demand accommodations in the nearby residential market. It is more likely there will be *greater demand and increase in prices for rental housing than owner-occupied housing*. Renters in the United States are more mobile than are homeowners. Therefore, it is very likely that those renting and living far from their new workplace will try to move closer, exerting some pressure on the local rental housing market.

b.2) <u>Properties reasonably close to prospective shopping and recreational destinations</u>
A house in a neighborhood that is conveniently served by a shopping center (neighborhood or community) is valued more than a house in a similar neighborhood without convenient access to a shopping center. A national study found that 42% of household trips are to and from entertainment and shopping destinations. Therefore, properties that gain convenient access to new shopping and entertainment centers should appreciate in value because of the *significant transportation savings (time and money)* that will be able to provide.

The reader is cautioned when considering properties located in municipalities in which a regional shopping center is about to be developed. Properties within *adjacent municipalities* are likely to benefit more from their improved accessibility to this new large shopping and entertainment destination. Empirical studies by Burnell (1985) and Stull (1978) found that housing values were lower in municipalities characterized by excessive commercial development.

In the case that the upcoming development represents a community shopping center, which in my opinion can be hardly considered as excessive development, properties within the municipality that will house the new development should benefit more than properties in adjacent municipalities.

b.3) Commercial properties adjacent to prospective large high-rise residential developments
The clientele of stores and businesses located close to new high-rise residential developments will increase considerably, since a great number of new customers will pour in after the buildings are completed and occupied. As a result, the tenants of these commercial establishments will be willing to pay higher rent, and commercial property values will increase. It is emphasized, that for commercial property values to increase at a non-negligible rate, the residential development should be large enough to bring a substantial number of new households in the vicinity of a commercial cluster.

b.4) Properties in the vicinity of a new university or hospital
The development of a large institution, such as a hospital or a university, represents a significant land use change, at least in the immediate area of these developments. Businesses and retailers providing goods and services associated with the operation of a *hospital* may demand commercial space in adjacent properties. In addition, many of the doctors that will be working in the new hospital may demand high-quality residences in the closest high-income neighborhoods. An unpublished study found that there is strong relationship between high housing values and the presence of a hospital within the same census tract.

In the case of the development of a *new university*, nearby rental housing will be in demand by students, as the university begins operations. In addition, vacant sites zoned for multi-family housing will be in great demand by developers, as they realize that rental housing is in high demand in such neighborhoods.

One important element of profitable investing in properties with complementarity upgrading potential is timing. Theoretically, the investor has three choices: 1) buy the property expected to benefit from the construction of large nearby developments before they break ground (I refer to this stage as pre-construction stage); 2) buy as soon as they break ground; and 3) buy as soon as they are completed. The first choice is the more risky because at this point, it is not certain that the project will start, let alone be completed. However, it will be the most profitable stage, if the project is indeed completed, because the investor can purchase the property at the lowest price, as he/she will be competing with fewer investors willing to take the risk to invest at this stage.

To minimize risk, when investing at the pre-construction stage, the investor needs to carefully assess whether:
   I. the project that will benefit the target property is certain or almost certain to break ground very soon
   II. it is not expected to take a very long time to be completed; a very long construction period increases the risk that something will prevent the project's completion.

The second choice, in terms of the investor's timing of entry, is to buy the property expected to benefit from the new development just *after it breaks ground*. As construction activities move from the earlier to the later stages, the chances that the project will not be completed are reduced. Because of the reduced uncertainty and risk, additional investors will become interested in acquiring properties in the vicinity of the new development as they anticipate the potential for property value appreciation. This would raise prices for such properties, thereby reducing the profit potential from future price increases.

Finally, the third choice, in terms of timing of entry, is to invest *after the completion* of the nearby development—during the stage of lease-up and operation. The demand pressures, but also the locational benefits from the new development will become more tangible during this stage. Investing at this stage involves less risk on the part of the investor, and that is why she/he will have to pay a higher price, compared to entering in previous stages. However, there may be some potential for further appreciation in the medium-term, even at this stage, because large developments tend to attract additional development around them, which should boost values even more in the future.

7) PROPERTIES WITH POTENTIAL FOR SIGNIFICANT IMPROVEMENT OF THEIR ACCESSIBILITY, VISIBILITY, AND TRAFFIC EXPOSURE

Large urban transportation projects, such as new light transit systems, or the expansion of existing ones, new freeways, highways, and bridges change considerably urban traffic patterns, creating new heavy-traffic corridors and intersections. Properties found on either side of these new heavy-traffic corridors and intersections will experience a dramatic improvement of their accessibility, visibility, and vehicular traffic exposure. If these properties are commercial buildings/sites or non-commercial buildings/sites that can be converted easily and at low cost to commercial use, they should appreciate considerably as they become exposed to heavy traffic and, as they become more accessible from every location in the metropolitan area. Be aware that residential properties about to be exposed to heavy traffic will lose value and should be avoided, unless they can be easily converted to commercial.

The positive effect of newly created transportation corridors on values will be significant, not only in the case of commercial properties that are on the corridor, but also in the case of clusters of uses and sites that are in close proximity to it. For example, office building clusters and vacant commercial sites that gain proximity to newly constructed freeways, major transportation arteries, and light rail stations should also appreciate considerably, as their accessibility to clients and labor within the metropolitan area improves significantly. Jonathan (2002) reports that office rents at locations adjacent to Toronto's light rail transit stations climbed 30% above the city average. Similarly, *residential areas*, whose broader access improves significantly, as a result of close proximity to such new corridors, should also register significant gains in value.

8) Vacant Lots with Potential for Becoming Suitable for Development

In this category, I include vacant lots that are about to experience developments that will make them more suitable or attractive for development. For example, vacant lots that cannot be easily and cheaply serviced by public utility lines, such as electricity, water, gas, telephone, and sewer, have low value because they are not typically demanded by developers. Sites that are served by such utilities have higher value. These sites are in demand by developers because they can be readily developed without time delays or additional expenses. Therefore, vacant sites not currently easily serviced but about to be serviced by utility lines in the immediate future may provide opportunities for significant profits if they are bought at the right price before public utility lines actually reach them.

Public utility companies and local government agencies can be of great help in identifying sites that will be serviced with utility lines. A vacant site has many chances of being serviced with utility lines in the immediate future if it shows up on the *projection reports and extension maps* prepared by utility agencies and local government agencies. One of the major responsibilities of the companies and agencies that provide public utilities is to anticipate, as accurately as possible, what areas will have to be served in both the short- and the long-term. Projection periods and plans range from one to ten years, and in some cases, even more. Also, notice that sometimes the possibility of utility servicing is just a matter of annexation within the city limits and a short extension of nearby utility lines, which the city may gladly undertake.

A word of caution when looking for vacant sites with value growth potential: beware of development moratoria! Many cities in the United States have been imposing development moratoria on new developments within their limits in the light of overloaded sewage lines and treatment facilities. A vacant site is of little value if it cannot be developed.

9) Properties with Potential for Upgrading Zoning Change

The value of a vacant site or a property depends on the income that can be earned by developing or using it at the most profitable use allowed by its zoning classification. For example, the value of a vacant site that can be developed with several apartment units is most likely greater than the value of a similar site at the same location that can be developed with a single-family house because the landlord can earn a higher income from the apartment development. Therefore, sites that can be re-zoned to uses that earn higher income per square foot offer opportunities for big profits *if they are bought at a price that reflects their original use.*

According to Carn (1984), a change in the allowable use of a site is more likely to be approved if the adjacent sites are zoned for the requested use change. Thus, a request for rezoning from single-family housing to multifamily housing is more likely to be approved if the site for which rezoning is requested borders a site that is zoned or already developed to such use. A site surrounded by single-family houses is unlikely to receive approval for such a change. Similarly, a request for rezoning of a site currently designated for residential use to a commercial use is more likely to be approved if an adjacent site is already developed in a commercial use.

The use of bordering sites is not the only criterion that determines the probability of approval of a rezoning request. Another important concern of zoning officials is that the requested zoning change does not severely violate the guidelines of the municipality's comprehensive land-use plan. A final consideration is the impact of the project associated with the rezoning request on the community. If significant benefits for the community, such as a great number of jobs are at stake, zoning officials are more likely to approve the requested zoning change.

Undeveloped sites zoned for non-commercial uses, or developed sites with non-commercial structures that can be converted to commercial use at low cost may provide big profits if they are bought under the residential-use regime and get rezoned to commercial use that can earn a higher income. Notice that this strategy will work only if the commercial structure that can be developed, after re-zoning is approved, produces *considerably higher income than the residential use for which the site was originally zoned.*

Investing in properties with potential for upgrading zoning change is *risky* because the investor cannot know with certainty whether the request for zoning change will be approved. Within this context, in evaluating such properties, the investor needs to thoroughly assess whether the property under consideration:

- ➢ represents a viable investment with an acceptable return *under its current use*
- ➢ can allow for big profits, after taking into account its purchase cost and any demolition and construction costs that may be required in order to develop the site to the use for which the zoning change is requested

10) OWNER-OCCUPIED HOUSING DURING PERIODS OF SHARP DECREASES IN INTEREST RATES

Given that most housing purchases are financed through borrowed money, sharp decreases in interest rates will make debt service payments considerably lower, making housing affordable to many households that are renting a house. Given that homeownership is the preferred mode of tenancy for many households, sharp decreases in interest rates should stimulate significant increases in the demand and prices of owner-occupied housing. As Figure 31 indicates, housing prices were rising at a faster rate over the period 2000-2004, when the 30-year fixed mortgage rate fell from 8% below 6%.

Within this framework, purchasing an owner-occupied housing unit as soon as interest rates start decreasing may prove profitable, assuming that the market is not oversupplied and no adverse demographic changes affecting negatively demand for housing are taking place. However, there is a significant risk involved with this strategy—interest rates may rise sharply after the property is purchased, in which case, the value of the property will likely decline. Increased rates contribute to reduced housing demand, which in turn triggers property value losses (all else being equal).

As the behavior of mortgage rates over the last 33 years shows, when mortgage rates (and interest rates) start declining, they continue doing so mostly for about 3-4 years (see Figure 31). Over the period 1972-2005, however, there were two periods during which mortgage rate declines lasted for only two years, 1981-1983 and 1984-1986. Notice though that these two-year declines were interrupted by a one-year rise, and that over the entire 1981-1986 period, they registered an amazing drop of about 700 basis points (from about 17% to about 10%).

Figure 31 – Annual Mortgage Rates and Housing Prices

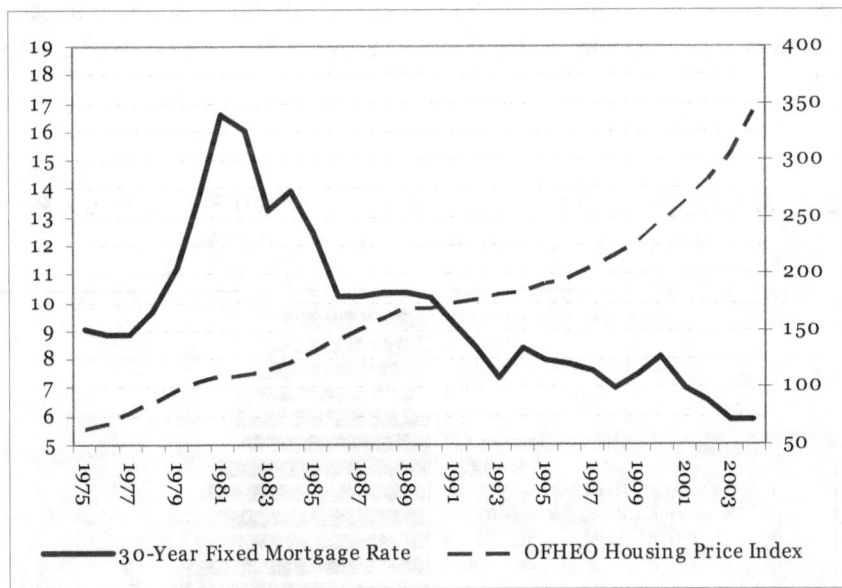

Sources: Freddie Mac and OFHEO

Another important point about the behavior of mortgage/interest rates is that, with the exception of the period 1978-1986, they seem to have been changing *relatively slowly*. The historical behavior of mortgage rates suggests that if investors buy at the beginning of sharp interest rate declines and hold for two-three years, they may realize significant profits. In any case, investors that apply this strategy should closely follow interest-rate developments and be ready to sell if they realize that interest rates are getting on a path of sharp increases, or the property is not expected to register any significant value gains due to other developments in its immediate or broader environment.

The *very strong effect of low interest rates* on housing demand in the first half of the 2000s is clearly reflected in the very strong 5-year appreciation rates for single-family houses reported by the Office of Federal Housing Enterprise Oversight (OFHEO). Figure 32 portrays the 20 top markets in terms of *annualized* 5-year growth rates in single-family housing prices as of the third quarter of 2005. These rates range from 18.9% in Merced, CA, the nation's top housing market, to 16.7% in Santa Ana-Anaheim-Irvine, CA, the nation's twentieth best market. These rates imply that from the third quarter of 2000, until the third quarter of 2005, single-family housing prices in Merced and Santa Ana-Anaheim-Irvine increased by 137.6% and 116.4%, respectively.

Figure 32 – Markets that Experienced the Strongest 5-Year House Price Increases in US, as of 3rd Quarter of 2005

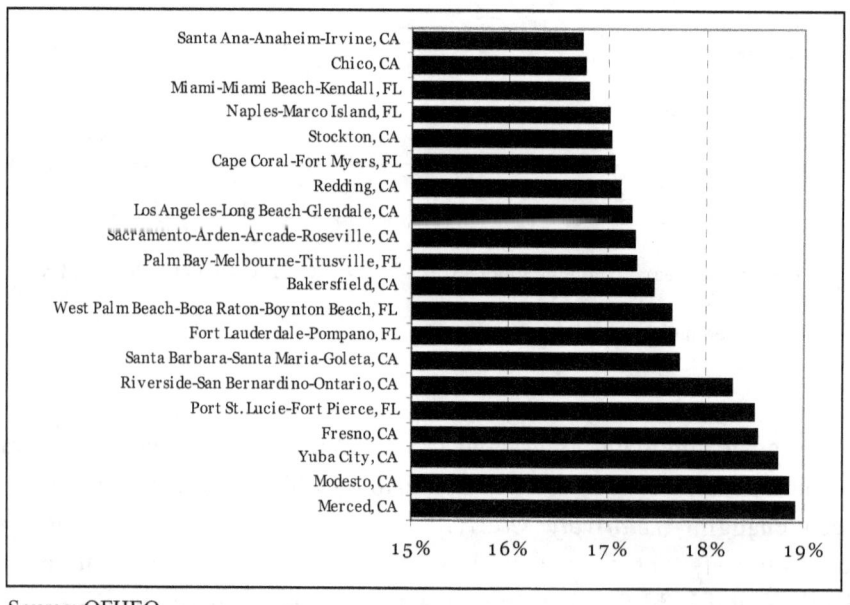

Source: OFHEO

The most important insight from Figure 32 is that the 20 locations that registered the strongest increases are located within *only two states*, Florida and California, which are considered among the most attractive in the country. This fact is consistent with my hypothesis that the locations that benefit the most in terms of value gains from aggregate increases in demand, such as the one caused by very low interest rates, are the most attractive ones (as long as they are not oversupplied).

Notice that the broader effect of interest rate decreases is independent of location–at least in terms of direction–because the capital markets are nationally and internationally integrated. The dramatic decreases in interest rates in the early 2000s in America and Europe have triggered double-digit housing price increases on both continents.

11) MONOPOLY PROPERTIES

In many cases, an extreme result of growth controls and regulations is the creation of *properties with monopoly status*, that is, existing properties of a particular use that become scarce because growth controls and regulations prohibit further development of similar properties. This means that properties that are bought *before they revert to monopoly status* and sold after they gain monopoly status should allow for big profits, since monopoly implies extreme scarcity, which in turn can lead to significant price increases. Furthermore, prices of monopoly properties tend to rise faster than average property prices.

Berry (1984) suggests that the number of monopoly properties has grown rapidly, due to *widespread downzoning and outright prohibition of land uses*. He cites numerous examples of monopoly properties, such as existing residences, motels, apartments, and mobile home parks on unique ocean frontages, where such uses have been restricted; existing high-rise apartments in districts where height restrictions have been imposed; and industrial plants in areas where newly adopted environmental regulations restrict the further development of such uses. Berry indicates that the level of price increases that may take place after a property acquires monopoly status will depend on *how long the property is likely to maintain such a status, the nature of events that may cause its termination, and the magnitude of demand for such a property.*

Berry's example of high-rise apartment buildings in districts where height restrictions have been imposed entails a notion of localized scarcity, but in my view, it may not approach the level of scarcity implied by the term "monopoly" if other high-rise apartments can be found in other districts within the urban area. Continuing improvements in communications and transportation have expanded significantly the *geographic extent of property markets*, and therefore, concepts such as monopoly and scarcity should be examined within the scope of the entire urban area, as opposed to a small geographic scale. Within this context, real estate investors need to think very carefully before attributing monopoly status to any given property.

Given significant locational substitutability within an urban area, and the fact that any type of property can be reproduced (except historical monuments, districts, and buildings perhaps), true scarcity and monopoly status may lie at the location level and not the property level. In other words, what may be *truly monopolistic* within an urban area are unique and scarce locational characteristics that can not be easily replicated. Think, for example, of a large coastal city, which has a few beaches of unique physical beauty, which are also suitable for swimming. I would argue that these few beaches qualify as monopoly locations, and the properties at these locations must qualify as monopoly properties by virtue of the monopoly status of those locations. To understand this, consider that while there are many hotels in a large urban area, there will be few located on uniquely attractive beaches.

Within this context, the characterization "monopoly property" would be warranted only based on unique (and therefore, scarce) characteristics of the location, combined with unique characteristics of the property. Maybe one way to locate such properties is to first identify locations of *unique and long-lasting advantages* that guarantee long-term high demand for its real estate. Subsequently, one needs to identify the types of properties in high demand due to the unique advantages of those locations, and investigate whether there are zoning and growth controls that prohibit or will prohibit further development of such uses in the future.

Chapter 10

Mismanaged Properties

The third category of properties with big profit potential includes mismanaged, or underperforming (as they are often referred to) properties. This category includes two subcategories of properties:

   a) properties that are not used in their highest and best use

   b) properties that are being used in their highest and best use but their earning capacity is well below their true potential given the advantages of their immediate and broader location

There are various slightly differing definitions of the highest and best use. The substance of all definitions, however, is that the highest and best use is the legally permissible use that will secure *the highest profit to the owner of the property*. Notice that the substantial difference between this category of properties and the first two categories is that the source of the big profit potential is not an upcoming change in the property's macroeconomic or microeconomic environment, but the *underutilization* of the property within its existing environment and market conditions, and the potential for significantly increasing its income by utilizing it to its full capacity.

Properties not being used at their highest and best use can provide high investment returns if the transition from their current use to the most profitable one is not very costly. In most cities and municipalities in the US, the general uses of land—agricultural, residential, commercial, industrial, and variations of these-- are determined by the local city planning office.[22] Nor-

---

[22] The Los Angeles planning and zoning code designates the following general-use zones: agricultural, suburban, residential estate, one-family, residential urban, residential zero side yard, residential waterways, two-family, restricted-density multiple dwelling, multiple dwelling,

mally, the local government will produce a comprehensive plan for the city/municipality, or update the existing one. The comprehensive plan is accompanied by the zoning ordinance, which usually designates which areas will be developed with single-family housing, multi-family housing, commercial, and industrial uses. The zoning ordinance includes, among others, height and density restrictions for the different zones.

Although the general use of a site is, in most cases, predetermined by local regulations, the principle of highest and best use is still applicable. The reason is that properties are developed in very specific uses. For example, the designation of a site as multifamily residential does not give a definite clue to the question of how the site should be developed, since it is possible to develop various structures of differing size, quality, and amenities that fall within this category. Such structures may be designed as high-income apartments, upper moderate-income apartments, moderate-income apartments, and so on. Even the designation high-income apartments is not specific enough, since the total size of each unit, as well as the number, sizes, function, and quality of the different spaces/rooms composing the unit still need to be determined. In order to do that, a highest and best use study needs to be carried out.

A highest and best use analysis for a specific site usually consists of the following major stages:

1) Identification of alternative uses suitable for the site given its physical characteristics and accessibility advantages

2) Collection of information regarding prevailing rental levels, sales prices, and vacancy rates in the neighborhood and the broader market for similar uses

3) Analysis of the feasibility and profitability of each of the permissible alternative uses, taking into account projected revenues, development costs, principal and interest payments, taxes, broker's fees, and operational costs for rental properties

---

automobile parking, parking building, limited commercial, commercial, commercial manufacturing, restricted industrial, limited industrial, light industrial, heavy industrial, and ocean submerged land.

4) Ranking of alternative uses in terms of profitability and risk. The profitability criterion usually used is the internal rate of return (see note 9 in Chapter 3 for a more detailed discussion of this measure).

Notice that the use that commands the highest rent or sales price per square foot is not necessarily the most profitable one, since construction and development costs differ among the different uses.

In trying to evaluate whether a specific property falls under the category of mismanaged properties, one needs to ask the following questions:

a) What is the strength of a specific location?

b) Are properties at this location being used in a way that takes full advantage of their immediate environment and accessibility advantages to surrounding communities and to the broader urban area?

c) Given the mix of people and activities in the neighborhood and conveniently accessible locations within its area of influence, what kind of use would earn the highest income?

The possibility and potential for *repositioning* is the key for identifying mismanaged properties that can be turned around successfully. Repositioning is the key concept because these properties usually require improvements in order to be brought to a qualitative and functional status that will allow them to attract tenants and increase income. Hence, a typical group of mismanaged properties across all types of real estate includes class-B and C structures at class-A locations. These properties usually require capital expenditures in order to be brought to a status that would capitalize on the full potential of their location. Examples of such properties are *class-B office buildings at class-A commercial locations, or low- and medium-quality houses and* apartments in *high-quality neighborhoods*.

Investors need to have in mind, though, that not all class-B or C structures at class-A locations offer opportunities for big profits. For example, some structures may have remained at a poor and dysfunctional condition simply because the cost of improvement is too high, compared to the expected increase in income. For such buildings to truly qualify as mismanaged properties, the anticipated increase in income as a result of the property's upgrade must be significantly greater than the cost of improvements. For this reason, in assessing the extent of mismanagement and the true value-increase potential of the property, extra caution is needed, with respect to assumed figures for occupancy, achievable rental rates, and required capital expenditures. The latter may involve façade work, renovation of lobby and common areas, updating of the mechanical equipment and building technology, the elevators, the parking structure, or even more serious and more costly structural modifications depending on the condition of the building under consideration.

An example of properties that may fall under the category of mismanaged properties include under-maintained, dysfunctional, and under-equipped single-family, multifamily, or apartment units in nice residential communities. These are housing units and multifamily residential buildings with deteriorated external and internal appearance, but without severe structural problems. It may be easier to find such properties in nice middle-income neighborhoods than in high-income neighborhoods, since high-income households are likely to spend considerably higher amounts for the maintenance of their homes than middle-income households. Improvement of these properties is likely to increase their value more than the cost of improvements, as long as they are located in nice neighborhoods.

The most important thing that needs to be done before buying deteriorated housing units in nice neighborhoods is an accurate estimation of the cost of renovating the property. This cost needs to be compared with a conservative estimate of the expected increase in the value of the property, taking into account the prices at which houses in very good condition sell in the neighborhood. Having in mind a conservative estimate of the required improvement costs and the price at which the house can sell once renovated, the investor can determine whether the property can allow for substantial profits.

Another category of mismanaged properties includes *shopping centers* of any size (from neighborhood to super-regional), whose sales are *well below their potential* because of poor tenant mix, poor-quality and under-maintained structures, unattractive environment, and poor management and marketing policies that fail to attract sales and tenants. Buying and turning around such centers could prove a very profitable venture. In fact, a number of private equity funds have pursued and successfully applied such strategies. A particular real estate investment trust (REIT) that uses this strategy is Feldman Mall Properties, Inc. In particular, Feldman specializes in buying under-performing malls and turning them into more attractive and profitable venues, by applying renovation programs that include architectural redesign, change of layout, square footage increase, and the addition of in-demand tenants.

Turning around mismanaged and underperforming retail centers situated in high traffic, in-fill areas requires, in most cases, some renovation which can be extensive. Investors need to evaluate the *post-renovation potential* of the property through meticulous analysis of the area's demographics, market research, and financial feasibility studies, taking into account planned renovations and lease-up costs. Before proceeding, the feasibility study needs to clearly establish that the implied value of the property, based on its projected revenue, will allow for significant profits on total invested capital after taking into account all costs (acquisitions, renovation, lease-up and operating).

Mismanaged properties include also rental apartments and office buildings, which do not seem to have any obvious locational or qualitative disadvantages compared to competing properties, yet their *vacancy rate is considerably higher* than the average for the local market in which they directly compete for tenants. In such cases, the most likely reason for the high vacancy is mismanagement, which means that the use of skillful leasing managers to fill the vacant space could help considerably increase the income-earning capacity and the value of these properties.

SUMMARY

> Mismanaged properties include two categories of structures: a) those that are not used at their highest and best use, and b) those that are used at their highest and best use, but their income-earning capacity is well below their potential, given the advantages of their location.

> The general use (single-family, multi-family, commercial, industrial) at which a site can be developed is pre-determined by the comprehensive plan of the municipality or city the site is located within, but the principle of highest and best use is still applicable, since many structures of differing size, quality, and amenities can be developed within each general use.

> Mismanaged and underperforming properties include class-B and C structures at class-A and B locations, such as poor-quality office and retail structures at strong commercial locations; office, multi-tenant industrial, and apartment buildings with high vacancy rate in low-

vacancy sub-markets; and poor-quality houses in nice residential communities.

- Retail centers with low income earning capacity due to poor tenant mix and poor management practices fall also within the category of mismanaged properties.
- Since, in many cases, turning around mismanaged properties involves significant capital expenditures, investors need to carefully assess the cost of planned improvements and the expected timing and magnitude of additional revenue, once the improvements are completed.
- Several private investment funds have achieved high returns by focusing on turning around mismanaged and underperforming properties.

CHAPTER 11

BARGAIN PROPERTIES

I define as bargain properties those properties that, because of *special circumstances*, such as tax delinquency, default on mortgage payments, or bankruptcy, *can be bought at a price considerably below their fair market value*. For this reason, many of these properties can provide high returns independently of market conditions. Furthermore, there is no need to wait for these properties to appreciate in order to profit from them. Usually, most of the properties that can be bought at low prices, due to the aforementioned circumstances, need some or a lot of fixing up before they can be functional. However, the low prices at which many of these properties can be bought can allow for big profits when sold at or near market prices, even after taking into account the cost of repairs. Some investors may do minor cosmetic repairs and resell these properties fast to other investors, at prices that are still well below market for quick profits. Of course, if the property has potential for market-driven or development-driven appreciation potential, the investor will stand to earn much higher returns by holding the property for a couple of years and then selling it.

Another investment strategy in dealing with these properties is fixing them up and renting them, instead of selling them. This strategy makes sense as long as the investor has a *decent cash flow*. This requires that the rental income of the property covers comfortably all operating and other expenses, including all loans that may have been undertaken by the investor in order to buy and repair the property.

Investors focusing on bargain properties, which are usually sold through public or private auctions, should:

1) Carefully and *conservatively* estimate all costs involved with assuming ownership of the property, repairing it, and reselling it. According

to Hicks (1992), acquisition costs may include cost of purchase, cost to bring loan to current, title insurance, transfer fee, documentary stamps, property insurance, any junior mortgages burdening the property, and encumbrances or liens. Costs to resell may include commission, title insurance, legal cost, cleanup cost, repair cost, escrow fees, pro-rata insurance, pro-rata taxes, points (if the Federal Home Administration or Veterans Administration is involved) etc.

2) Investigate thoroughly the financial obligations associated with the ownership of the property, such as junior liens (second or third mortgages, or other debt subordinated to the first mortgage). Otherwise, the buyer may end up buying a property heavily indebted and assuming responsibility for those loans.

3) Once the decision has been made to buy a bargain property, it is wise to get title commitment and title insurance before the purchase in order to avoid any responsibilities for undiscovered junior liens. In this way, any responsibility for undiscovered junior liens is transferred to the insurance company.

4) Ask for the mortgage contract and read it carefully to understand the obligations undertaken by buying the property.

5) Evaluate carefully properties with severe functional and/or structural problems that are very costly to repair, properties that are difficult to resell or rent because of locational or other irreversible problems, and properties located in markets or submarkets where property values are declining rapidly due to unfavorable developments in their immediate environment or unfavorable market conditions.

6) Have in mind that most types of bargain properties sold through public auctions have a redemption period that varies across states. This is a period during which the original owner, or the holders of junior liens, can gain ownership of the property by paying any taxes or other dues associated with the property, as well as the purchaser's expenses. In these cases, the investor will gain ownership only after the end of the redemption period.

7) Check information sources for bargain properties frequently, because good opportunities go away quickly.

TAX DELINQUENT PROPERTIES

Very often cities and counties advertise in the legal section of the local newspapers the sale or public auction of properties that have been taken over in default of real estate taxes. In many cases, these properties can be bought very cheaply by paying the taxes and sometimes a small amount for legal and advertising fees. If the local government wants very badly to put a property back into the tax roll it may dispose it at a very low price and certainly *considerably below its market value.*

As I emphasized earlier, investors need to be careful when buying tax delinquent properties because they may be quite deteriorated due to under-maintenance. It is likely that the owners of such properties stopped maintaining them some time after they stopped paying taxes. Furthermore, a number of these properties belong to absentee landlords who have neglected them.

According to the redemption laws that some states may have, the original owner of a tax delinquent property has the right to redeem his property within a pre-determined period by paying the unpaid taxes and the new owner's expense. Although this happens rarely, the investor should be aware of this possibility.

Properties that have been seized by the Internal Revenue Service in default of income or other taxes also belong in the category of tax delinquent properties that can be bought at prices considerably below market. These properties are sold through public auctions, and the rule of the redemption period does apply. Notices announcing the sale of such properties are posted in the legal section of local newspapers and at the local IRS office.

FORECLOSURE PROPERTIES

The second category of properties that can be bought below market price includes foreclosure properties. These are properties the owners of which have defaulted on their mortgage payments and have been taken over by the lender. Foreclosure properties may need significant improvements before they can be put on the market because of under-maintenance. These properties are usually auctioned, and their sales price is determined through competitive bidding.

Kyle and Perry (1979) suggest that a rational owner who cannot afford to pay the mortgage payments will want to sell the property before the actual foreclosure process begins. In this way, he/she will avoid attorney's fees and other expenses that accumulate as the foreclosure process moves to the final stages. As Conover (1975) suggests, this pre-foreclosure stage may be a good time for the investor to get in, for two reasons. First, the investor can assume the existing loan or re-finance, and second, he/she can avoid the auction process, where he/she may have to pay a higher price in order to outbid other interested buyers. When setting his/her maximum bid, the investor needs to keep in mind that the cost of the foreclosure is added to the remaining mortgage balance.

The most profitable strategy probably is the one that involves the purchase of a junior lien of a small amount and filing a notice of redemption towards the end of the redemption period. McLean (1988) suggests that foreclosure properties that are not sold during the auction, and eventually revert to a financial institution that happens to be the lender, offer the most attractive investment opportunities. These properties are handled by special departments, entitled REO, which stands for "Real Estate Owned," and may be sold at below-market prices because financial institutions are primarily in the lending business, not in the real estate business. As such, they only want to transfer ownership and get their money back as soon as possible.

Kyle and Perry (1979) suggest that foreclosure properties that have been held for more than 10-15 years may offer significant profit opportunities. These properties may have *accumulated a significant amount of equity*, because their owners may have repaid a significant amount of the loan principal. If these properties are bought by repaying just the remaining balance of the loan, the accumulated equity will be the investor's profit. The investor, however, needs to make sure that the property has no serious structural or functional deficiencies and that the amount of equity accumulated is considerably higher than the cost of any improvements that may be needed. For this reason, it is important to examine the loan origination date, to figure out how much principal has been repaid, and if possible verify the amount with the lender. Kyle and Perry point out that a property held up to 15 years may still be burdened with 95% of the original loan balance. This percentage, however, varies considerably, depending on the terms of the loan, and that is why the investor needs to examine and understand these terms very well.

Extra caution should be taken when estimating the cost of improvements that may be required to upgrade the property. McLean (1988) suggests that usually these properties are more run down than they appear. For this reason he suggests the investor adjust estimates of improvement costs upwards by 25%, in order to avoid unpleasant surprises. Furthermore, it should be taken into account that purchase costs may include, in addition to the balance of the first mortgage, delinquencies, advances, and fees for first and second mortgages, the balance of a second mortgage, title and escrow expenses, property taxes, insurance, and loan origination fees.

Besides looking at the legal section of the local newspaper, investors can inquire at government agencies that hold public auctions. These are the Federal Housing Administration (FHA), the Small Business Administration (SBA), the General Services Administration (GSA), and the Veterans Administration (VA). Properties sold through auctions by the FHA range from single-family houses to multiunit apartment buildings, while the VA sells mostly single-family units. The SBA sells real estate and business equipment through auctions, while the GSA sells all types of properties, including land.

One easy way to learn about upcoming auctions is to get on these agencies' mailing lists. Finally, another good source of information for foreclosure properties is the REO department of financial institutions. Information regarding the specific address, location, and legal description of foreclosure properties can be obtained from the county recorder's office.

BANKRUPTCY-SALE PROPERTIES

Bankruptcy sales are part of liquidation and distribution of assets by an appointed trustee. These are sold through private auctions. Bankruptcy-sale properties offer greater opportunities for big profits because the bids are sealed, the competition is limited, and there is the possibility of lower asking prices by the sellers. To be notified when bankruptcy sales take place, investors need to get on the mailing list of bankruptcy courts. If there is no such thing as a mailing list, investors can communicate with the bankruptcy trustees. Information about an area's bankruptcy courts and trustees can be obtained from the Federal District court.

SUMMARY

- Bargain properties are properties that can be bought at a price considerably below their market value due to special circumstances, such as tax delinquency, foreclosure, or bankruptcy.

- In dealing with bargain properties, investors need to exercise caution, since they may be in poor condition due to neglect and under-maintenance.

- Investors need to carefully evaluate repair and other costs (including any senior and junior liens that may burden the property), as well as the revenue that can be earned by selling or renting the property after renovating it.

- Investors need to make sure the property is not burdened by other loans, such as a second and third mortgage, as well as other claims.

- Some investors may do minor cosmetic repairs and resell at low (below market) prices for quick profits.

- Investors may be able to acquire tax delinquent properties cheaply by paying the amount of taxes burdening the property and a small amount for legal and advertising fees.

- In the case of foreclosure properties, it may be better for the investor to enter the scene at the pre-foreclosure stage in order to gain ownership of the property by assuming the existing loan, thus avoiding the auction process, where he/she may need to pay a higher price to acquire the property.

- Properties that have been held for more than 10-15 years may offer significant profit opportunities because they may have accumulated a significant amount of equity, which will translate to profit, if the property is acquired by paying the remaining loan balance and repair costs are relatively low.

CHAPTER 12

BUILDING HIGH-RETURN PORTFOLIOS

A *real estate portfolio* is a collection of properties held by an individual or a firm. Property portfolios targeting high returns and big profits are referred to in the real estate community as "opportunity" or "opportunistic funds." These investment vehicles emerged in the early 1990s, targeting returns in excess of 20% and have since grown rapidly. The basic investment strategy of these funds is pretty much the one discussed extensively in this book—acquiring properties with significant value-increase potential, capturing this added value using skillful managers, and then reselling the properties in two to four years to take advantage of the increases in value (Hahn, Geltner, and Gerardo-Lietz, 2005). Hahn, Geltner, and Gerardo-Lietz point out that such funds have often focused on development and turnaround properties. The term turnaround property is used in association with distressed or problematic properties. Within the framework developed in this book, such properties can be classified mainly under the category of "mismanaged" properties or under the category of bargain properties if they have been confiscated because of the inability of their owners to meet certain financial obligations.

As opportunities for distressed properties become more difficult to find, opportunity funds have turned to niche strategies in an effort to capitalize on opportunities within particular sectors. Opportunity funds are classified as high risk ventures since they consist of taking advantage of the yet unrealized potential of a property for big value increases. The risk lies with the uncertainties of the future and the occurrence of developments that may impede the realization of such potential.

APPLYING MODERN PORTFOLIO THEORY (MPT) IN STRUCTURING HIGH-RETURN PORTFOLIOS

Investments in portfolios of properties have *advantages over single-property investments* because they provide possibilities for diversification. Diversification is the allocation of investment funds across assets (properties, in the case of real estate portfolios) whose performance is driven by different factors. This is desirable because it reduces the uncertainty (risk) regarding the future performance of the portfolio. Portfolio risk can be reduced by including differently-behaving assets because any unexpectedly bad performances by a few of the properties are less likely to be imitated by the other properties that compose the portfolio.

The concept of diversification, and its application to portfolio structuring, have been refined by Markowitz (1952) who has presented a very particular quantitative model for constructing investment portfolios. Markowitz's model, which is the foundation of modern portfolio theory (MPT), focuses on the selection of the group of assets that will maximize the portfolio's expected return and minimize risk (uncertainty). This group of assets is selected from a set of possible investments referred to as the investment universe. In doing so, the constraining factor is the amount of funds available for investments, as well as investor preferences in terms of focusing on or avoiding certain types of investments. For example, a small amount of investment funds will allow the purchase of only a small number of properties, while a larger amount of funds will allow the purchase of a greater number of properties.

Application of MPT requires the estimation of return and risk measures for each asset/investment that can be potentially included in the portfolio. The second component of MPT applications in structuring real estate portfolios is the use of measures indicating how movements in the performance of one property type or market relate to movements in the performance of other property types or markets that will potentially be included in the portfolio.[23] The underlying rationale of using these meas-

---

[23] This can be done through a statistical procedure referred to as correlation analysis, which calculates the so-called "correlation coefficients." These measures indicate how synchronized, parallel, or opposite are the movements of an indicator (employment for example) in one market compared to the movements of the same indicator in another market. Correlation

ures is to diversify the portfolio across markets and property types whose performances are related as little as possible or, even better, in a negative fashion (see note 23). The negative performance links between investments that compose a portfolio are sought with the hope that not only will poor performance in one investment not be transferred to other investments, but also that it will be counterbalanced by better performances of investments negatively related to it.

When it comes to real estate, the Markowitz model is not applicable at the specific-property level, since one cannot estimate return and risk measures for all potential real estate investments at any location within the country or even within a single metropolitan market. It can be applied, however, at the market and property-type selection stage, since forecasts of average market performance (returns), and estimates of risk measures can be produced along these dimensions by firms specialized in real estate forecasting and risk analysis (Sivitanides, Southard, Torto, and Wheaton, 2000).

Describing the specific models and methodologies that can be used to apply Markowitz's model in structuring real estate portfolios is out of the scope of this book. However, understanding the broader guidelines and substance of the diversification principle, as well as how the four categories of value-gain potential fit within this framework, do fall within the scope of the book.

The broad guideline we can draw from MPT is that real estate investors can diversify their property portfolios along two dimensions: 1) metropolitan areas, and 2) property types. The discussion presented in this book has introduced *another dimension*, along which investors can diversify their holdings in structuring high-profit portfolios. This diversification perspective can be applied at the property-specific level *across*

---

coefficients can be positive or negative, and range in value between 1 and -1. A correlation coefficient of 1 would suggest that the two markets are moving in exactly the same way in terms of the indicator examined, while a correlation coefficient of -1 would suggest that the two markets are moving in exactly the opposite way in terms of the indicator examined. The ideal composition of a portfolio from a diversification point of view is to include markets that are negatively correlated (pair wise), so that bad economic performance in one market will be counterbalanced by good performance in another market.

the four types of sources of value gains. Figure 33 presents all three major diversification dimensions; the related aspects are discussed below.

Figure 33 – High-Return Portfolio Diversification Dimensions

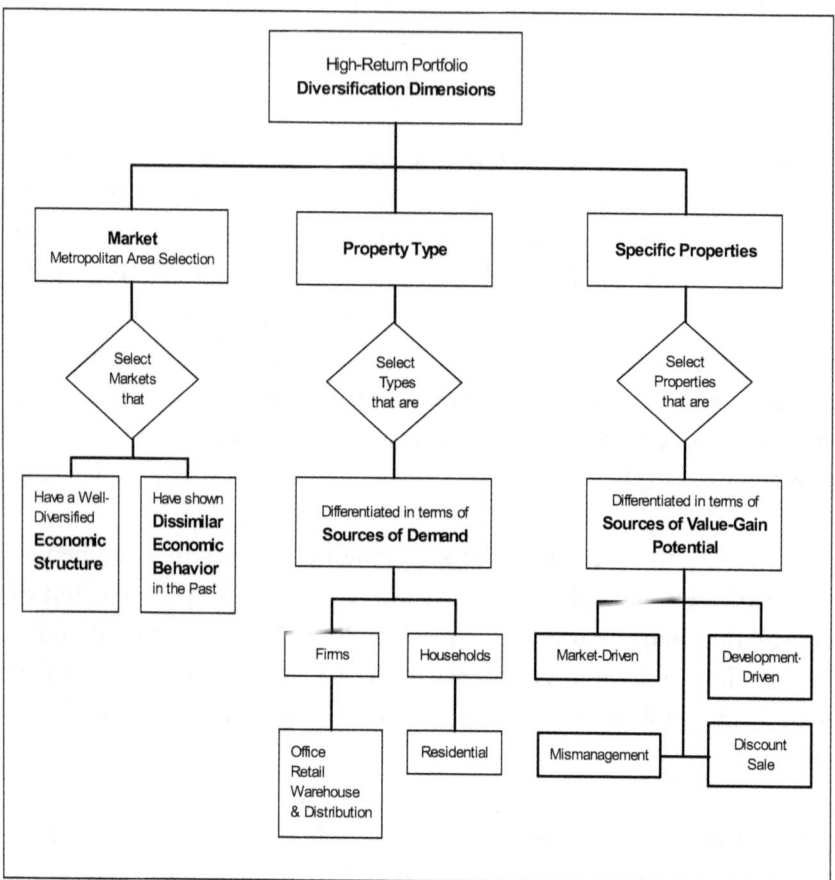

Markowitz's work demonstrates that two risk concepts are important in determining portfolio risk: a) *the risk level* of each investment included in the portfolio, and b) *performance links* among the investments included in the portfolio. Thus, in selecting a group of metropolitan markets and a group of property types or subtypes to be targeted for property investments, it is important to consider how these concepts apply.

The selection of *metropolitan markets* for a high-return portfolio has to start from those predicted to register the *strongest rent growth*. If rent growth forecasts are not available then investors should focus on markets predicted to register the strongest economic growth and relatively low vacancy rates. Once this step is completed, the selected metropolitan markets can be reduced to a smaller target group based on risk level and performance links. Since the objective of diversification is to reduce risk, metropolitan markets that appear less risky and have minimal or negative performance links with other markets are more suitable to be targeted for investments.

The risk-level consideration is valid since uncertainty regarding future economic performance varies across metropolitan markets. Risk is often associated, in the minds of investors, with the *volatility of the economy of a market*. Sivitanides and Sivitanidou (1996) found that metropolitan markets with greater historical volatility of employment growth commanded a greater risk premium, as reflected in variations in market capitalization rates. Sivitanidou and Sivitanides (1999) also found that metropolitan markets with a more diverse office tenant base were considered less risky by office property investors.

In terms of performance links, diversification benefits may be achievable by selecting metropolitan markets whose *sources of economic growth are different*. However, this may run against the objective of selecting markets with a diverse economic structure, since if the latter is true, sources of growth will be also diversified and not very different across such markets.

As was the case for choosing metropolitan markets for targeting investments, the selection of *property types* or subtypes for a high-return portfolio has to start with those predicted to register *strong rent and value increases*. Once this step is completed, if there is need to narrow down the selection, investors can use the risk levels of each type, and performance links, as criteria. Based on the historical fluctuations of the value of the different property types examined in Chapter 2, one could argue that office and warehouse properties, as well as super-regional shopping centers, are more risky, while apartments and neighborhood/community centers are less risky.

In terms of performance links, investors should focus on including types and/or subtypes of property types whose demand comes from *distinct groups that are likely to exhibit different behavior*. For example, the inclusion in the portfolio of office and apartment properties seems logical from a diversification point of view since demand for office space comes from firms, while demand for apartments comes from households.

Analysis of the relationship between historical property-value movements over the period 1984-2004 among the different property types (as represented by the correlation figures shown in Table 8) verifies this proposition. Notice that office and apartments have the smallest correlation of 0.05, which suggests that value movements of these two property types were unrelated. Overall, the numbers presented in Table 7 suggest that office, retail, and apartments compose the group that has the weakest performance links in terms of value behavior. Warehouse seems to have strong performance links with both office and retail.

Table 8 – Correlations among the Four Property Types Based on Historical Value Movements (1984-2004)

	Office	Retail	Warehouse	Apartments
Office	1.00			
Retail	0.35	1.00		
Warehouse	0.84	0.64	1.00	
Apartments	0.05	0.26	0.46	1.00

Source: Calculated by the author based on NCREIF data.

Econometric forecasts of real estate demand, supply, vacancy, and *rent growth* by metropolitan market and property type, from reputable forecasting firms, can provide the best basis for selecting metropolitan markets and property types to be targeted for profitable real estate investments during the first stage of the portfolio construction process. Such forecasts can provide the basis for developing expected *return measures by market/property type*.[24]

---

[24] Ideally, the estimation of such measures should be based on rent growth forecasts and forecasts of capitalization rates.

If rent growth forecasts are available, investors should use them as the basis for selecting markets to be included in high-return portfolios, as opposed to using economic growth forecasts. Economic growth forecasts reflect only the demand side of the market, while rent growth forecasts take into account both demand and supply conditions expected to prevail in a specific metropolitan area and property type. Furthermore, econometric rent growth forecasts take into account how *rent adjustment speeds* vary across markets. Sivitanides (1997) has presented empirical evidence suggesting that office rents adjust at different speeds in various metropolitan markets.

If rent growth forecasts by market and property type are not available, investors should use economic growth forecasts and information on vacancy rates by market and property type. Up-to-date vacancy rate information can be obtained from large brokerage companies that carry out quarterly vacancy rate surveys. With this information at hand, investors need to focus on markets that combine the strongest economic growth prospects and relatively low vacancy rates. In the second stage of the portfolio structuring process, they should try to identify within these markets assets that fall within the four categories of properties with big profit potential.

THE ROLE OF SOURCES OF PROFIT POTENTIAL IN STRUCTURING HIGH-RETURN PORTFOLIOS

To examine the implications of the diversification principle within the context of allocating investments across the four types of properties with significant profit potential identified in this book, we need to focus on the two key concepts of diversification—risk levels and performance links. Before discussing these aspects, let us revisit the four major categories of properties with significant profit potential:

1) Properties with *significant* market-driven value-increase potential due to anticipated developments in the broader market forces, such as *strong* employment, income and/or population growth, which are expected to boost considerably values at: a) office clusters best positioned to attract new and expanding firms, b) the most attractive shopping destinations bound to benefit the most from increased consumer spending, and c) residential communities best positioned to attract the additional demand for owner-occupied housing and rental units

2) Properties with *considerable* development-driven value-increase potential due to anticipated significant favorable changes in their locational advantages and attractiveness

3) Mismanaged properties, which can be brought up to their full income-earning potential using skillful managers

4) Bargain properties that can be bought at a *significant discount* due to special circumstances and can be sold at regular market transactions at considerably higher prices after some improvements

With respect to the question of risk levels, I would argue that these four categories of properties are *not equally risky*. For example, mismanaged and bargain properties should entail less risk because their profit potential is not based on future changes that may occur in the market or the property's immediate and broader environment, but on their unexploited potential *given their current environment and circumstances*. Thus, the only prediction involved in these types of properties is that of the successful unleashing of their existing potential, which is more a matter of thorough analysis and evaluation of the possibilities, and less of a forecast. The role of prediction versus evaluation will be greater in cases where the turnaround time of a mismanaged property is expected to be long. Within this context, I would argue that mismanaged properties (at least those with short turnaround times) and bargain properties entail less risk than properties with market and development-driven value-increase potential.

If the four categories of properties were equally risky and profitable, the diversification principle would dictate that the investor's funds be equally allocated to each of the four types (putting aside any allocation implications dictated by pairwise correlations of performance between these asset classes). If, however, my hypothesis that mismanaged and bargain properties are less risky is accepted, it would suggest that managers who want to construct big-profit portfolios with lower risk profile should include these two types in greater proportions.

In terms of performance links, the four categories of properties are, by definition, *largely independent*, which means there are minimal, if any, performance links. For example, by definition, the development-driven potential for value growth stems from expected significant locational developments that are likely to increase considerably the locational advantages of a property, independently of whether broader economic growth in the metro area will occur. Likewise, the market-driven potential for value growth at specific locations stems from expected strong increases in aggregate demand in the metro area due to economic growth, independently of whether the locations will benefit from urban development projects. Furthermore, the source of the profit potential embodied in bargain properties stems from the considerable discount in their sales price, and has nothing to do with the market's prospects for economic growth or any locational developments. Likewise, the source of the profit potential in the case of mismanaged properties, as defined in this book, has little to do with the area's economic growth prospects, urban development projects, or discount sales.

The most important implication of the diversification principle is that investors building high-return portfolios should strive to include all four categories of value-increase potential in their portfolios in proportions that will result in a balanced mix. Since the sources of the value-gain potential of these categories of properties are different, such a portfolio structure will serve the purpose of protecting the rest of the portfolio in case one of these sources does not materialize as expected.

Although the four sources of value-gain potential identified in this book are independent, *they are not mutually exclusive*, in the sense that we cannot rule out the possibility of finding locations that will capitalize on the combined benefit from both broader economic growth and large development and transportation projects. Furthermore, we cannot rule out the possibility that an investor may be able to find bargain and/or mismanaged properties at such locations. Such properties would stand to benefit from at least three or four of the sources of profit potential identified in this book—broader metro growth, increases in locational advantages, mismanagement correction, and/or discount sales.

Within this context, I would argue that managers striving to build portfolios targeting high returns and big profits should try to include in their portfolios only properties that stand to benefit from *at least two sources of value growth*. Such properties are, in theory, both less risky and more profitable than properties whose value growth potential stems from only one source, because first, they are likely to get a greater boost in value, and second, if one source of value growth is not realized as expected, the property has still a good chance to benefit from the second source. If this logic is adopted by the portfolio manager, it can be applied by first limiting investments to selected markets with strong economic growth potential, and then finding in those markets properties that stand to benefit from both this metropolitan growth and another source of value-gain potential. This may not be easy to apply, but it may worth trying, to the extent allowed by the opportunities presented.

SUMMARY

> ➤ Structuring high-return real estate portfolios is not a new idea; such investment vehicles emerged under the label "opportunity" or "opportunistic funds" in the early 1990s, and since then, they have grown rapidly.

> ➤ The core strategy of real estate opportunity funds has been focusing on finding properties with strong appreciation potential, using skillful managers to realize this potential, and then selling quickly, in two to four years, to take advantage of strong value increases. This is very similar to the basic strategy discussed in this book.

> ➤ Investors structuring high-return portfolios can reduce risk and increase returns by selecting assets that stand to benefit from two or more sources of value growth, as discussed in this book, since these sources are, largely, independent of each other.

> ➤ National investors structuring high-return portfolios can gain valuable insight and foresight about the potential for achieving big profits in the different markets and property types around the country by obtaining econometric demand, supply, vacancy, and especially, rent growth forecasts from reputable forecasting firms.

> ➤ Rent-growth forecasts constitute a better indicator than economic-growth forecasts for selecting markets and property types for a high-return portfolio because the latter reflect only the demand side of the real estate market while the former summarize not only the demand side, but also the supply side and the idiosyncratic behavior of rent

- Investors structuring high-return portfolios can mitigate risk by diversifying their investments across the four sources of profit potential identified in this book; this can be achieved by spreading the investments, in a balanced fashion, across the four categories of properties with big profit potential.

- National investors can mitigate risk by diversifying their investments across metropolitan markets whose economies and real estate markets have historically behaved differently.

- The four categories of properties with significant profit potential are not equally risky; mismanaged and bargain properties should entail less risk since their potential exists mostly in their current status and is not based on a forecast/expectation of economic and physical growth, as is the case for properties with market-driven and development-driven appreciation potential.

- Investors that want to structure high-return portfolios with lower risk may want to include mismanaged and bargain properties with increased weights, if available investment opportunities allow it.

- For national investors, the best way to go about structuring high-return portfolios is to obtain econometric rent growth forecasts from reputable forecasting firms, select markets with the strongest rent growth prospects, and then identify properties that can be classified under the four categories of properties with significant profit potential, as defined in this book.

Glossary

Appreciation Rate The percentage change in value over a given period.

Bargain Properties Properties that can be bought significantly below their market value due to special circumstances, such as foreclosure, tax delinquency, and bankruptcy.

BBST Abbreviation for the "Buy at Bottom and Sell at the Top" strategy.

BBSS Abbreviation for the "Buy at Bottom and Sell Soon" strategy.

Capital Gain The dollar difference between the purchase and the sales price of a property.

Capitalization Rate The ratio of NOI of the property at the time of sale over its sales price. This ratio represents the required income return by investors active in the marketplace. However, due to the lack of transaction data, market capitalization rates are often estimated using actual NOI over the property's fair market value.

Compatibility Recovery Potential The potential of a property for value gains due to the removal of nearby incompatible uses that undermine its value.

Complementarity Improvement Potential The potential of a property to become more complementary to neighboring uses. Improvement of complementarity does not necessarily imply increases in values if it is associated with a downgrade of the property.

Construction Lag The time that it takes to perceive, plan, and construct a project. This time can range from 18 months to several years, depending on the size and nature of the project.

Correlation A statistical measure indicating the extent to which movements in one variable are related to movements in another variable.

Development-Driven Value Increases Property-value gains triggered by major urban and transportation development projects, or developments specific to the location of a property, which improve its attractiveness and income-earning potential.

Discounted Cash Flow (DCF) Model A mathematical formulation that takes into account all cash flows expected to be earned by a property over a given holding period, as well as the resale price at the end of the holding period, and discounts them to the present using an appropriate rate in order to estimate the property's investment value.

Equity Investment The amount of investor's own money used to finance investments in real estate (purchase and/or development).

Encumbrances Encumbrances include claims of use (not ownership) or monetary claims that may burden a property, such as right of way, maintenance agreements, homeowner association assessments, and utility easements.

Highest and Best Use The most profitable use to which a site can be legally developed.

FAR Abbreviation for the ratio of buildable floor area over land area (floor/area ratio).

Internal Rate of Return The periodic (annual, quarterly, etc.) rate of return of an investment. This is calculated as the discount rate that equalizes the purchase price with the present value of all cash flows expected to be received over a given holding period, including the resale price at the end of the holding period.

Leveraged Return The return of an investment, taking into account the effect of borrowed funds.

Liens The term "lien" refers to any charge or encumbrance against a property that secures the payment of a debt. For example liens may include past due property taxes, judgments, and other mortgage loans that may burden a property.

Market-Driven Value Increases Value increases triggered by increases in demand because of economic growth in the broader market area of a property.

NOI Abbreviation for net operating income, calculated as the total income earned by the property (rental income, plus other income) minus operating expenses.

NCREIF National Council of Real Estate Investment Fiduciaries.

Outbidding The phenomenon during which one user is involuntarily displaced by another user who is willing and can afford to pay a higher price.

Positive Leverage The use of borrowed funds to increase the investor's rate of return. Positive leverage is possible when the loan used to finance the purchase of a property is such that the mortgage constant is smaller than the investment's unleveraged return.

Migration Relocation across jurisdictional boundaries, the definition of which varies, depending on the geographic scope and context of the analysis. Within the context of this book, the more appropriate boundaries for examining migration patterns are the metropolitan area boundaries.

Mortgage Constant The percent of the original loan amount that needs to be paid periodically in order to fully repay the loan over the term of the loan.

Net Migration The difference between immigration and outmigration.

Price Elasticity of Demand The sensitivity of quantity demanded to changes in prices. It is measured as the ratio of the percentage change in quantity demanded over the percentage change in price. If the absolute value of this ratio is less than one, then demand is characterized as price inelastic. Investors looking for markets that will allow for greater price increases in response to increases in demand should be looking for areas and property types with price inelastic demand.

Price Elasticity of Supply The sensitivity of quantity supplied to changes in prices. It is measured as the ratio of the percentage change in quantity supplied over the percentage change in price. If the absolute value of this ratio is less than one, then supply is characterized as price inelastic. Investors looking for markets that will allow for greater price increases in response to increases in demand should be looking for areas and property types with price inelastic supply.

Primary Trade Area The area from which a retail center or cluster draws primarily its customers.

Private Urban Renewal Inner-city neighborhood revitalization primarily originated and carried out by private population and business groups.

Public Urban Renewal Inner-city neighborhood revitalization primarily originated and encouraged by the local government.

Second Mortgage Loan using as collateral a property that has already been used as collateral for another loan.

Structural Vacancy Rate The minimum vacancy rate needed to allow normal search processes by buyers/renters looking for properties, and landlords looking for buyers/renters. According to empirical studies, this should vary across metropolitan markets, but it is difficult to accurately quantify.

Title Insurance Insurance policy issued by a title insurance company that protects the buyer against liens and encumbrances not discovered in the title search. Its cost is typically based on the value of the property under consideration.

Unleveraged Return is the return of an investment, assuming that no borrowed funds are used.

REFERENCES

Abel, A. and B. Bernanke. 1995. Consumption, Saving, and Investment. Chap. 4 in *Macroeconomics*. Reading, MA: Addison-Wesley Publishing Company.

Bartik, T. 1985. "Business Location Decisions: Estimates of the Effects of Unionization, Taxes, and Other Characteristics of States." *Journal of Business and Economic Statistics*, Vol. 3, No. 1, pp:14-22.

Benjamin, J. and S. Sirmans. 1996. "Mass Transportation, Apartment Rent, and Property Values." *The Journal of Real Estate Research*, Vol. 12, No. 1.

Berry, H. 1984. "Monopoly Property-Monopoly Value." *Appraisal Journal*, October.

Burges, E. 1925. *The City*. Chicago: University of Chicago Press.

Burnell, J. 1985. "Industrial Land Use Externalities and Residential Location." *Urban Studies*, Vol. 22, No. 5.

Burns, L. and Grebler, L. 1986. *The Future of Housing Markets*. New York, NY: Plenum Press.

Carlton, D. 1979. "Why Firms Locate where they Do: An Econometric Model." *In Interregional Movements and Regional Growth*, edited by W. Wheaton. Washington, DC: The Urban Institute.

Carn, N. 1984. "Is Highest and Best Use Justification for Zoning?" *Appraisal Journal*, April.

Carn, N., J. Rabianski, R. Racster, and M. Seldin. 1988. *Real Estate Market Analysis: Techniques and Applications*. Englewood Cliffs, NJ: Prentice-Hall, Inc.

Conover, J. 1975. *How to Make Big Profits from Land in Transition.* Englewood Cliffs, NJ: Executive Reports Corp.

Daniels, P. 1975. *Office Location: An Urban and Regional Study.* London, UK: G. Bell and Sons Ltd.

DiPasquale, D. and W. Wheaton. 1996. *Urban Economics and Real Estate Markets.* Englewood Cliffs, NJ: Prentice Hall.

Correll, R., J. Lillydahl and L. Singell. 1978. "The Effects of Greenbelts on Residential Property Values: Some Findings on the Political Economy of Open Space." *Land Economics*, Vol. 54, pp: 207-217.

Di, Z. and X. Liu. 2003. "How Local Rent Change and Earning Capacity Affect Natural Household Formation by Young Adults." Joint Center of Housing Studies, Working Paper, W03-3.

Elliott, M. 1981. "The Impact of Growth Control Regulations on Housing Prices in California." *American Real Estate and Urban Economics Association Journal*, Vol. 9, pp: 115-33.

Erickson. R. and M. Wasylenko. 1980. "Firm Relocation and Site Selection in Suburban Municipalities." *Journal of Urban Economics*, Vol. 8, pp: 69-85.

Ferguson, B., M. Goldberg, and J. Mark. 1988. "The Pre-Service Impacts of the Vancouver Advanced Light Rail Transit System on Single-Family Property Values." In *Real Estate Market Analysis*, eds J. Clapp and S. Messner, New York, NY: Praeger Publishers.

Frieden, B. 1979. *The Environmental Protection Hustle.* Cambridge, MA: MIT Press.

Geltner, D. 1991. "Smoothing in Appraisal-Based Returns." *Journal of Real Estate Finance and Economics*, Vol.4, No.3, pp: 327-345.

Gerking, S. and W. Boyes. 1980. "The Role of Functional Form in Estimating Elasticities of Housing Expenditures." *Southern Economic Journal*, XLVII, No. 2.

Goodall, B. 1979. *The Economics of Urban Areas*. Oxford, UK: Pergramon Press.

Greer, G. and M. Farrell. 1993. *Investment Analysis for Real Estate Decisions*. Chicago: Dearborn Financial Publishing, Inc.

Hack, J. 2002. "Regeneration and Spatial Development: a Review of Research and Current Practice." IBI Group, Toronto.

Harris, C. and E. Ullman. 1959. "The Nature of Cities." In *Readings in Urban Geography*, eds. H. Mayer and C. Kohn. Chicago: University of Chicago Press.

Harter-Dreiman, M. 2003. "Drawing Inferences about Housing Supply Elasticity from House Price Responses to Income Shocks." OFHEO Working Paper 03-2.

Hartshorn, T. and P. Muller. 1992. "The Suburban Downtown and Urban Economic Development Today." In *Sources of Metropolitan Growth*, eds E. Mills and J. McDonald, New Brunswick, NJ: Center for Urban Policy Research.

Hicks, T. 1992. *Big Money in Real Estate in the Tighter, Tougher '90s Market*. Englewood Cliffs, NJ: Prentice Hall.

Hoyt, H. 1939. *The Structure and Growth of Residential Neighborhoods in American Cities*. Washington, D.C.: FHA.

Hurd, M. R. 1924. *Principles of City Land Values*. New York: The Record and Guide.

Ingene, C. 1984. "Structural Determinants of Market Potential." *Journal of Retailing*, Vol. 60, No. 1, pp: 37-64.

Kau, J. and C.F. Sirmans. 1988. "Urban Residential Land Markets: An Analysis of Changes, 1966-78." in *Real Estate Market Analysis*, ed. J. Clapp, New York: Praeger Press Inc.

Kyle, R. and J. Perry. 1988. *How to Profit from Real Estate.* Chicago, IL: Longman Financial Services Publications.

Lourgant, M. 1989. "Apartment Earnings and Regional Economic Diversification." Working Paper, M.I.T. Center for Real Estate Development.

Markowitz, H. 1952. "Portfolio Selection." *Journal of Finance*, Vol. 7, pp: 77—91.

McLean, A. 1988. *Investing in Real Estate.* New York, NY: John Wiley & Sons.

Malpezzi, S. 1996. "Housing Price Externalities, and Regulation in US Metropolitan Areas." Journal of Housing Research, Vol. 7, pp: 209-241.

Rice Center Community Research Development Corp. 1979. *Research Briefs.* Houston, TX: Rice Center Community Research Development Corp.

Rosen, K. 1983. Towards a Model of the Office Building Sector. *American Real Estate and Urban Economics Association Journal*, Vol. 12, No. 4.

Rosen, K. and L. Smith. 1983. The Price Adjustment Process for Rental Housing and the Natural Vacancy Rate. *American Economic Review*, Vol. 73, pp: 779-786.

Rosen, K. and L. Smith. 1986. The Resale Housing Market. *American Real Estate and Urban Economics Association Journal*, Vol. 14, No. 4.

Saiz, A. 2001. "Room in the Kitchen for the Melting Pot: Immigration and Rental Prices." Joint Center for Housing Studies, Working Paper W01-7.

Schmitz, A. and D. Brett. 2001. *Real Estate Market Analysis: A Case Study Approach*. Washington, D.C.: ULI-the Urban Land Institute.

Shenkel, W. 1980. *Modern Real Estate Principles*. Dallas, TX: Business Publications, Inc.

Shilling, J. D., C. F. Sirmans, and J. B. Corgel. 1987. "Price Adjustment Process for Rental Office Space." *Journal of Urban Economics*, Vol. 22, pp: 90-100.

Sivitanides, P. 1997. "The Rent Adjustment Process and the Structural Vacancy Rate in the Commercial Real Estate Market." *The Journal of Real Estate Research*, Vol. 13, pp: 195-209.

Sivitanides, P., J. Southard, R. Torto, W. Wheaton. 2000. "Strategic Portfolio Analysis: A New Approach." *Real Estate Issues*, Vol. 24, No. 4, pp: 23-32.

Sivitanides, P. and R. Sivitanidou. 1996. "Office Capitalization Rates: Why Do they Vary across Metropolitan Office Markets?" *Real Estate Issues*, Vol. 21, No. 2, pp: 34-39.

Sivitanidou, R. 1996. "Do Office Firms Value Access to Office Employment Centers? A Hedonic Value Analysis in the Los Angeles PMSA." *Journal of Urban Economics*, Vol. 40, No. 2, pp: 125-149.

Sivitanidou, R. and P. Sivitanides. 1999. "Office Capitalization Rates: Real Estate and Capital Market Influences." *Journal of Real Estate Finance and Economics*, Vol. 18, No. 3, pp: 297-322.

Stull, W. 1975. "Community, Environment, Zoning and the Market-Value of Single-Family Homes." *Journal of Law and Economics*, Vol. 18, pp: 535-558.

Sweeny, J. 1974. "A Commodity Hierarchy Model of the Rental Housing Market." *Journal of Urban Economics*, Vol. 1, No. 3, pp: 288-323.

US Census Bureau. 2003. *Domestic Migration across Regions, Divisions, and States: 1995 to 2000*. Census 2000 Special Reports.

Weicher, J. and R. Zerbst. 1973. "The Externalities of Neighborhood Parks: An Empirical Investigation." *Land Economics*, Vol. 49, No. 1, pp: 99-105.

Wheaton, W. 1983. "Theories of Urban Growth and Metropolitan Spatial Development." In *Research in Urban Economics*, ed. J. Henderson, Greenwich: JAI Press, pp: 3-39.

Wheaton, W. 1987. "The Cyclic Behavior of the National Office Market." *American Real Estate and Urban Economics Association Journal*, Vol. 15, pp: 289-299.

Wheaton, W. and R. Torto. 1988. "Vacancy Rates and the Future of Office Rents." *American Real Estate and Urban Economics Association Journal*, Vol. 16, No. 4.

Wheaton, W. and R. Torto. 1990. "An Investment Model of the Demand and Supply of Industrial Space." *AREUEA Journal*, Vol. 18. No. 4, pp: 530-546.

Wheaton, W. and R. Torto. 1994. "Office Rent Indices and their Behavior through Time." *Journal of Urban Economics*, Vol. 35, pp: 121-139.

Wurtzebach, C. and M. Miles. 1994. *Modern Real Estate*. New York: John Wiley & Sons.

Zeitz, E. 1979. *Private Urban Renewal*. Lexington, MA: D.C. Heath and Company.

www.ingramcontent.com/pod-product-compliance
Lightning Source LLC
Chambersburg PA
CBHW071419170526
45165CB00001B/324